MW00931142

STRATEGIC SYNERGY

Mastering the Art of Leadership in the
Modern Business World

Joel R. Klemmer

not assume responsibility for any consequences, losses, or damages resulting from reliance on the information presented herein.

Content Sensitivity Disclaimer: This book may contain discussions on sensitive or potentially triggering topics. Readers are advised to be aware of the nature of the content and exercise discretion when reading. It is essential to take necessary precautions and seek appropriate support or guidance if you find any content distressing or challenging. The author acknowledges the potential sensitivity of these topics and encourages readers to prioritize their emotional well-being.

Endorsement Disclaimer: Mention of products, services, organizations, or other entities in this book is for illustrative purposes only. It does not constitute an endorsement, recommendation, or affiliation with these entities. The author and publisher have no formal association with the mentioned products, services, or organizations, and the content should not be interpreted as an endorsement or sponsorship of any kind. Readers should conduct their research and assessments independently when considering such entities or offerings.

First Edition: 2023

ISBN: 9798883672636

This book is dedicated to my parents, Robert and Kimberlee, who have always supported me through life's toughest challenges and encouraged me to pursue my dreams. Your unwavering belief in me has been my greatest inspiration.

I would also like to express my deepest gratitude to my wife, Victoria, whose love and unwavering support continually encourages me to be a better person every day. Your presence in my life is a source of immense strength.

To Milan, Blake, Luke, Belle, and Joel, I want to impart this message: Always pursue your dreams, no matter what adversity may be bestowed upon you. Your limitless potential inspires me, and I believe in each of you wholeheartedly.

Lastly, I extend my heartfelt thanks to the countless authors, leaders, and professors who have played a significant role in shaping my journey, encouraging me to reach new heights, and challenging me to grow. Your wisdom and guidance have been invaluable.

Simply stated – Thank you!

Table of Contents

Chapter 1
Introduction to Leadership

"Leadership is the strategic alignment of diverse talents
towards a common vision, turning individual efforts into
a collective success."

- Joel R. Klemmer

Chapter 1
Introduction to Leadership

In the professional realm, understanding the essence of leadership is pivotal for fostering effective teams and driving organizational success. Leadership, in its most functional form, is the art and science of guiding individuals or groups toward achieving shared objectives. It is much more than just management or directive authority; it involves the strategic orchestration of diverse talents, aligning them with the organization's vision and goals. This process demands a leader's ability to not only inspire and motivate but also to recognize and utilize the unique strengths of each team member.

This definition lays the groundwork for our exploration into the facets of leadership within a business context. It shifts our focus from conventional perceptions of leadership as a mere position of power, emphasizing its role as a catalyst for collaborative success. It underscores the importance of inclusivity, highlighting how a leader's effectiveness is amplified by their ability to harness diverse perspectives and skills towards a unified strategy. The inspirational aspect of leadership is also pivotal, requiring a blend of creativity, strategic thinking, and an understanding of organizational dynamics. Throughout this book, this nuanced comprehension of leadership will illuminate our discussion on various leadership theories, styles, and practices, offering practical insights for their application in the business world.

Leadership, often visualized within the corridors of corporate power or the halls of political influence, extends far beyond these conventional arenas. Its essence, inherently universal, permeates through various dimensions of our daily lives, manifesting in contexts as diverse as community building, education, sports, and even within the familial sphere.

Consider the impact of leadership in community development. Here, leadership is not just about decision-making; it is about inspiring collective action and nurturing a shared vision. Leaders in community projects demonstrate this by rallying people together for common causes, be it neighborhood improvement initiatives or local fundraising events. Their ability to connect, engage, and motivate individuals towards a common goal is a vibrant display of leadership in action.

Shifting focus to the educational sector, leadership here transcends administrative duties. It is about molding young minds and guiding educators. School principals, for instance, do more than oversee operations; they set the educational tone and ethos of the institution. They are instrumental in fostering an environment that encourages innovative teaching methods and inclusive learning, thereby shaping the future leaders of society.

In the world of sports, leadership dynamics are equally intriguing. The role of a coach or a team captain is not limited to strategy and tactics. It is about building team spirit, resilience, and the will to surpass limits. The way a coach guides a team through difficulties, or how a captain rallies their team members on the field, mirrors the quintessence of leadership - motivating individuals to achieve a collective excellence that transcends individual capabilities.

The subtlety of leadership within family structures is often underappreciated. Family leadership involves guiding by example, setting values, and creating a nurturing environment. The influence parents and guardians have in shaping attitudes and behaviors is profound. Their everyday actions and decisions lay the groundwork for the development of future societal leaders.

Leadership is a versatile and dynamic force, not confined to a single definition or domain. Its principles, when applied across various facets of life, have the power to bring about meaningful change and progress. Understanding this versatility of leadership is not just enlightening; it is empowering. It allows us to recognize and appreciate the different forms and impacts of leadership in our surroundings and beyond.

When we think about the impact of leadership, it is like looking at two sides of the same coin. Leadership can either propel us towards remarkable achievements or lead us down a path of unfortunate consequences. It is a powerful force, and history, along with modern-day stories, is brimming with examples that bring this to life.

Colin Powell's leadership journey epitomizes the essence of principled leadership combined with pragmatic decision-making. As a military leader and statesperson, Powell's career was marked by a steadfast commitment to ethical values and a clear, strategic vision. His role during the Gulf War and his tenure as Secretary of State under President George W. Bush highlight his adeptness in handling complex international situations. Powell was known for his doctrine of overwhelming force, yet his leadership was also characterized by a thoughtful approach to diplomacy and conflict resolution. His principles of leadership, including the importance of gathering solid information, remaining focused under pressure, and maintaining a moral compass, offer invaluable lessons. Powell's ability to lead with a blend of strength and integrity, while navigating the intricate corridors of military and political power, sets a benchmark for leaders aiming to make a positive impact in high-stakes environments.

In stark contrast, Kenneth Lay's leadership at Enron serves as a somber reminder of the consequences of ethical failure. Lay's tenure at Enron was marked by fraudulent practices and a culture that prioritized profits over ethical considerations. The Enron scandal, one of the most infamous corporate collapses in history, unfolded as a direct result of leadership that fostered an environment of deceit and financial manipulation. This scandal not only led to the company's bankruptcy but also resulted in significant financial losses for employees and shareholders, and a loss of trust in corporate America. Lay's leadership and the Enron debacle underscore the vital importance of ethical integrity in leadership. It serves as a cautionary tale about the destructive potential of leadership that disregards moral principles and prioritizes personal gain over collective well-being.

The transformative journey of Nelson Mandela stands as a testament to the power of resilient, inclusive, and morally grounded leadership. From his early days as an anti-apartheid activist to his later years as South Africa's first Black president, Mandela's life story is a narrative of extraordinary leadership under the most challenging conditions. His approach to leadership, characterized by a deep commitment to justice, reconciliation, and the unification of a divided nation, offers profound lessons in leading through adversity. Mandela's ability to forgive his oppressors and focus on building a unified South Africa, rather than seeking retribution, exemplifies his extraordinary emotional intelligence and visionary leadership. His leadership style, marked by humility, empathy, and an unwavering commitment to democracy and human rights, continues to inspire leaders worldwide. Mandela's story is not just about leading a nation through a period of transformation; it is about demonstrating how leaders can effect lasting change by adhering to principles of justice and inclusivity.

The dark shadow cast by Joseph Stalin's authoritarian leadership during his reign over the Soviet Union illustrates the destructive impact of tyrannical leadership. Stalin's regime, characterized by totalitarian control, political purges, and a disregard for human life, resulted in widespread atrocities and suffering. His leadership style, rooted in fear, oppression, and personal glorification, led to catastrophic outcomes, including famines, mass executions, and labor camps. Stalin's rule serves as a grim reminder of how leadership, when divorced from ethical and moral considerations and focused solely on the accumulation of power, can lead to dire consequences. It highlights the critical need for leaders to balance power with responsibility and to prioritize the well-being of the people they serve over personal or ideological ambitions.

In the realm of technology and innovation, Steve Jobs' leadership at Apple demonstrates the transformative power of visionary leadership. Jobs' return to Apple in 1997 marked the beginning of a period of unprecedented innovation and success for the company. His leadership was characterized by an unwavering focus on design aesthetics, user experience, and product excellence. Jobs was known for his demanding leadership style, pushing his team to achieve levels of creativity and performance that they often did not think possible. His ability to foresee market trends and his relentless pursuit of innovation led to the development of groundbreaking products like the iPhone and iPad, which not only revolutionized the technology industry but also changed the way people interact with technology. Jobs' legacy at Apple illustrates how visionary leadership, coupled with a commitment to innovation and excellence, can drive an organization to achieve remarkable success.

However, the story of Elizabeth Holmes and Theranos presents a starkly different narrative in the tech industry. Initially celebrated as a revolutionary leader in healthcare technology, Holmes' fall from grace was precipitous. The Theranos scandal, marked by exaggerated claims about the company's technology and capabilities, became a textbook case of fraudulent leadership. Holmes' initial portrayal as a visionary entrepreneur soon unraveled, revealing a disturbing pattern of deception and overambition. The Theranos debacle highlights the dangers of leadership that prioritizes personal ambition and public image over factual accuracy and ethical standards. It serves as a cautionary reminder of the importance of transparency, integrity, and the ethical responsibilities that come with leadership positions.

These diverse leadership stories, spanning various fields and historical contexts, provide rich lessons in the power and responsibility inherent in leadership roles. They demonstrate that effective leadership is not just about achieving goals, but also about adhering to ethical standards, empathizing with others, and positively impacting society. As we reflect on these examples, they challenge us to contemplate the type of leaders we aspire to be and the legacy we wish to leave.

As we reflect on the diverse range of leadership stories that span various fields and historical contexts, we are reminded of the rich lessons embedded in the power and responsibility inherent in leadership roles. These narratives, highlighting both the triumphs and tribulations of leadership, underscore that true leadership is more than just achieving goals; it involves a deep commitment to ethical standards, empathy, and a positive societal impact. This exploration challenges us to think deeply about the type of leaders we aspire to be and the legacy we wish to leave behind. It is a journey that not only enlightens us about the qualities of effective leadership but also invites us to question and reevaluate our perceptions and beliefs about what truly constitutes leadership.

In venturing further into this exploration, we encounter a realm riddled with myths and misconceptions about leadership. This domain is layered with traditional beliefs and popular notions that often misguide our understanding of the true nature of leadership. Diving into this realm is like embarking on a quest to uncover hidden truths, a quest that promises to enrich our understanding of leadership in profound ways. By meticulously unraveling these myths and misconceptions, we do more than just correct false narratives; we democratize the concept of leadership, opening the possibility that leadership potential resides in each of us. This process of demystification is not merely an academic exercise; it is a crucial step towards recognizing and nurturing the diverse expressions of leadership that exist all around us. It challenges us to expand our view beyond conventional images of leaders and to embrace a more inclusive and varied understanding of what leadership can look like.

As we journey through these misconceptions, it becomes increasingly clear how they can steer us away from appreciating the true essence of what makes a leader. This journey is not just about debunking myths; it is about discovering the multifaceted nature of leadership and acknowledging that there are many paths to effective leadership. In doing so, we begin to see leadership not as a distant ideal embodied by a select few, but as a quality that is accessible and achievable by many. This newfound understanding not only deepens our appreciation of leadership but also invites each of us to explore our own potential to lead in various capacities. It is a revelation that transforms our perception of leadership from a fixed trait to a dynamic and evolving skill set, one that can be cultivated and nurtured over time.

The debate over whether leaders are born or made is as old as the concept of leadership itself. This age-old question suggests that leadership is an innate quality, gifted only to a select few from birth, as if pre-ordained for greatness. It paints a picture of leadership as a rarefied trait, accessible only to those with the right genetic makeup or familial pedigree. But when we really delve into the stories of renowned leaders, this notion begins to unravel.

Let us take a closer look at Nelson Mandela's journey, for example. His story is not one of predestined leadership; rather, it is a tale of transformation through adversity. Mandela was not born into a life of leadership; he was born into a society steeped in inequality and oppression. His path to becoming a world-renowned leader was paved with challenges, struggles, and a relentless pursuit of learning and personal growth. He did not emerge as a fully formed leader but developed his leadership qualities over time, shaped by his experiences and the context of his struggle. This evolution highlights a crucial aspect of leadership - it is often forged in the crucible of life's challenges, not simply inherited at birth.

Similarly, consider Colin Powell's trajectory. One might argue that Powell had a natural propensity for leadership. However, a closer examination reveals that his leadership skills were honed over years of military service and political involvement. Powell's journey was one of continuous learning, adapting, and growing. His experiences, from the battlefields to the halls of government, were not just stops along the way but were integral to shaping his leadership style. This journey underscores the idea that leadership is not a static quality, but a dynamic skill set that evolves over time, cultivated through experience and reflection.

This concept of leaders being made, not born, is further exemplified by countless other figures in history and contemporary society. Across different industries and fields, from business to science, from activism to the arts, leaders have emerged not because they were preordained to lead but because they developed the necessary skills, adapted to their circumstances, and embraced the mantle of leadership.

Therefore, the narrative that leadership is an exclusive club, only accessible to those born with certain traits, does a disservice to the true nature of leadership. It overlooks the potential for leadership that exists in each of us. By recognizing that effective leadership is a product of personal development, experience, and the ability to adapt to one's context, we open the door to a more inclusive and empowering understanding of what it means to lead. This perspective invites us to consider leadership as a journey of continuous growth, where the seeds of potential can be nurtured and cultivated in anyone willing to embark on the journey.

The myth that leadership is synonymous with high-ranking positions or formal authority is one that often limits our understanding of what true leadership entails. We tend to associate leadership with the top tiers of corporate or political hierarchies, but leadership is about influence, impact, and the ability to inspire action, irrespective of one's official title.

My personal experience in the military vividly illustrates this. As an enlisted E-4 Specialist, I was not high up in the ranks, but I found myself in a position where leadership was not just required but was crucial. I was tasked as the battle captain for a field exercise, a role that typically would not fall to someone of my rank. Suddenly, I found myself in a situation where individuals up to the rank of General were looking to me for answers and direction. It was a scenario that completely flipped the traditional hierarchy on its head. The success of the exercise depended not on my rank, but on my ability to effectively coordinate, make decisions, and lead the team.

The exercise turned out to be a resounding success, not just in achieving its objectives but also in demonstrating how leadership can emerge from any level. It was an eye-opening experience for many, including myself, as it shattered preconceived notions about where leadership should originate. My efforts were recognized with the 'Hero of the Battlefield' award, but the real victory was the invaluable lesson in leadership it provided. It underscored that leadership is about stepping up, taking responsibility, and guiding others toward a common goal, regardless of one's position or rank.

This experience echoes the story of Rosa Parks and her act of defiance on the Montgomery bus. Like Parks, who was not in a position of formal authority but whose actions spoke volumes about her leadership, my role in the military exercise demonstrated similar principles. Leadership is about the actions we take and the impact we create. It is about inspiring and guiding others, whether you are a recognized leader or an unsung hero behind the scenes.

Furthermore, leadership is vividly present in our everyday lives, from the teachers who inspire their students to the community volunteers leading local initiatives. These individuals may not have high-ranking titles, but their influence and ability to drive change is undeniable. Their actions exemplify true leadership – guiding, inspiring, and making a difference.

In rethinking leadership, we begin to see it as an inclusive and accessible quality. It is not confined to the boardrooms or the halls of government but can be found in every walk of life, at every level. By expanding our understanding of leadership, we open ourselves to recognizing and embracing the potential for leadership within us all, regardless of where we stand in a traditional hierarchy. This broader perspective not only enriches our understanding of leadership but also empowers each of us to step into our own potential as leaders, in whatever capacity we might find ourselves.

Another myth that often clouds our perception of leadership is the idea that it is all about charisma. We have all heard stories of charismatic leaders like Martin Luther King Jr. and Steve Jobs, whose magnetic personalities and compelling speeches have left an indelible mark on history. There is no denying the powerful influence of their charisma in their leadership. However, the notion that charisma is a prerequisite for effective leadership does not capture the whole picture.

Let us consider Angela Merkel, for instance. Her leadership style is often described as the opposite of charismatic – pragmatic, unemotional, and decidedly low-key. Merkel, often known as the 'Iron Lady' of contemporary politics, does not fit the charismatic leader mold, yet her impact and effectiveness in leading Germany through numerous challenges have been undeniable. Her approach, characterized by rational decision-making, a no-nonsense attitude, and a remarkable ability to build consensus, demonstrates that charisma is not the only path to effective leadership. Merkel's leadership, particularly in times of crisis, has been marked by stability, resilience, and a focus on long-term solutions rather than short-term popularity. This highlights an essential aspect of leadership – the ability to inspire trust and confidence through actions, decisions, and a commitment to values, rather than just through eloquent speech or personal charm.

This is not to say that charisma is not valuable. Charismatic leaders like President Barack Obama, with his exceptional oratory skills, have inspired millions and driven significant change. However, equating leadership solely with charisma overlooks the myriad other ways in which leadership can manifest. There are leaders who inspire through quiet determination, like Greta Thunberg, whose stoic commitment to climate activism has galvanized a global movement. Her leadership is not about grand speeches; it is about the power of conviction and the ability to mobilize action through steadfast commitment.

Leadership, therefore, is more nuanced than simply captivating an audience. It is about how you inspire confidence and trust, whether it is through words, actions, or the integrity of your decisions. It is about understanding the needs of your team, your organization, or your cause, and finding the most effective way to guide them towards a goal. Leaders like New Zealand's Prime Minister Jacinda Ardern exemplify this. Ardern's empathetic and transparent approach, especially in the face of national crises, has been lauded not just for its effectiveness but for the sense of unity and resilience it fostered.

In broadening our understanding of leadership beyond the charisma myth, we open ourselves to a spectrum of leadership styles, each with its own strengths. We begin to appreciate that effective leadership can be as much about listening and empathizing as it is about inspiring and directing. This more inclusive view allows us to recognize and value different forms of leadership, understanding that the best leaders may not always be the most charismatic ones, but those who can connect, inspire, and lead in a way that resonates with their unique context and challenges.

Finally, let us tackle the widespread belief that to be a leader, one must be the most knowledgeable person in the room, or an absolute expert in every area. It is a common misconception that suggests leadership is synonymous with having all the answers. However, true leadership is often less about personal expertise and more about the ability to harness and channel the collective knowledge and strengths of a team.

Take Tim Cook's journey at Apple as an example. When he took over from Steve Jobs, he was stepping into some very big shoes. Jobs was a visionary, a charismatic leader known for his groundbreaking ideas. Cook, on the other hand, had a background steeped in operational expertise. He could have tried to emulate Jobs' style, but instead, he chose to leverage his own strengths. More importantly, Cook recognized the wealth of talent and expertise within Apple and focused on fostering that collective strength. Under his leadership,

Apple continued to innovate and grow, not because Cook was an expert in all things, but because he knew how to bring together the best in his team to keep Apple at the forefront of technology.

This approach to leadership – recognizing and utilizing the expertise of others – is not limited to the corporate world. Consider the field of scientific research. Here, leaders of research teams might not be the most knowledgeable in every single aspect of their projects. Instead, their strength lies in bringing together a team of experts in various subfields, facilitating collaboration, and guiding the project towards its goals. This style of leadership demonstrates the power of collective intelligence over individual expertise.

Moreover, the idea that leaders must know everything is not just unrealistic; it can be detrimental. It can create a culture where leaders feel the need to have all the answers, leading to burnout or poor decision-making. Great leaders acknowledge their limitations. They are not afraid to say, "I don't know, but let's find out together," or "You have more expertise in this area; what do you think?" This humility and willingness to learn from others not only strengthens the team's respect for the leader but also fosters a more collaborative and innovative environment.

Leadership, therefore, is as much about asking the right questions and listening as it is about providing answers. It is about understanding that the collective capabilities of a team often outweigh the knowledge of a single individual. In embracing this concept, leaders can harness the full potential of their teams, creating an environment where ideas can flourish, and innovation is a collective endeavor. This approach also allows for more diverse and inclusive leadership styles, recognizing that the best leaders may not always be the most knowledgeable, but those who can effectively harness the knowledge, skills, and abilities of those around them.

As we delve into the heart of these long-standing myths surrounding leadership, we uncover a profound truth: leadership is far more intricate and ever-changing than many have believed. It is not merely a matter of being born with a certain set of traits or holding a prestigious title. Instead, it is a dynamic, multifaceted journey that is accessible to anyone eager to nurture their ability to inspire, influence, and create a positive impact.

This revelation is nothing short of empowering. It means that the canvas of leadership is vast and diverse, like an artist's palette filled with various styles, approaches, and personalities, each capable of leaving a unique imprint. As we embark on this exploration, we come to realize that the potential for leadership resides within every one of us, patiently waiting to be nurtured and brought to life. It is a thrilling realization that opens doors to endless possibilities, and we are here to uncover them together. So, let us embark on this enriching journey, unlocking the incredible potential that lies within each of us to be a leader in our own right.

Chapter 2

The History and Evolution of Leadership

"Leadership, drawing wisdom from the past, fuels the
flame of progress for a brighter future."

- Joel R. Klemmer

Chapter 2
The History and Evolution of Leadership

Embarking on a captivating journey through time unravels the fascinating history and evolution of leadership. The rich tapestry of leadership's past will uncover how leadership has evolved into the complex concept we understand today. This exploration will take us from the cradle of ancient civilizations to the intricacies of contemporary leadership theories.

Imagine stepping into the past, where cultures like Egypt, Mesopotamia, and China had their unique ways of leadership. It is like opening a time capsule of leadership practices and seeing how they have shaped our modern understanding of it.

Let us transport ourselves to the captivating realm of ancient Egypt, a civilization steeped in mystique and grandeur, where leadership was a complex amalgamation of political prowess and divine authority. Picture the vast and fertile landscapes, with the mighty Nile River flowing through the heart of the land.

In this extraordinary setting, leadership transcended the ordinary; it became an embodiment of the divine. The pharaoh, the paramount leader of Egypt, was not just a ruler but an earthly deity. They were believed to be imbued with the very essence of the gods themselves, a living conduit between the mortal realm and the divine cosmos. This divine kingship bestowed upon the pharaoh an unparalleled level of power and influence that extended across all spheres of life.

At the heart of this leadership model was an intricate interplay between politics and religion. The pharaohs held sway over not only the political governance of Egypt but also the spiritual beliefs and practices of the populace. Their authority extended to matters of statecraft, where they presided over crucial decisions related to governance, law, and diplomacy. Simultaneously, they played a pivotal role in religious rituals, ensuring the favor of the gods and the prosperity of the kingdom.

The leadership landscape in ancient Egypt was characterized by a hierarchical and authoritarian structure. Beneath the pharaoh, a pyramid-like structure of officials, nobles, and priests governed various aspects of society. Loyalty to the pharaoh was paramount, and dissent was met with severe consequences. This centralized and authoritarian leadership model was intricately tied to the divine order, with the pharaoh as the ultimate guardian of Ma'at, the concept of cosmic balance and harmony. The divine kingship of ancient Egypt serves as a testament to the profound ways in which leadership can be shaped by culture, spirituality, and the beliefs of a society.

Now to the ancient land of Mesopotamia, often hailed as the cradle of civilization, where the very foundations of organized society were laid. In this vast and fertile landscape, we encounter a fascinating tapestry of city-states, each presided over by its own monarchs and revered priests. These leaders held the reins of power in their respective domains, shaping the destiny of their city-state and its inhabitants.

Now, imagine these rulers holding in their hands ancient legal codes, the likes of which the world had never seen before. One of the most renowned among them is the famous Code of Hammurabi, a veritable cornerstone of governance in Mesopotamia. These legal codes were not mere compilations of rules; they were the rulebooks for leadership itself. They provided the framework upon which the city-states operated, delineating rights, responsibilities, and consequences. These codes became the bedrock of justice, defining how disputes were settled and how order was maintained in a world teeming with complexities.

Intriguingly, these ancient leaders, in their roles as both rulers and religious figures, occupied a unique position in society. They were not only responsible for the practical affairs of their city-states but also served as intermediaries between the earthly realm and the divine. This dual role lent a spiritual aura to their leadership, emphasizing the profound intertwining of politics and religion in ancient Mesopotamia.

As we embark on this exploration of Mesopotamian leadership, one can see the intricacies of these legal codes and their enduring legacy on leadership principles. The echoes of Mesopotamian governance can still be heard in the corridors of power today, underscoring the enduring influence of this ancient civilization on our understanding of leadership. These are the layers of history that reveal the profound impact of Mesopotamian leadership on the tapestry of human civilization.

As we embark further on our historical voyage, we can set our course eastward, where ancient China awaits us with its captivating blend of emperors, philosophers, and dynasties. In this realm, leadership was intricately interwoven with profound philosophies that continue to echo through the annals of history. Among these philosophical currents, Confucianism, Daoism, and Legalism stood as towering pillars that shaped the very essence of leadership.

In the heart of this vast empire, emperors reigned as the ultimate authority, their rule guided by the tenets of these philosophies. Confucianism, with its emphasis on moral rectitude, benevolence, and social harmony, held a profound sway over the imperial court. Emperors aspired to rule with benevolence, striving to embody the Confucian ideals of virtuous leadership. Their reigns were marked by a commitment to the welfare of their subjects, an unwavering dedication to ethics, and a vision of a harmonious society.

Contrastingly, the doctrine of Legalism advocated for a different approach to governance—one characterized by strict laws, rigorous control, and a belief in the inherent flawed nature of humanity. Legalist rulers recognized the necessity of strong central authority to maintain order, and they did not shy away from employing strict measures to achieve it.

In this intricate tapestry of philosophies and leadership styles, embarked a journey into profound philosophical differences manifested in the corridors of power. It provided the core dynamics between emperors and their advisors, the impact of philosophical ideals on policy decisions, and the enduring legacy of these ancient philosophies on contemporary leadership practices.

The intricate maze of ancient Chinese leadership uncovered where the wisdom of Confucianism, the tranquility of Daoism, and the rigor of Legalism converged and collided, leaving an indelible mark on the history of leadership. The intricate dance between philosophy and power, we can gain deeper insights into the rich tapestry of leadership principles that continue to shape the world today.

One prevailing theme became abundantly clear—an era characterized by hierarchical and authoritative leadership. In these ancient epochs, leaders stood atop unassailable pedestals of authority, their rule flowing from the summit down to the farthest reaches of their domains. This overarching theme, reverberating through the corridors of time, underscored a crucial facet of our exploration.

Intriguingly, this historical backdrop served as a crucial backdrop for comprehending the evolution and transformation of leadership into the multifaceted and dynamic field it is today. By peering into the depths of this historical reservoir, we could glean profound insights into the very foundations upon which contemporary leadership has been erected.

Our journey into the past was akin to unraveling the intricate threads of leadership's historical tapestry. It was a voyage through the ages when leadership was marked by unwavering authority, and decision-making flowed from the apex of power downward. This hierarchical and authoritative structure was the bedrock upon which societies were built, and its echoes continue to resonate in our modern leadership paradigms.

As we journey deeper into history, we now find ourselves in the remarkable epochs of ancient Greece and Rome. These were times when leadership took on distinctive and philosophical dimensions, enriching our understanding of what it means to lead. In this chapter of our historical odyssey, we will embark on a captivating journey to unveil the profound insights and principles that left an indelible mark on leadership during classical antiquity.

Picture the vibrant agora of Athens, where philosophers like Plato and Aristotle contemplated the essence of leadership and its connection to the greater good. These thinkers did not just ponder leadership; they sought to define its very nature. We will delve into their philosophical contributions and explore how their ideas on virtue, ethics, and governance continue to reverberate in contemporary leadership discourse.

Then, let us transport ourselves to the grandeur of Rome, where orators like Cicero articulated the art of rhetoric and persuasion, essential skills for leaders of the time. Their teachings on eloquence and diplomacy have left a legacy, and we will uncover how these lessons remain relevant in modern leadership communication.

Throughout our journey, we will encounter the concept of virtuous leadership, where character, morality, and civic duty were at the forefront of leadership principles. We will reflect on how citizenship played a pivotal role in shaping leaders' responsibilities and explore the enduring wisdom that emanated from these classical civilizations.

So, join us as we navigate the philosophical landscapes of ancient Greece and Rome, where the foundations of leadership were not only laid but also carved with intellectual precision. The insights from this chapter will not only enrich your historical perspective but also provide valuable lessons for leadership in our contemporary world.

Ancient Greece, often celebrated as the cradle of democracy and philosophy, offers us a profound understanding of leadership that continues to influence contemporary thought. In this remarkable civilization, the seeds of philosophical leadership were sown by visionaries such as Plato and Aristotle, leaving an indelible mark on our perception of leadership.

Plato's "Philosopher-King" concept was nothing short of revolutionary. It introduced the notion of leaders as philosopher-guides, emphasizing the paramount importance of wisdom and virtue in governance. Plato envisioned a society where rulers were not merely administrators but also seekers of truth and wisdom. Their leadership was founded on the principle that those with the deepest understanding of justice and morality should guide the state. This idea has endured through the ages, reminding us of the significance of intellectual and moral leadership in the modern world.

Aristotle, a towering figure in ancient philosophy, delved into the ethical dimensions of leadership. His profound exploration led to the elucidation of the concept of "eudaimonia," often translated as human flourishing. Aristotle posited that the goal of leadership should be the well-being and flourishing of individuals and the broader community. This emphasis on the ethical responsibility of leaders to promote greater good has resonated across centuries and remains a cornerstone of contemporary leadership theories.

Ancient Greece bequeathed us with the enduring legacy of philosophical leadership, where wisdom, morality, and the pursuit of human flourishing lie at the heart of effective leadership. These timeless principles continue to inspire and guide leaders in their quest to make meaningful and ethical contributions to society.

Our expedition through the annals of history now carries us to the formidable Roman Empire, a time when the remarkable Cicero further enriched leadership principles. This celebrated orator, philosopher, and statesperson left an indelible mark on leadership theory with his profound insights.

Cicero's writings serve as a beacon of wisdom, emphasizing the foundational virtues that underpin effective leadership. His principles revolved around wisdom, justice, courage, and self-discipline, forming the bedrock of virtuous leadership. In Cicero's view, a leader's wisdom was essential for sound decision-making, while justice guided fair and equitable governance. Courage enabled leaders to face challenges with fortitude, and self-discipline ensured the restraint needed for responsible leadership.

Cicero's ideals of the "orator-statesman" embodied a fusion of rhetoric, diplomacy, and ethical leadership. He believed that leaders should not only possess the ability to communicate effectively but also adhere to the highest ethical standards. Cicero's influence extended far beyond his time, resonating with subsequent generations of leaders who recognized the enduring value of his principles.

Cicero's legacy endows us with a profound understanding of leadership as a virtuous endeavor, one guided by wisdom, justice, courage, and self-discipline. These timeless virtues continue to inform and inspire leaders in their pursuit of ethical and impactful leadership in the modern world.

In the tapestry of ancient civilizations, leadership was intricately woven into the fabric of citizenship, a concept quite distinct from our contemporary understanding. In those times, citizenship carried not only a mantle of rights but also a profound tapestry of responsibilities, chief among them being active engagement in the governance of the polis or republic.

Leaders were not simply rulers, but they embodied the ideals of virtuous citizenship. They were entrusted with the noble duty of guiding their fellow citizens toward the common good. This perspective fundamentally diverges from our modern concept of leadership, which often revolves around authority and decision-making vested in a select few.

Ancient leaders, with their intertwined roles as states people and exemplars of virtuous citizenship, exemplified a form of leadership that transcended personal power. Their mission was to serve as stewards of collective well-being, setting a standard of ethical conduct for all to follow. This philosophy underscores the deep-rooted connection between leadership and the greater good, a concept that, while transformed in modern times, still echoes through the corridors of leadership philosophy.

Our journey through the annals of history, guided by the philosophical currents of ancient Greece and Rome, has unveiled a treasury of timeless wisdom that resonates with profound relevance in the realm of leadership today. As we continue to delve deeper into these philosophical depths, we illuminate the enduring principles that have left an indelible mark on the very essence of leadership.

In this quest, the radiant wisdom imparted by philosophers like Plato, Aristotle, and Cicero beckons to us from across the ages. It reminds us that leadership is a tapestry intricately woven with threads of virtue, wisdom, and moral excellence. These philosophical luminaries, each in their unique way, have lent their insights to craft a definition of leadership that transcends the limitations of time and culture.

Plato's "Philosopher-King" concept beckons us to consider the profound impact of wisdom and virtue in governance and leadership. Aristotle's exploration of eudaimonia, the flourishing of human potential, calls upon leaders to consider the holistic well-being of those they lead. Cicero's ideals of ethical leadership, grounded in wisdom, justice, courage, and self-discipline, resound as a clarion call to contemporary leaders.

These foundational principles are not relics of the past but timeless beacons that guide our way forward. They affirm that, regardless of the era or societal evolution, the pursuit of wisdom and moral excellence remains at the very heart of effective leadership. Thus, our journey through the philosophical currents of antiquity not only enriches our understanding of leadership's past but also illuminates the path toward leadership's enduring future.

As we embark on our historical journey, we find ourselves standing at the threshold of a momentous era—the Industrial Era, a time of profound transformation in leadership theories and paradigms. It is within this intriguing historical context that we encounter a concept of great significance, the "Great Man Theory," which emerged as a cornerstone of leadership thought during this pivotal period.

The Industrial Era, characterized by unprecedented technological advancements and societal changes, brought forth a reevaluation of leadership and its underlying principles. The Great Man Theory, which emerged as a prominent perspective, posited that leaders were not ordinary individuals; they were exceptional, possessing innate qualities and traits that set them apart from the masses. These exceptional individuals were seen as the architects of history, influencing the course of events through their remarkable abilities.

In our exploration of this theory, we will delve into its foundational concepts, understanding how it perceived leadership as an inherent quality that only a select few possessed. We will illuminate this perspective with examples of leaders who were regarded as "great men" during this era, individuals whose extraordinary qualities and actions left an indelible mark on history.

By delving into the Great Man Theory, we gain valuable insights into the evolution of leadership thought and the changing perceptions of leadership during the Industrial Era. This theory not only reflects the historical context of its time but also invites us to contemplate the broader implications of leadership as an innate and exceptional quality—a perspective that has shaped our understanding of leadership in the modern world.

The Great Man Theory, a pivotal concept in the realm of leadership thought during the 19th century, presented a unique perspective on leadership. It viewed leadership as an innate quality, a divine endowment bestowed upon a select and extraordinary few. According to this theory, leaders were not products of circumstance or education; rather, they were born with exceptional traits and qualities that destined them for greatness.

This perspective held leaders in high esteem, elevating them to a revered status as individuals who possessed inherent qualities that set them apart from the masses. It suggested that these exceptional individuals emerged at critical junctures in history to shape the course of events through their extraordinary abilities and leadership prowess.

The Great Man Theory reflected its time, a period marked by significant societal changes and the industrial revolution. It was a response to the need for strong and visionary leaders in a rapidly evolving world. While this theory has been critiqued and evolved over time, its influence on shaping early leadership thought cannot be denied.

In examining the Great Man Theory, we gain valuable insights into how leadership was perceived during the 19th century and how this perspective has contributed to the broader discourse on leadership. It reminds us of the enduring fascination with the idea of innate leadership qualities and their impact on the course of history.

The Great Man Theory painted a vivid portrait of leaders as heroic figures, often rising to prominence during times of crisis or significant change. These individuals were perceived as natural-born leaders, endowed with innate characteristics that set them apart. Traits such as courage, charisma, intelligence, and unwavering determination were seen as their defining qualities.

In the eyes of proponents of the Great Man Theory, these exceptional leaders were destined to shape the course of history, guiding society towards progress and prosperity. They were celebrated as figures of immense influence, capable of making pivotal decisions and leading with authority and conviction.

This theory captured the imagination of many during the 19th century, reflecting the societal yearning for strong and visionary leaders in an era of rapid industrialization and transformation. It offered a compelling narrative that emphasized the significance of individual leadership in the grand sweep of history.

While the Great Man Theory has been subject to critique and evolved over time, its legacy endures in the broader discourse on leadership. It reminds us of the enduring fascination with the concept of innate leadership qualities and their potential to shape the destiny of nations and societies.

The Industrial Era witnessed the rise of leaders who were celebrated as prime examples of "great men," lending credence to the premise of the Great Man Theory. Abraham Lincoln, who led the United States through the American Civil War, and Queen Victoria, who presided over the British Empire during a period of vast expansion, are notable figures from this era.

Indeed, Abraham Lincoln's leadership during the American Civil War is a testament to his exceptional qualities as a leader. His commitment to preserving the Union and his moral stance against slavery set him apart as a visionary leader. Lincoln's ability to communicate his vision effectively through speeches like the Gettysburg Address, which emphasized the principles of liberty and equality, resonated deeply with the American people.

One of his most significant leadership actions was the Emancipation Proclamation, which declared the freedom of enslaved individuals in Confederate territory. This bold move not only changed the course of the war but also represented a monumental step toward ending slavery in the United States. Lincoln's leadership during this turbulent period demonstrated not only his political acumen but also his unwavering dedication to principles of justice and human rights.

Abraham Lincoln's legacy as a transformational leader who navigated a nation through one of its darkest periods continues to inspire leaders today. His leadership qualities of integrity, resilience, and visionary thinking serve as a timeless example of effective leadership in times of crisis and change.

On the other side of the Atlantic, Queen Victoria's reign marked a significant period in the history of the British Empire. The Victorian Era, named after her, was a time of immense growth and transformation, not only for Britain but for the entire world. As a leader, Queen Victoria played a symbolic yet essential role in the expansion and influence of the British Empire.

During her lengthy reign, the British Empire reached its peak, with territories spanning across continents and oceans. The sun never set on the British Empire, highlighting the extent of its global dominance. Queen Victoria became a symbol of this imperial power and cultural influence, despite the constitutional constraints on her role as a monarch.

While her leadership was primarily symbolic, Queen Victoria's reign was characterized by stability and continuity. Her commitment to her role as a unifying figure for the empire contributed to a sense of identity and purpose among her subjects. Additionally, her support for the British military and her interest in foreign affairs played a role in shaping the empire's policies and actions during this era.

Queen Victoria's legacy as a leader is intertwined with the expansion and influence of the British Empire. Her era remains a pivotal chapter in world history, and her leadership, though different in nature from other leaders of her time, left an enduring mark on the global stage.

Both leaders, in different contexts and roles, exemplified qualities associated with the Great Man Theory of leadership. Their impact on their respective nations and the world at large continues to be studied and celebrated, further cementing their places as significant historical figures. Both Lincoln and Queen Victoria faced formidable challenges during their leadership tenures, and their ability to navigate these challenges with determination and wisdom earned them a place in history as exemplary leaders. Their leadership seemed to align with the Great Man Theory's premise that extraordinary leaders emerged when the world needed them the most.

These leaders demonstrated the impact that individuals with exceptional qualities could have on the course of history, inspiring future generations and contributing to the ongoing fascination with the concept of great leaders.

Our journey through the Industrial Era and the Great Man Theory provides us with valuable insights into the evolution of leadership perceptions. The Great Man Theory, prevalent during the 19th century, portrayed leaders as exceptional individuals born with innate qualities that destined them for greatness. It celebrated heroic figures who emerged during times of crisis or significant change.

Leaders like Abraham Lincoln and Queen Victoria were seen as prime examples of these "great men." Lincoln's unwavering commitment to preserving the Union and abolishing slavery, coupled with his eloquence and vision, made him a revered leader. Queen Victoria's symbolic role during the Victorian Era represented an era of British imperial power and cultural influence.

However, as we reflect on this theory, we also recognize its limitations. The Great Man Theory had a narrow view of leadership, overlooking the role of followers, context, and the possibility of leadership development. It placed leaders on a pedestal, portraying them as superhuman figures, which is an oversimplification of leadership dynamics.

Our exploration of this theory prompts us to consider how our understanding of leadership has evolved. Contemporary leadership theories emphasize the importance of context, situational factors, and the idea that leadership can be developed and nurtured. While the

Great Man Theory highlights the exceptional qualities of certain leaders, it is crucial to recognize that leadership is a complex and multifaceted phenomenon influenced by various factors.

As we move forward in our exploration of leadership history, we will continue to uncover the diverse perspectives and theories that have shaped our understanding of leadership, leading us to a more comprehensive and nuanced view of this essential aspect of human society.

In our ongoing journey through the annals of leadership history, we now arrive at a pivotal juncture—the Industrial Era. This era marked a time of profound change in the way leadership was perceived and studied. Within this transformative period, a notable theory emerged, known as the Trait Theory of Leadership, which gained prominence in the early 20th century. This theory introduced a novel perspective on leadership by shifting the focus towards identifying the specific traits that were believed to define effective leaders.

Indeed, as we delve deeper into the Trait Theory of Leadership, we find that it represented a notable departure from the prevailing Great Man Theory. The Great Man Theory had long held sway, emphasizing that leaders were extraordinary individuals blessed with innate qualities that destined them for greatness. It was a perspective that looked up to leaders as unique and exceptional, born with traits that set them apart from the ordinary.

In contrast, the Trait Theory of Leadership ushered in a change in basic assumptions in how leadership was conceptualized. It steered away from the notion of leadership as a rare and innate quality possessed by a select few. Instead, it turned the spotlight towards a more systematic and scientific examination of leadership, focusing on the specific traits and attributes that could be identified, studied, and potentially cultivated.

This shift in focus marked a pivotal moment in the evolution of leadership thought. It signaled a departure from the realm of mysticism and the belief in an exclusive cadre of "born leaders." Instead, it encouraged a more inclusive and methodical exploration of what made leaders effective in their roles. Researchers and scholars of the Trait Theory sought to create a taxonomy of leadership traits, aiming to uncover the common denominators among successful leaders.

Within the Trait Theory framework, these identified traits ranged from intelligence and decisiveness to charisma and integrity. The theory operated on the assumption that individuals possessing these specific traits were more likely to excel in leadership positions. It was a departure from the notion that leadership was solely the result of destiny or chance.

The Trait Theory of Leadership did indeed initiate a systematic exploration of leadership traits, seeking to identify and catalog those characteristics believed to be pivotal for effective leadership. Researchers within this framework embarked on a quest to pinpoint the essential traits that set apart successful leaders from others. These traits encompassed a spectrum of qualities, including intelligence, decisiveness, charisma, integrity, and self-confidence, among others.

The underlying assumption of the Trait Theory was that individuals possessing a specific combination of these traits were more likely to excel in leadership roles. This perspective marked a significant shift away from the notion of leadership as a mysterious and innate quality reserved for a select few. Instead, it heralded a more structured and empirical approach to understanding leadership.

As our exploration continues, we will delve deeper into the specifics of these traits and how they were assessed and evaluated within the Trait Theory framework. Additionally, we will examine the limitations and challenges that researchers encountered as they sought to identify a definitive list of leadership traits.

While the Trait Theory of Leadership has its share of criticisms and shortcomings, it undeniably played a crucial role in advancing our understanding of leadership. It laid the groundwork for subsequent theories that would further refine and expand our comprehension of what makes an effective leader. Our journey through the evolving landscape of leadership thought will continue to unveil these developments and shed light on how they have shaped the practice of leadership in modern times.

However, as we delve into the depths of this theory, it becomes evident that it, too, had its limitations. The Trait Theory of Leadership faced criticism for its inability to provide a comprehensive explanation of leadership. It became increasingly clear that leadership was a complex and multifaceted phenomenon that could not be boiled down to a mere checklist of traits.

Nonetheless, the Trait Theory of Leadership played a crucial role in the evolution of leadership studies. It laid the foundation for subsequent research and theories, contributing to a deeper understanding of leadership. While it may not offer a complete picture of leadership, it marked an important step in the ongoing journey to unravel the intricacies of this essential aspect of human society.

As we proceed with our exploration of leadership history, we will continue to unearth the diverse theories and perspectives that have shaped our understanding of leadership. Each theory, including the Trait Theory, has left its mark, bringing us closer to a more comprehensive and nuanced view of leadership in all its dimensions.

At the core of the Trait Theory is the notion that leadership is not solely dependent on one's position or external circumstances. Instead, it proposes that leadership is, at least in part, a result of inherent traits and characteristics that individuals possess. Proponents of this theory embarked on a quest to pinpoint a specific set of key traits that were consistently linked to successful leaders. Their belief was that by identifying these traits, it would be possible to predict an individual's leadership potential.

This perspective represents a departure from earlier theories that portrayed leadership as an elusive quality reserved for a select few. The

Trait Theory introduced a more systematic and scientific approach to understanding leadership, emphasizing the importance of certain inherent qualities. It marked a significant shift in thinking, laying the foundation for the development of subsequent leadership theories.

As we continue our exploration, we will delve into the specific traits that researchers associated with effective leadership within the Trait Theory framework. We will also critically examine the theory's strengths and limitations, shedding light on how it contributed to the broader evolution of leadership thought. Through this journey, we will gain a deeper understanding of how the study of leadership has evolved over time, with each theory building upon the foundations of its predecessors.

Within the Trait Theory of Leadership, researchers turned their attention to a range of specific traits that were believed to be critical for effective leadership. Traits such as self-confidence, intelligence, decisiveness, integrity, and charisma were among the key qualities scrutinized in the quest to unlock the secrets of leadership success.

The underlying objective was to identify the distinctive characteristics that distinguished leaders from followers. Researchers sought to create a blueprint for leadership success by pinpointing these essential traits. They hypothesized that individuals possessing a particular combination of these traits would be more likely to excel in leadership roles.

Critics of the Trait Theory of Leadership raised valid concerns about its limitations. While the theory offered valuable insights into the qualities associated with effective leadership, it faced criticism for oversimplifying the intricate nature of leadership. Detractors argued that reducing effective leadership to a fixed set of traits failed to account for the contextual and situational aspects that play a crucial role in leadership effectiveness.

Leadership, they contended, was not a one-size-fits-all endeavor. Instead, it depended on various factors, including the specific circumstances, the individuals involved, and the goals of the organization or group being led. What constituted effective leadership could vary significantly from one situation to another.

Despite its limitations, the Trait Theory of Leadership left an indelible mark on the field of leadership studies. Its influence cannot be underestimated, as it initiated a significant shift in how leadership was perceived and explored. By redirecting attention from a narrow focus on innate qualities to a more comprehensive view that considered traits, behaviors, and situational factors, the Trait Theory laid the groundwork for a more nuanced understanding of effective leadership.

While the Trait Theory laid important groundwork by highlighting key leadership qualities, it became increasingly clear that understanding leadership required more than just a list of traits. The evolving landscape of organizational dynamics and the complexity of human behavior called for a more nuanced approach. This realization paved the way for the emergence of behavioral theories. These theories shifted the focus from inherent traits to observable behaviors, actions, and interactions between leaders and their teams, addressing some of the limitations of the trait-based approach.

Behavioral theories of leadership marked a significant departure from trait-focused perspectives. They emphasized the actions and behaviors of leaders, rather than their innate qualities. Pioneering studies like the Ohio State and University of Michigan research explored how different leadership styles, like consideration and initiating structure, influenced team dynamics and performance. These studies highlighted that effective leadership was not just about who a leader was intrinsically, but how they acted and reacted in various situations, bringing a more adaptable and practical understanding to the field of leadership.

One of the prominent strands of behavioral theories includes the Ohio State Studies and the University of Michigan Studies. These studies aimed to understand leadership behaviors by categorizing them into specific dimensions. The Ohio State Studies, for example, identified two major dimensions of leadership behavior: consideration (concern for people) and initiating structure (concern for task). On the other hand, the University of Michigan Studies focused on employee-oriented and production-oriented behaviors. The Ohio State and University of Michigan studies were instrumental in this shift, as they introduced a more systematic and structured approach to understanding leadership behaviors.

In the Ohio State Studies, the first dimension, known as consideration, emphasized the leader's concern for the well-being and needs of their followers. Leaders who exhibited consideration were seen as supportive and focused on building positive relationships within their teams.

The second dimension, initiating structure, focused on the leader's ability to define roles, set clear expectations, and establish structured work processes. Leaders who excelled in initiating structure were viewed as task-oriented and effective in organizing and managing tasks.

Consideration, with its focus on interpersonal relationships and support, acknowledged the importance of empathy and rapport in leadership. Leaders who exhibited consideration were seen as approachable and caring, fostering a positive work environment where team members felt valued.

On the other hand, initiating structure acknowledged the necessity of clear direction and organization within a team or organization. Leaders who excelled in initiating structure were skilled at setting goals, defining roles, and ensuring that tasks were well-organized and managed efficiently.

The recognition that both dimensions were essential for effective leadership laid the foundation for more comprehensive leadership models and theories in the modern era, acknowledging that leaders needed to be versatile in their approach to meet the diverse needs of their teams and organizations.

Similarly, the University of Michigan Studies introduced the concepts of employee-oriented and production-oriented leadership behaviors. Employee-oriented leaders were those who prioritized the human needs of their team members, fostering a supportive and collaborative work environment. Production-oriented leaders, on the other hand, were more focused on achieving task goals and productivity.

Employee-oriented leaders were concerned with creating a supportive and positive work environment. They prioritized the well-being and satisfaction of their team members, fostering a sense of camaraderie and trust. Such leaders were often approachable and empathetic, valuing the needs and concerns of their team.

On the other hand, production-oriented leaders were task-focused and driven to achieve results. They emphasized productivity, efficiency, and goal attainment. These leaders were skilled at organizing work processes, setting clear objectives, and ensuring that tasks were completed effectively.

The key insight from these studies was that effective leaders did not adhere rigidly to one style but adapted their behavior based on the situation and the needs of their team. This adaptability became a hallmark of modern leadership theories, recognizing that leadership effectiveness was contingent on the context and the individuals being led.

The Ohio State and University of Michigan studies collectively laid the groundwork for behavioral theories of leadership, emphasizing the importance of a leader's actions and behaviors in influencing team performance and satisfaction. These studies were pivotal in shaping the evolving landscape of leadership research and practice, guiding leaders to adopt more flexible and situationally appropriate leadership approaches.

These studies provided valuable insights into the different dimensions of leadership behavior and highlighted that effective leadership could manifest in various ways, depending on the leader's emphasis on either consideration or initiating structure, or a balance of both. This shift in perspective laid the groundwork for more nuanced and adaptable approaches to leadership in the

Effective leaders, according to these studies, were those who could strike a balance between building positive relationships and providing structure and guidance to their teams. This approach recognized that leadership effectiveness was not a one-size-fits-all concept, and leaders needed to adapt their behavior to suit the needs of their followers and the specific situation at hand.

Indeed, the shift from trait-based theories to behavioral theories represented a profound transformation in the understanding of leadership. It fundamentally challenged the notion that leadership was solely dependent on certain innate traits possessed by a select few. Instead, these behavioral theories proposed that leadership was a set of behaviors that could be learned, developed, and refined over time.

This shift in perspective is significant because it democratizes leadership. It suggests that effective leadership is not limited to a privileged few but is attainable through the cultivation of specific actions and behaviors. It empowers individuals to take an active role in their leadership development and encourages organizations to invest in leadership training and development programs.

Leadership, under this new paradigm, becomes more accessible and inclusive. It emphasizes the importance of continuous learning and growth, allowing individuals at all levels of an organization to aspire to leadership roles. It also underscores the importance of adaptable leadership, where leaders can adjust their behaviors to suit the needs of different situations and teams.

As we continue our journey through the modern era of leadership, the significance of leadership actions and behaviors takes center stage. It becomes increasingly evident that leaders are not bound by a fixed set of traits but can adapt and refine their behaviors to suit the dynamic needs of their teams and organizations. This evolving perspective on leadership opens the door to a deeper exploration of leadership theories that encompass a broader range of factors, behaviors, and circumstances.

Leadership in the modern era is characterized by its adaptability and responsiveness to the complexities of today's world. It acknowledges that effective leadership is not a one-size-fits-all concept but a dynamic interplay of behaviors, actions, and situational factors. Leaders must be agile and attuned to the ever-changing landscape of their organizations and industries.

Moreover, this shift in perspective places a greater emphasis on the role of emotional intelligence, communication skills, and interpersonal relationships in leadership. Leaders are not just taskmasters; they are facilitators of collaboration, innovation, and team cohesion. Their behaviors set the tone for organizational culture and employee engagement.

As we journey deeper into our exploration of modern leadership theories, we encounter the intriguing concept of contingency theories. Unlike earlier theories that aimed to establish a universal approach to leadership, contingency theories embrace the idea that leadership effectiveness is contingent upon various situational factors.

Contingency theories challenge the notion of a one-size-fits-all leadership style and emphasize that what works in one situation may not work in another. They recognize that leadership is not static but adaptable, requiring leaders to assess the context they are in and adjust their leadership behaviors accordingly.

One prominent contingency theory, Fiedler's Contingency Model, posits that the effectiveness of a leader depends on the match between their leadership style and the situation they are in. Fiedler categorized leaders as either task-oriented or relationship-oriented and argued that the favorability of a situation determined which type of leader would be most effective. In highly favorable or highly unfavorable situations, task-oriented leaders were seen as more effective, while in moderately favorable situations, relationship-oriented leaders were deemed more successful.

Proposed by Fred Fiedler in the 1960s, this model provides valuable insights into the dynamic relationship between leadership styles and situational favorableness. The essence of Fiedler's Contingency Model lies in its recognition of the role that situational factors play in determining leadership effectiveness. According to this theory, not all leadership styles are universally effective; their success is contingent upon the favorableness of the situation.

In a highly favorable or highly unfavorable situation, task-oriented leadership tends to be more effective. For instance, in a well-structured environment where tasks are clearly defined and team relationships are not a significant concern, a leader who focuses on task achievement is likely to excel. Similarly, in a crisis where quick decisions and structured tasks are paramount, a task-oriented leader may shine.

On the other hand, relationship-oriented leadership is deemed more suitable in moderately favorable situations. In scenarios where team cohesion, collaboration, and interpersonal relationships are critical, a leader who prioritizes building strong relationships with team members is likely to thrive. This style of leadership fosters trust and cooperation, which can be invaluable in achieving team goals.

Fiedler's Contingency Model underscores the importance of aligning leadership styles with the specific demands of the situation. It challenges the notion of a one-size-fits-all leadership approach and highlights the need for leaders to assess the favorableness of their environment and adapt their leadership behaviors accordingly.

Another influential contingency theory is the Hersey-Blanchard Situational Leadership Model, which emphasizes the importance of adapting leadership styles to the developmental level of team members. This model proposes that leaders should vary their leadership approach based on the competence and commitment of their followers. Leaders can adopt different styles, including directing, coaching, supporting, or delegating, depending on the readiness of their team members.

This model presents an intriguing approach to leadership, emphasizing the importance of tailoring your leadership style to the developmental level of your followers. Imagine you are leading a diverse team with varying levels of expertise and commitment to a particular task. The Situational Leadership Model provides you with a valuable toolkit for effectively guiding your team through different stages of development.

Imagine you are leading a team, and within that team, each member is at a different stage of readiness or development for a particular task. Some might be new to the task and need clear guidance, while others are more experienced and can manage more responsibility. This is where the Hersey-Blanchard model comes into play.

Developed by Paul Hersey and Ken Blanchard, this model is all about matching your leadership style to the needs of your team members. It recognizes that one-size-fits-all leadership does not work in today's dynamic workplaces.

The model categorizes leadership into four primary styles:

Directing: Think of this as the teaching mode. It is when your team members are new to a task, and they need your clear instructions and close supervision. You are guiding them step by step.

Coaching: As your team members gain some competence but still need guidance, coaching comes into play. You are still providing direction, but it is more of a collaborative approach. You are acting as a mentor, helping them develop their skills.

Supporting: Sometimes, your team members might be enthusiastic and committed, but they are not there in terms of skills. In this scenario, you are in a supporting role. You are encouraging them, giving them the confidence, they need, and providing recognition for their efforts.

Delegating: When your team members are both competent and committed, it is time to delegate. Here, you are stepping back and letting them take the lead. They have the skills and the motivation, so you trust them to get the job done.

The beauty of this model is that it recognizes that people are different, and their needs change depending on the task. It is about being flexible as a leader, knowing when to provide clear direction and when to step back and let your team shine.

By understanding and applying the Hersey-Blanchard model, you can become a more versatile and effective leader. You will be better equipped to guide your team to success, no matter what challenges or opportunities come your way.

Contingency theories, by acknowledging the dynamic interplay between leadership and situational variables, provide a more nuanced understanding of leadership effectiveness. They empower leaders to be flexible and responsive, making informed decisions about their leadership approach based on the specific circumstances they face. Contingency theories mark a pivotal departure from the traditional one-size-fits-all approach to leadership. They underscore the importance of adaptability and responsiveness in leadership. Instead of a fixed leadership style, these theories highlight the need for leaders to adjust their approach based on the specific context and the individuals they are leading. Situational factors, such as the complexity of the task, the skill level of team members, and the overall work environment, become critical determinants in selecting the most effective leadership style for a given situation.

Imagine you are in a leadership role, facing various projects with diverse challenges. In one scenario, you encounter a well-structured task, and your team members are seasoned professionals who require minimal guidance. Here, you may opt for a more hands-off, delegating style, entrusting your team's expertise.

Now, picture another scenario where you are dealing with a complex, high-stakes project, and your team consists of individuals who are new to the task. In such cases, they rely on you for clear guidance and support. This is when you pivot your leadership style, adopting a directing or coaching approach to provide the necessary structure and assistance.

These theories highlight a fundamental principle: effective leadership is not a rigid, one-dimensional concept. Instead, it is a dynamic process that hinges on the interplay between your leadership style and the specific demands of the situation. It is about recognizing that leadership is not just about you as a leader; it is about understanding the context and the unique needs of your team members. As we journey deeper into the realm of leadership theories, keep in mind that great leaders are those who can flexibly adapt to the ever-changing landscape of leadership challenges. Contingency theories remind us that effective leadership is not a one-size-fits-all formula; it is a dynamic interplay between the leader, the followers, and the context.

As we venture further into the realm of contemporary leadership theories, we arrive at the captivating concepts of transformational and transactional leadership. These ideas introduce a dynamic and influential dimension to the study of leadership.

At its very core, transformational leadership represents a profound shift in the traditional understanding of how leaders influence their teams. This concept, which emerged prominently through the groundbreaking work of James MacGregor Burns in his 1978 book "Leadership," offers a visionary perspective on leadership dynamics.

Transformational leaders, as envisioned by Burns, are not merely taskmasters or transactional managers. They are visionary inspirers who have a remarkable ability to stimulate their followers to achieve far more than they initially thought possible. These leaders possess a unique capacity to tap into the aspirations and motivations of their team members, igniting a sense of purpose and passion that transcends the ordinary.

Burns contrasts transformational leadership with transactional leadership, which he sees as a more conventional form of leadership focused on exchange and compliance. Transactional leaders operate within established systems of rewards and punishments, using a straightforward "give and take" approach to motivate their teams. In contrast, transformational leaders challenge the status quo, encouraging creativity and innovation while fostering a deep sense of commitment and loyalty among their followers.

At the heart of transformational leadership are four key components: idealized influence, inspirational motivation, intellectual stimulation, and individualized consideration. These elements collectively create a compelling leadership style that elevates both the leader and the followers to new heights of achievement and personal growth.

Idealized influence involves the leader serving as a role model, embodying the values and ethics that inspire others. Inspirational motivation entails creating a compelling vision of the future and inspiring commitment to that vision. Intellectual stimulation encourages followers to think creatively and critically, fostering a culture of innovation. Lastly, individualized consideration recognizes the unique needs and strengths of each team member, providing personalized support and guidance.

Transformational leadership's profound impact extends beyond immediate outcomes, leading to enhanced job satisfaction, increased organizational commitment, and improved overall performance. Its principles have reverberated through the fields of business, education, and beyond, leaving an indelible mark on contemporary leadership theory and practice.

Transactional leadership is a pragmatic approach to leadership that revolves around a clear exchange between the leader and their followers. This exchange is rooted in the concept of rewards and punishments, where leaders use incentives and consequences to encourage compliance with established goals, standards, and rules within an organization or team.

In a transactional leadership model, leaders set specific expectations and guidelines for their followers. They provide rewards, which can range from financial bonuses to recognition, when these expectations are met or exceeded. Conversely, there are consequences for failing to meet these expectations, which may include reprimands or other forms of disciplinary action.

While transactional leadership has its merits, particularly in contexts where tasks are routine, and the expectations are well-defined, it may not be the most effective approach in situations that demand innovation, creativity, and intrinsic motivation. This leadership style tends to focus on maintaining the status quo and ensuring that established processes are followed, but it may not necessarily inspire individuals to go beyond their prescribed duties.

In contrast to transactional leadership, transformational leadership represents a more profound and inspirational approach to leading teams and organizations. Transformational leaders are visionaries who transcend mere transactional exchanges and engage with their followers on a deeper, more meaningful level. They operate by appealing to the higher ideals and values of their team members, fostering an environment of growth and personal development.

At the heart of transformational leadership lies the ability to create a compelling vision of the future. Transformational leaders articulate a clear and inspiring vision that paints a vivid picture of what can be achieved. This vision serves as a beacon, guiding the actions and aspirations of the entire group. It instills a sense of purpose and direction, motivating individuals to strive for excellence and work collaboratively toward common goals.

Transformational leaders also set exceptionally grand expectations for their followers. They believe in the potential of their team members and challenge them to reach beyond their perceived limitations. By establishing ambitious goals, they encourage individuals to push their boundaries, fostering personal and professional growth.

Creativity and innovation are key components of transformational leadership. Leaders in this category not only welcome but actively promote innovative ideas and approaches. They recognize that progress often arises from innovative thinking and provide the support and encouragement necessary for creative problem-solving.

Crucially, transformational leaders rely less on external rewards and punishments and more on fostering a sense of intrinsic motivation and engagement among their followers. Rather than focusing on tangible incentives, they inspire individuals to find fulfillment and satisfaction in their work through a shared sense of purpose and accomplishment.

Understanding transformational leadership can provide valuable insights for leaders seeking to inspire and empower their teams to reach new heights. To truly grasp the essence of transformational leadership, it is valuable to examine real-life examples of leaders who have embodied this approach and left an enduring impact on history. One such iconic figure is Martin Luther King Jr., a man whose vision, charisma, and unwavering commitment ignited a transformative force within the civil rights movement in the United States.

Martin Luther King Jr.'s "I Have a Dream" speech is not merely a historical address; it stands as a testament to his profound transformational leadership. In that iconic moment on the steps of the Lincoln Memorial in 1963, King not only articulated a vision for change but also kindled a spark within the hearts of millions. His words resonated with the deep-seated aspirations of people from all walks of life, transcending racial boundaries and igniting a collective desire for a more just and equitable society.

At the core of King's transformational leadership was his ability to inspire. He possessed the unique gift of connecting with people on a deeply emotional and moral level. By appealing to their higher ideals and shared values, he evoked a sense of purpose and unity that transcended the immediate challenges of the civil rights struggle. His vision was not limited to the alleviation of racial injustice but extended to the broader aspiration of a society founded on equality and love.

Moreover, Martin Luther King Jr. set exceptionally high expectations for himself and those who followed his lead. He challenged individuals to rise above the prevailing norms of prejudice and discrimination, urging them to embody the principles of nonviolence and civil disobedience. His leadership demanded courage, resilience, and unwavering commitment to a cause larger than oneself.

King's transformative influence went beyond mere rhetoric; it inspired action. His leadership fostered a groundswell of activism and civic engagement, propelling the civil rights movement forward with remarkable momentum. Through peaceful protests, marches, and acts of civil disobedience, individuals across the nation became active participants in the struggle for justice.

Martin Luther King Jr.'s legacy as a transformational leader extends far beyond his lifetime. His ability to inspire change, unite diverse communities, and elevate the human spirit serves as a timeless example of the profound impact that transformational leadership can have on individuals and society. It underscores the enduring power of visionary leadership to bring about meaningful and lasting transformation.

Another exemplary illustration of transformational leadership can be found in the life and leadership of Nelson Mandela, a towering figure in the struggle against apartheid in South Africa. Mandela's journey from prisoner to president is a testament to his extraordinary ability to inspire, unite, and transform a nation.

Nelson Mandela's commitment to reconciliation and forgiveness, even after enduring 27 years of imprisonment, stands as a hallmark of his transformational leadership. Upon his release from prison in 1990, he could have chosen a path of vengeance and retaliation, given the profound injustices he and his fellow South Africans had suffered under apartheid. However, Mandela's vision was rooted in something far more profound – the healing of a deeply wounded nation and the forging of a new, inclusive South Africa.

Mandela's leadership was characterized by his unwavering belief in the power of forgiveness and reconciliation as instruments of change. He recognized that lasting transformation could only be achieved by transcending the bitterness and divisions of the past. His ability to convey this vision to a nation marked by racial strife was a testament to his exceptional communication skills and moral authority.

One of the most iconic moments in Mandela's leadership journey was his presidency, which began in 1994 after the first multiracial democratic elections in South Africa. During his presidency, he championed a policy of reconciliation, which included the Truth and Reconciliation Commission. This commission allowed victims and perpetrators of apartheid-era crimes to come forward, share their stories, and seek forgiveness. Mandela's leadership in implementing such a process demonstrated his commitment to healing the wounds of the past.

Mandela's leadership style also emphasized inclusivity and the importance of unity in diversity. He recognized the strength of South Africa's diversity and actively worked to build a nation where all races and ethnicities could coexist harmoniously. His presidency marked a significant departure from the divisions of apartheid, as he sought to create a more just, equal, and unified South Africa.

Nelson Mandela's transformational leadership was about more than just political change; it was about the profound transformation of hearts and minds. His ability to inspire hope, courage, and forgiveness in the face of adversity exemplified the highest ideals of leadership. Mandela's legacy lives on as a testament to the enduring power of transformational leadership to bring about reconciliation, unity, and lasting change.

Indeed, the examples of Martin Luther King Jr. and Nelson Mandela vividly illustrate the transformative potential of leadership that goes beyond the transactional, inspiring individuals and entire nations toward positive change.

As we transition into the realm of contemporary leadership theories, we find ourselves amidst a shift towards leadership approaches that prioritize ethics, values, and the well-being of individuals. Let us explore two prominent models that embody these principles: authentic leadership and servant leadership. These models represent a departure from earlier, more transactional approaches, and they underscore the growing recognition of the importance of genuine, people-centric leadership in today's complex and interconnected world.

Authentic leadership, a model gaining prominence in contemporary leadership discussions, is centered on the concept of leaders being true to themselves and maintaining transparency in their actions and decisions. At its core, authentic leadership requires self-awareness, the capacity for self-regulation, and a commitment to staying aligned with one's values and principles. Leaders who embrace this approach are regarded as credible and trustworthy, attributes that arise from their commitment to leading with integrity and remaining faithful to their core beliefs. This emphasis on authenticity reflects the growing recognition of the importance of personal integrity and genuine interactions in leadership practices today.

Authentic leadership acknowledges that leaders, like all individuals, are fallible. It encourages leaders to exhibit vulnerability and humility, thus fostering trust and open communication within their teams. Leaders who embrace authentic leadership inspire their followers to also embrace their authentic selves, cultivating an environment characterized by honesty and genuineness. In this context, authenticity is not just a personal trait but a leadership philosophy that promotes self-awareness, emotional intelligence, and ethical behavior. It underscores the idea that leaders who are true to themselves can lead others more effectively by building authentic and trusting relationships.

Servant leadership represents a departure from traditional leadership paradigms by inverting the hierarchy. In this model, leaders are positioned as servants to their followers, prioritizing the needs of their team members. The primary objective of a servant leader is to empower and support their followers in achieving their goals and personal development. This leadership style is characterized by humility, empathy, and a strong commitment to the well-being of others. It fosters a culture of collaboration, trust, and mutual respect within organizations. Servant leaders are not driven by personal ambition or the desire for power; instead, they find fulfillment in serving others and helping them reach their full potential. This approach has gained traction in contemporary leadership discussions, emphasizing the importance of a leader's ethical and moral responsibilities to their team members and society.

In practice, servant leaders embody empathy and active listening, striving to genuinely understand the perspectives and needs of their followers. They prioritize the personal growth and development of both them and their team members, fostering an environment of continuous improvement. This approach promotes collaboration and teamwork, often resulting in higher job satisfaction and enhanced organizational performance. Servant leadership aligns with the values of ethical and socially responsible leadership, emphasizing the broader impact of leadership on individuals, organizations, and society. It underscores the idea that leadership should extend beyond personal gain and power, focusing instead on making a positive difference in the lives of others.

What unites these contemporary leadership theories is their unwavering commitment to ethical and values-based leadership. Leaders who embrace these approaches prioritize principles like honesty, compassion, and fairness in their decision-making processes. They understand the significance of making choices that not only benefit the organization but also extend their positive impact to employees and the larger community. These leadership models underscore the idea that leadership is not just about achieving organizational objectives but also about fostering a culture of responsibility, empathy, and social consciousness.

The transition towards ethical and values-based leadership in the modern era is indicative of a heightened awareness regarding leadership's influence on individuals and society at large. This shift acknowledges that leadership encompasses more than just the attainment of organizational objectives; it is equally about achieving them in a manner that resonates with moral and ethical principles. Leaders today are increasingly being called upon not only to drive performance and profits but also to uphold a sense of responsibility, fairness, and social consciousness in their actions. As we proceed in our exploration of contemporary leadership theories, we will gain a deeper understanding of how these principles are put into practice and their profound implications for leadership in our intricate and interconnected world.

Today, leaders are expected to wear many hats, and adaptability is at the forefront. The pace of change is relentless, so leaders must be ready to pivot and adjust their strategies on the fly. Inclusivity is another vital aspect; leaders are now tasked with creating diverse and inclusive environments where everyone's voice is heard. Transparency has become non-negotiable in this digital age, as stakeholders demand openness and honesty. Ethical leadership is a must; leaders are expected to uphold high moral standards in all their actions. Digital literacy is essential too, given the technology-driven nature of our world. Having a global perspective is increasingly important, as leaders deal with diverse cultures and international markets. Environmental and social responsibility is on the rise, with leaders needing to consider the impact of their decisions on the planet and society. Empathy and emotional intelligence are highly valued, as they foster strong relationships. Leaders are also expected to foster innovation, promote resilience, adapt to remote leadership demands, commit to lifelong learning, and excel in crisis management. These evolving expectations reflect the multifaceted nature of leadership in the 21st century and meeting them is crucial for effective leadership in our interconnected world.

Throughout history, leadership has undergone significant changes in its conceptualization and practice. In ancient civilizations like Egypt, Mesopotamia, and China, leadership was often characterized by hierarchical structures and an authoritarian style. Leaders held divine or monarchic authority, and their rule was unquestioned. The emphasis was on maintaining order and control.

As we moved forward in time, we encounter the philosophical foundations of leadership in ancient Greece and Rome. Thinkers like Plato, Aristotle, and Cicero introduced ideas that emphasized virtue and ethics in leadership. This marked a shift towards a more philosophical and values-based approach to leadership.

The Industrial Era brought forth theories like the Great Man Theory and Trait Theory, which suggested that leadership was an innate quality possessed by a select few individuals. These theories focused on identifying specific traits or characteristics that made a leader. However, they had limitations and were criticized for oversimplifying the complex nature of leadership.

In the Modern Era, behavioral theories emerged, emphasizing leadership actions and behaviors over traits. The Ohio State and University of Michigan studies, for example, explored leader behavior and its impact on group dynamics and productivity. This shift marked a move away from the notion that leaders were born and towards the idea that leadership could be learned and developed.

Contingency theories, such as Fiedler's Contingency Model and Hersey-Blanchard's Situational Leadership Model, considered situational factors that influenced leadership effectiveness. These theories highlighted that there was no one-size-fits-all leadership style and that leaders needed to adapt their approach based on the circumstances.

Transformational and transactional leadership theories emerged, with James MacGregor Burns introducing the concept of transformational leadership. This approach emphasizes inspiring and motivating followers through a shared vision and values. Transformational leaders aimed to bring about meaningful change and improvement.

In the contemporary landscape, recent leadership theories, including authentic leadership and servant leadership, reflect a shift towards ethical, values-based, and people-centric approaches. Authentic leaders prioritize self-awareness and transparency, while servant leaders focus on serving the needs of their team members.

Throughout this journey, we have witnessed a democratization of leadership and an increasing recognition of the importance of followers in the leadership process. Leadership is no longer solely about top-down authority; it involves collaboration, communication, and adaptability. In the modern era, leaders are expected to engage with and empower their teams, fostering a more inclusive and participatory approach to leadership.

Understanding these shifts in leadership models and theories provides valuable insights into the dynamic nature of leadership. It illustrates how leadership has evolved from rigid and authoritarian structures to more flexible and inclusive paradigms, where leaders are expected to embody values, adapt to situations, and collaborate with their followers. This evolution reflects the changing needs and expectations of organizations and society.

Amidst the ever-evolving landscape of leadership, certain core principles and qualities have remained constant, transcending time and cultural boundaries. These enduring elements of leadership continue to be relevant and essential in shaping effective leaders.

One of the timeless qualities of leadership is integrity. Integrity encompasses honesty, ethics, and moral principles. Leaders who act with integrity inspire trust and confidence in their followers. Whether in ancient Egypt, classical Greece, or the modern era, leaders who displayed unwavering integrity were often revered and respected. This principle of ethical conduct has consistently defined great leaders throughout history.

Another enduring element is vision. Effective leaders possess a clear and compelling vision that guides their actions and inspires others. Whether it was the pharaohs of Egypt envisioning a prosperous kingdom or contemporary leaders charting the course for a global organization, a strong vision serves as a beacon, rallying individuals towards a common goal. Visionary leaders are often transformative, leaving a lasting impact on their organizations and society.

Adaptability is a quality that has persisted as a hallmark of leadership. Leaders who can adjust to changing circumstances and remain resilient in the face of challenges have consistently demonstrated their effectiveness. This adaptability has been evident in leaders from various eras, including those who navigated the complexities of ancient city-states, the industrial revolution, or the fast-paced technological advancements of the modern world.

While leadership models and theories have evolved over time, these fundamental leadership principles endure. Integrity, vision, and adaptability are not bound by historical context or cultural differences. They remain the cornerstones of effective leadership, providing a stable foundation upon which leaders can build and adapt their leadership styles to meet the demands of the ever-changing world. As we explore the rich history of leadership, we recognize that these enduring elements serve as a timeless guide for leaders seeking to make a positive impact in their respective fields and eras.

As we bring this chapter to a close, we have embarked on a fascinating journey through the annals of history to explore the evolution of leadership. We have witnessed how leadership models and theories have shifted and adapted in response to the evolving needs of societies and organizations. Yet, amidst the transformations, we have uncovered the enduring qualities and principles that consistently characterize effective leadership in the modern world of business.

The pages of history have revealed that leadership is not a static concept but a dynamic force that responds to the challenges and opportunities of each era. The leadership landscape has witnessed the divine authority of ancient Egypt, the philosophical wisdom of classical antiquity, the great men of the industrial era, and the behavioral and contingent approaches of the modern age. Through it all, integrity, vision, and adaptability have remained unwavering touchstones of leadership excellence.

As we transition to the following chapters, we will delve deeper into these timeless qualities and explore how they apply to the leadership demands of today's dynamic and complex business environment. The journey of leadership continues, and our exploration of its facets will equip you with the knowledge and insights needed to thrive as a leader in the contemporary world

Chapter 3

Core Qualities of Effective Leaders

"Effective leaders, guided by their core values and a vision
for positive change, illuminates the path to success not
only for themselves, but for their teams."

- Joel R. Klemmer

Chapter 3
Core Qualities of Effective Leaders

Let us explore the fundamental qualities that distinguish effective leaders in the modern business world. These core qualities serve as the bedrock of leadership excellence, shaping the actions and decisions of leaders. We will delve into essential traits such as vision, empathy, integrity, and resilience, and examine how they contribute to the success of leaders.

Vision is like a North Star, guiding leaders, and their teams toward a shared and inspiring future. It is not just a lofty idea; it is a powerful force that shapes the course of organizations and ignites the spirit of teams.

Imagine a leader who can vividly paint a picture of what lies ahead, a future filled with possibilities and purpose. This vision acts as a compass, providing direction in a complex and ever-changing world. It clarifies not just the "what" but also the "why" of the journey. Without this guiding light, individuals and teams may wander aimlessly, unsure of their destination or the significance of their efforts.

But vision does more than point the way; it brings people together. When a leader communicates a compelling vision, it unites individuals under a common purpose. This alignment is vital for achieving collective goals and harnessing the collective power of a group. It fosters a sense of belonging and shared identity, something that is deeply motivating.

This motivation, stemming from a shared vision, can be transformative. It has the potential to kindle passion and enthusiasm within teams. When people see the bigger picture and understand how their contributions fit into the grander scheme, they become more engaged and willing to invest their energy and creativity.

Furthermore, a vision does not just focus on the status quo; it calls for progress and innovation. Effective leaders often include a commitment to continuous improvement within their vision. This emphasis on growth encourages individuals to think beyond boundaries, explore new horizons, and seek innovative solutions to challenges.

But one of the most remarkable aspects of a vision is its ability to provide resilience. In the face of adversity or setbacks, a well-crafted vision serves as a source of strength and determination. It reminds individuals of the goal, helping them persevere through difficult times. It kindles hope, which can be a powerful force during tough moments.

Vision is not a mere concept; it is a dynamic force that can transform individuals, teams, and organizations. It is not about empty words but about aligning actions with aspirations. When a leader's vision is rooted in authenticity and aligned with their core values, it becomes a beacon of credibility and trust.

Moreover, a vision is not rigid; it is adaptable. It should be able to flex and evolve as circumstances change, all while staying true to its core purpose. A leader who can navigate this balance between steadfastness and adaptability harnesses the true power of vision.

So, as we explore the multifaceted realm of leadership, remember that vision is more than a buzzword; it is a cornerstone. It is a quality that leaders can cultivate, refine, and utilize to drive change, inspire teams, and achieve remarkable outcomes.

Picture this: a team of individuals, each with their unique skills and perspectives, coming together under the banner of a well-articulated vision. It is akin to an orchestra, with each member playing their part in harmony to create a beautiful symphony.

In the world of leadership, this harmonization is achieved through the power of vision. When a leader communicates a vision that resonates with team members, it transforms a group of individuals into a cohesive unit. Suddenly, they are not just working side by side; they are working towards a shared destiny.

This sense of shared destiny is a potent motivator. It taps into the human desire for purpose and meaning. When people understand that their work has a broader significance and contributes to something larger than themselves, it infuses their efforts with passion and dedication. It is as if they have found a reason to pour their hearts and souls into what they do.

A compelling vision acts as a source of inspiration during both ordinary days and challenging times. On regular days, it keeps the team focused and driven. It reminds them of the bigger picture when the details might seem overwhelming. It is a North Star that guides their daily actions and decisions, ensuring they stay on course.

In times of adversity, a powerful vision becomes a source of resilience. When setbacks occur, and obstacles loom large, the vision serves as a reminder of the goal. It fuels determination and perseverance. It encourages team members to rise above adversity, knowing that their collective efforts are building toward something significant.

Moreover, a compelling vision fosters a sense of belonging. It unites individuals from diverse backgrounds and experiences, forging a shared identity within the team. This sense of unity is not to be underestimated; it promotes collaboration, trust, and mutual support. It is the glue that holds the team together.

But a vision is not a one-time proclamation. Effective leaders continuously nurture and reinforce the vision. They keep it alive through regular communication, reminding the team of their shared purpose. This ongoing dialogue reinforces the importance of the vision, embedding it deep within the team's culture.

Furthermore, a visionary leader understands that a vision is not carved in stone. It must be adaptable to changing circumstances. As the external environment evolves, so too may the vision. The leader guides this evolution, ensuring the vision remains relevant and inspiring.

A compelling vision is like a magnetic force, drawing individuals together, infusing their efforts with meaning, and propelling them toward shared aspirations. It is a dynamic and transformative quality that effective leaders cultivate and harness to achieve remarkable outcomes. As we journey further into the world of leadership, we will continue to explore how vision interplays with other essential qualities, painting a comprehensive portrait of leadership excellence.

The role of vision as a guiding force cannot be overstated. Think of it as the captain of a ship charting a course through uncharted waters. The captain relies on navigational tools, maps, and a clear destination to steer the ship in the right direction. Similarly, a leader uses their vision as the compass that points the way forward.

In organizations, this compass aligns everyone's efforts. It answers essential questions: Where are we headed? What do we stand for? How do we want to get there? These questions may seem simple, but their answers are the building blocks of a successful journey.

A well-articulated vision does not just provide a destination; it also sets the tone for the journey itself. It establishes the values and principles that will guide every decision, every action. It is a beacon that reminds everyone of the organization's core beliefs, ensuring that even during change, certain things remain constant.

Imagine a sports team with a vision of becoming champions. This vision not only defines the goal of winning but also the values that will underpin their journey—values like teamwork, discipline, and perseverance. These values become the team's identity, shaping their interactions, practices, and games.

Moreover, a clear vision serves as a filter for decision-making. When faced with choices, leaders and team members can refer to the vision to evaluate which option aligns best with their long-term goals. It is a decision-making tool that simplifies complex choices by providing a clear framework.

A vision serves as a touchstone for every action, big or small. It is a constant reminder of the desired destination and the path to get there. This alignment is particularly critical in times of change or uncertainty when it is easy to lose one's way.

But a vision is not a mere document tucked away in a drawer. Effective leaders breathe life into their vision by consistently communicating it and integrating it into the organizational culture. They infuse it into the daily conversations, making it a part of the team's collective consciousness.

Furthermore, a visionary leader understands that a vision should not be rigid. It must be adaptable to changing circumstances. The leader knows when to recalibrate the compass, ensuring that the organization remains on course, even in turbulent seas.

So, in the grand tapestry of leadership, vision is the loom that weaves together purpose, direction, values, and decision-making. It is the force that propels organizations and teams toward their desired futures. As we delve deeper into leadership, we will continue to explore how vision intertwines with other essential qualities, painting a more comprehensive picture of leadership excellence.

Visionary leaders throughout history have made an indelible impact on their organizations and industries by crafting and executing compelling visions that inspired positive change. These leaders envisioned a brighter future, communicated their dreams effectively, and took decisive actions to turn their visions into reality.

Steve Jobs' vision, encapsulated in his statement "To make a contribution to the world by making tools for the mind that advance humankind," demonstrates the transformative power of visionary thinking. His influence extended far beyond the realm of technology, and his legacy continues to shape industries and user experiences. His visionary approach was not merely about selling products; it was about empowering individuals through innovation.

What is particularly compelling about Steve Jobs is his communication and execution prowess. Effective communication of a vision is as crucial as the vision itself. Jobs was an expert communicator, able to convey complex technological concepts in an understandable and engaging manner. His keynote presentations were legendary, captivating audiences with passion and clarity.

Furthermore, Jobs' firsthand approach ensured that every detail, from hardware design to software functionality, aligned seamlessly with his vision. This commitment to execution played a pivotal role in turning his vision into reality and achieving transformative results.

The legacy of Steve Jobs reminds us that visionary leadership is not confined to one industry or era. It serves as a beacon, guiding leaders in diverse fields to embrace visionary thinking, communicate their vision effectively, and execute it with unwavering dedication. As we explore the multifaceted dimensions of leadership, the power of vision remains a constant source of inspiration and guidance for leaders seeking to make a lasting impact.

Elon Musk, another visionary leader of our time, offers a compelling example of how a clear vision can transform industries and push the boundaries of human achievement. His vision statement, "To accelerate the world's transition to sustainable energy," underscores his commitment to addressing pressing global challenges.

Musk's impact on the automotive and aerospace sectors is profound. Through Tesla, he revolutionized the automobile industry by popularizing electric vehicles, making sustainable transportation a reality for millions. His audacious goal to make space travel more accessible through SpaceX has reignited interest in space exploration and redefined possibilities beyond Earth.

When it comes to communication and execution, Musk is known for his audacity and bold statements. He does not shy away from setting ambitious goals that align with his vision. His relentless pursuit of innovation and willingness to take calculated risks have been pivotal in driving his companies forward.

Musk's approach underscores that visionary leadership is not just about lofty ideas; it is about taking concrete actions to turn those ideas into reality. His commitment to sustainable energy and space exploration displays the transformative potential of visionary thinking in today's world.

As we explore the dynamics of visionary leadership, these real-life examples like Steve Jobs and Elon Musk illustrate how leaders who dare to envision a better future can inspire change, push boundaries, and leave a lasting impact on the world. Their stories serve as a testament to the enduring power of a compelling vision.

Another iconic figure in the realm of visionary leadership is Mahatma Gandhi, whose vision transcended borders and inspired a nation to reclaim its independence from British colonial rule. Gandhi's vision statement was simple yet profound: he aimed to lead India to freedom through nonviolent resistance, which he termed Satyagraha.

The impact of Gandhi's vision on India's struggle for independence is immeasurable. His unwavering commitment to justice and his embodiment of nonviolence inspired millions to unite against oppression. His vision became a rallying point for people from all walks of life, leading to India's liberation in 1947.

Gandhi's approach to communication and execution of his vision was deeply rooted in his actions. He lived out his principles of nonviolence, self-reliance, and simplicity, setting an example for others to follow. His speeches and writings served as a source of inspiration and guidance, galvanizing a diverse population in their pursuit of freedom. Notably, Gandhi's leadership was marked by humility and inclusivity, creating a sense of unity among the masses.

The story of Mahatma Gandhi underscores the transformative power of a visionary leader who can mobilize a nation through nonviolence and unwavering commitment to justice. His life and legacy serve as a testament to the enduring impact of visionary leadership in the face of formidable challenges.

Empathy, at its core, is a vital leadership trait that entails the capacity to understand and share the feelings and perspectives of others. It goes beyond sympathy, as it involves truly connecting with others on an emotional level, allowing leaders to grasp their concerns, needs, and motivations. Such a genuine connection forms the bedrock of trust and rapport within teams and organizations.

Empathy is like a bridge that connects leaders with their team members on a deeper level. It is not just about acknowledging someone's emotions; it is about genuinely feeling and understanding those emotions. When leaders can step into the shoes of their team members, it creates a sense of trust and openness that is invaluable in any organization.

Think about it this way: when you know that your leader cares about your well-being and genuinely understands your perspective, you are more likely to be motivated, engaged, and committed to your work. This not only boosts individual performance but also contributes to the overall success of the team and organization.

Moreover, empathy is not just a one-way street. It is also about leaders being open to feedback, listening actively, and showing that they value the input of their team members. In this way, empathy becomes a two-way channel for effective communication and collaboration.

Emotional intelligence, often mentioned in the context of empathy, is another critical aspect of leadership. Leaders with high emotional intelligence can navigate the complex landscape of human emotions, which is essential for resolving conflicts, making informed decisions, and creating a positive work environment.

Trust is the glue that holds a team together and allows it to function cohesively. Empathy acts as a catalyst for building this trust by creating a safe and supportive environment where team members feel seen, heard, and valued.

Imagine a workplace where your leader not only listens to your concerns but also takes the time to understand your perspective and emotions. In such an environment, you are more likely to feel secure and comfortable sharing your thoughts and ideas openly. This level of trust promotes open communication, which is essential for effective teamwork and problem-solving.

When team members trust their leader's intentions and believe that their leader genuinely cares about their well-being, they become more committed to their work and the team's goals. This commitment translates into higher levels of engagement and productivity. People are more willing to go the extra mile when they know their contributions are recognized and valued.

Moreover, empathy plays a pivotal role in conflict resolution. In any team, conflicts are bound to arise from time to time. An empathetic leader can navigate these conflicts with finesse by understanding the underlying emotions and concerns of those involved. This understanding enables the leader to find solutions that address the root causes of the conflict and promote reconciliation.

Empathy also contributes to a positive organizational culture. When leaders prioritize empathy, it sets a tone for the entire organization. Team members are more likely to emulate empathetic behavior, creating a culture of support, inclusion, and mutual respect.

This, in turn, attracts and retains top talent, as people are drawn to organizations where they feel valued and understood.

The constructive collaboration between empathy and emotional intelligence is a remarkable aspect of effective leadership. When leaders have a strong grasp of their own emotions and can empathize with the emotions of others, they become adept at managing relationships and fostering a positive workplace atmosphere.

Consider a leader who possesses high emotional intelligence. They not only understand their own emotional triggers and responses but also can recognize when their team members are experiencing certain emotions. This heightened awareness allows them to respond appropriately, offering support and understanding when team members are facing challenges or celebrating with them during moments of success.

Empathy becomes a bridge that connects leaders with their teams on an emotional level. It enhances communication and strengthens relationships, as team members feel heard, valued, and supported. When employees know that their leader is attuned to their emotional well-being, they are more likely to voice their concerns, seek guidance, and collaborate effectively.

Additionally, empathy plays a pivotal role in conflict resolution. Conflicts can arise in any workplace, and leaders who are empathetic are better equipped to oversee these situations with finesse. They can put themselves in the shoes of those involved in the conflict, understanding their perspectives and emotions. This understanding allows for more effective mediation and the development of solutions that address the root causes of the conflict.

Empathetic leaders also excel at providing constructive feedback. Rather than delivering feedback in a cold or critical manner, they approach it with sensitivity and consideration for the individual's feelings. This approach makes feedback more actionable and less threatening, encouraging team members to embrace growth and development.

Satya Nadella's leadership at Microsoft is a testament to the transformative power of empathy in the corporate world. When he took the reins as CEO, he inherited a company facing numerous challenges and needed to chart a new course. Recognizing the significance of empathy, he made it a central pillar of his leadership philosophy.

Nadella understood that for Microsoft to thrive in the rapidly evolving tech landscape, it needed to foster a culture of innovation, collaboration, and inclusivity. His empathetic leadership style emphasized the importance of listening to employees, understanding their perspectives, and valuing their contributions.

One of the key changes Nadella implemented was a shift away from the company's previous "know-it-all" culture to a "learn-it-all" culture. This change encouraged employees to embrace a growth mindset, be open to learning from failures, and continuously adapt to new challenges. By doing so, Nadella not only promoted empathy within the organization but also reinforced the idea that every employee's voice mattered.

Nadella's approach to empathy extended beyond the walls of Microsoft. He recognized the broader social and ethical responsibilities of the company. Under his leadership, Microsoft has committed to addressing important societal issues, such as accessibility, environmental sustainability, and digital inclusion. These initiatives reflect Nadella's empathetic leadership, as they prioritize the well-being of not only Microsoft's employees and customers but also the communities and world at large.

The impact of Nadella's empathetic leadership on Microsoft's success has been profound. The company's resurgence as an innovation powerhouse, particularly in cloud computing, is a testament to the positive changes he instilled. Microsoft's market value has soared, and it continues to be a leader in the tech industry.

Satya Nadella's journey as a leader underscores that empathy is not just a soft skill but a strategic imperative. It has the potential to drive innovation, foster employee engagement, and lead to organizational excellence. As we continue to explore empathy in leadership, we will delve into more examples and practical strategies for harnessing its power in various leadership contexts.

Yvon Chouinard's leadership journey with Patagonia is a compelling illustration of how empathy can be a catalyst for sustainable success in the corporate world. Chouinard, an enthusiastic outdoors person and environmentalist, founded Patagonia with a mission that extended far beyond just making profits. His empathetic approach to leadership is deeply intertwined with his commitment to environmental sustainability, social responsibility, and the well-being of both his employees and the planet.

One of the standout aspects of Chouinard's empathetic leadership is his genuine concern for the work-life balance of his employees. He understood the importance of creating an environment where employees could thrive both personally and professionally. To achieve this, he introduced progressive policies like flexible work hours and on-site childcare facilities, which provided practical support for his employees' daily lives.

Chouinard's empathy is not limited to his employees; it extends to the broader community and the environment. Patagonia's steadfast commitment to sustainability and environmental responsibility reflects his empathetic values. Under his leadership, the company has consistently advocated for environmental causes, supported grassroots environmental organizations, and worked to minimize its own ecological footprint.

The alignment between Chouinard's empathetic leadership and Patagonia's mission has had a profound impact on the company's success. The empathetic culture he cultivated within Patagonia has attracted like-minded and dedicated employees who share his values. This shared sense of purpose and empathy for the environment has, in turn, fostered a loyal customer base that values Patagonia not just for its products but for its commitment to sustainability and ethical business practices.

Chouinard's empathetic leadership has created a virtuous cycle where employees, customers, and the company itself all benefit from a shared sense of empathy and purpose. This example demonstrates that empathy can be a powerful force for good in the business world, driving success and positive impact simultaneously.

Indra Nooyi's leadership journey at PepsiCo provides a remarkable example of how empathy and inclusivity can drive success in the corporate world. As the former CEO of the multinational food and beverage giant, Nooyi embraced an empathetic and inclusive leadership style that left a lasting impact on the company and its stakeholders.

One of the standout qualities of Nooyi's leadership was her unwavering commitment to diversity and inclusion. She recognized that a diverse workforce and customer base required leaders to approach their roles with a deep sense of empathy. Nooyi understood that to understand the needs and perspectives of a diverse array of employees and consumers, empathy had to be at the core of her leadership philosophy.

Under Nooyi's guidance, PepsiCo actively promoted diversity and inclusion within its ranks. This commitment went beyond mere rhetoric; it translated into tangible initiatives and policies that fostered an inclusive workplace culture. Nooyi understood that an inclusive environment, where employees felt valued and heard, was essential not only for ethical reasons but also for business success.

Nooyi's empathetic leadership style had a cascading effect throughout the organization. It improved employee morale, engagement, and retention. When employees feel that their leaders genuinely care about their well-being and perspectives, they are more likely to be motivated and committed to their work. This, in turn, translated into positive business outcomes for PepsiCo.

PepsiCo's global success during Nooyi's tenure as CEO can be attributed, in part, to her empathetic and inclusive leadership style. It allowed the company to connect with a diverse customer base on a more profound level, understanding their preferences and needs. By fostering inclusivity within the organization, PepsiCo also attracted and retained talent from various backgrounds, bringing diverse perspectives to the table and enhancing innovation and decision-making.

Indra Nooyi's leadership at PepsiCo exemplifies the transformative power of empathy and inclusivity in the corporate world. Her empathetic approach not only improved the workplace culture and employee satisfaction but also contributed significantly to the company's global success. This example underscores the importance of empathy as a core leadership trait and its potential to drive positive outcomes for organizations and their stakeholders. As we continue to explore the role of empathy in leadership, we will uncover additional insights and strategies for cultivating empathy in diverse leadership contexts.

These examples underscore how empathy is not just a theoretical concept but a practical and powerful leadership trait. These leaders actively cultivated empathy within their organizations, creating workplaces where employees felt valued, motivated, and empowered. They demonstrate that empathy is not a sign of weakness but a strength that drives positive change and fosters a culture of trust and collaboration.

Integrity, often regarded as the essence of ethical leadership, is not merely a desirable trait; it serves as the very foundation upon which trust, and respect are constructed. It encompasses far more than just honesty; it encapsulates a steadfast commitment to a set of moral and ethical principles that not only guide one's actions but also define the character of a leader.

In the intricate realm of leadership, integrity emerges as a linchpin that wields the power to establish, sustain, or shatter trust among team members, stakeholders, and the broader community. When individuals perceive their leaders as individuals of unwavering principle and truthfulness, the seeds of trust and faith take root. These seeds germinate into loyalty, commitment, and a willingness to be guided and led. The influence of integrity extends beyond the immediate sphere of leadership; it ripples through the fabric of relationships, teams, and organizations, shaping their collective identity and reputation.

Furthermore, integrity extends its reach far beyond the confines of the workplace. It casts a long shadow over an organization's standing and reputation in the eyes of the public. Leaders who place ethical conduct and transparent decision-making at the forefront of their leadership not only foster an environment of trust but also contribute to the cultivation of a positive organizational image. This can yield tangible benefits, including increased customer loyalty, elevated stakeholder confidence, and a competitive edge within the market landscape.

The concept of integrity transcends individual actions and radiates throughout the organizational culture, becoming an integral part of an institution's DNA. When integrity is firmly entrenched in an organization's core values and behaviors, it reverberates as a guiding principle for ethical conduct at all echelons. This resonant harmony of values and actions establishes a harmonious and ethical environment, nurturing trust, and respect both within and beyond the organization's boundaries.

The far-reaching impact of an organization's integrity-infused culture is profound. It manifests itself as a profound and enduring influence on the organization's reputation, casting a positive light that beckons customers, partners, and top talent to align themselves with an entity known for its resolute dedication to moral rectitude. Integrity acts as a magnetic force, drawing stakeholders who seek to associate with an organization that consistently chooses the path of righteousness, reinforcing the belief that doing what is right is not just an aspiration but a way of life.

In this light, integrity emerges as an invaluable asset that can enhance an organization's competitiveness, bolster its market position, and engender a sense of pride and commitment among its employees. It is a beacon that illuminates the path to ethical leadership and underlines the interconnectedness of personal and organizational integrity. As we continue our exploration, we will delve into the lives of leaders who personified unwavering integrity, navigating complex ethical challenges with unwavering commitment, and leaving an indelible mark on the landscape of leadership.

Mother Teresa, in an extraordinary manner, upheld her unwavering values amid challenging circumstances. The slums of Calcutta, where Mother Teresa devoted her life to helping the destitute and suffering, presented a staggering ethical challenge. Confronted with limited resources and overwhelming poverty, she encountered the daunting task of deciding how to allocate these resources in a way that would have the most significant impact on those in dire need.

Imagine the weight of such a responsibility: choosing who among the countless impoverished individuals would receive food, shelter, and medical care. It was a moral dilemma of immense proportions, one that could have easily left many feeling helpless or paralyzed by the enormity of the suffering around them.

However, Mother Teresa's response was nothing short of remarkable. At the heart of her decision-making process was an unshakable commitment to her values, particularly the belief that every human life is sacred and deserving of dignity and compassion. This foundational principle served as her guiding light in the darkest and most challenging moments.

In the face of resource scarcity, she refused to compromise on her deeply held beliefs. Instead, she channeled her unwavering commitment into tireless efforts to provide sustenance, shelter, and medical attention to those in need. Her approach was characterized not only by practical assistance but also by a profound spiritual and ethical dedication to the well-being of others.

Mother Teresa's actions transcended mere charity; they were an embodiment of her core values. They reflected an unyielding belief in the sanctity of every human life, regardless of their circumstances. Her life's work became a testament to the incredible impact that one individual, driven by unwavering integrity and compassion, can have on the lives of countless others.

Her legacy continues to shine brightly as a beacon of hope and inspiration, reminding us that even in the face of insurmountable ethical dilemmas, it is possible to navigate a path guided by unshakable values. Mother Teresa's example challenges us all to examine our own values and the depths of our commitment to them in our leadership and everyday lives.

Eleanor Roosevelt provided a remarkable journey as the United States' First Lady and her subsequent role as a prominent human rights advocate. Eleanor Roosevelt was no stranger to controversy and opposition, especially when advocating for civil rights, women's rights, and refugee assistance during the tumultuous era of World War II.

As the First Lady of the United States, Eleanor Roosevelt faced an ethical dilemma that was as complex as it was significant. She recognized the profound injustices of racial segregation and discrimination that permeated American society. With an unwavering commitment to equality and justice, she felt compelled to use her position and influence to advocate for civil rights, even when it meant challenging the status quo and confronting powerful political forces that vehemently opposed such changes.

In the face of resistance and criticism, Eleanor Roosevelt stood firmly by her values. She believed in the inherent worth and dignity of every individual, regardless of their race or gender, and she was resolute in her belief that the United States could and should do better in upholding these principles. Her commitment to social and political change extended far beyond rhetoric; she took concrete actions to advance the causes she held dear.

During World War II, she confronted the ethical dilemma of addressing the plight of refugees fleeing the horrors of war and persecution. In the face of widespread public opinion against accepting refugees, Eleanor Roosevelt advocated passionately for providing refuge and assistance to those in desperate need. She saw the ethical imperative of offering compassion and support to those who had lost everything.

Eleanor Roosevelt's ethical compass guided her through these turbulent times. Her actions were not driven by political expediency but by a deep-seated commitment to her values. She used her platform and influence to bring about positive change, even when it was met with resistance.

One of the crowning achievements of her life's work was her instrumental role in drafting the Universal Declaration of Human Rights. This landmark document, adopted by the United Nations in 1948, remains a touchstone for the protection and promotion of human rights worldwide. Eleanor Roosevelt's unwavering dedication to human rights, even in the face of formidable ethical dilemmas, left an indelible mark on the world and continues to inspire leaders and advocates for justice and equality to this day.

Her legacy reminds us that ethical leadership is not defined by avoiding dilemmas but by confronting them with courage, integrity, and an unyielding commitment to the values that shape a more just and compassionate world. Eleanor Roosevelt's life and work serve as a powerful testament to the enduring impact of ethical leadership in even the most challenging of circumstances.

Strategic Synergy

Winston Churchill during World War II offers us a profound glimpse into the complexities of leadership in times of conflict and crisis. Churchill, as the Prime Minister of the United Kingdom, was tasked with making decisions that carried immense ethical weight, particularly in the context of military strategy and the targeting of civilian areas in Nazi-occupied Europe.

One of the most agonizing ethical dilemmas Churchill faced was the decision to engage in strategic bombing campaigns that targeted industrial and civilian areas in Nazi-occupied Europe. The bombings were intended to weaken the Nazi war machine and disrupt the German economy but often resulted in civilian casualties and extensive destruction.

In grappling with this dilemma, Churchill had to weigh the moral and strategic imperatives of his decisions. On one hand, he understood the horrific consequences of war and the tragic loss of innocent lives. On the other hand, he believed that defeating Nazi tyranny and preserving the democratic values of freedom and justice were paramount. He saw these values as worth defending at any cost, and he was resolute in his determination to do so.

Churchill's integrity shone through in his unwavering commitment to the larger principles of liberty and human rights. He believed that the Allied cause, which aimed to confront and defeat the oppressive Nazi regime, was a just and ethical one. While facing difficult choices and ethical dilemmas, Churchill remained steadfast in his conviction that the preservation of freedom and justice for future generations was a cause worth the sacrifices and tough decisions.

His leadership during World War II, marked by his principled stance and commitment to democratic values, not only played a pivotal role in the Allied victory but also left an enduring legacy of compassion, justice, and freedom. Churchill's ethical leadership in the face of profound ethical dilemmas serves as a testament to the enduring power of integrity and the ability of leaders to make principled choices even in the most challenging circumstances.

These three leaders exemplify unwavering integrity by making principled choices in the face of ethical dilemmas, staying true to their values, and leaving a legacy of compassion, justice, and freedom.

Resilience, at its core, is the remarkable ability to bounce back from adversity, setbacks, and even outright failures while keeping a steady gaze on long-term goals and objectives. It is akin to a cornerstone, a bedrock upon which great leaders stand, unwavering and unyielding in the face of adversity. Resilience, in its essence, is the remarkable ability to rebound from challenges, setbacks, and even outright failures, all while maintaining a steadfast focus on long-term objectives.

Think of it as the steel frame that reinforces a towering skyscraper, allowing it to withstand the fiercest of storms without swaying. In the realm of leadership, resilient individuals not only endure trials but emerge from them stronger, more determined, and better equipped to face the next challenge that lies ahead. It is a quality that encapsulates the very essence of a leader's mettle, their ability to weather storms, and their capacity to lead with poise and confidence even amidst the most demanding and unpredictable circumstances.

But why is resilience so critical for leaders in the contemporary world? The answer lies in the nature of the challenges and uncertainties that define today's global business landscape. Rapid technological advancements, economic volatility, and unforeseen disruptions like global pandemics have become hallmarks of the 21st century. In such an environment, leaders who lack resilience may find themselves overwhelmed by the sheer magnitude of change and uncertainty, unable to steer their organizations toward success.

However, leaders who embody resilience possess a unique ability to not only weather the storms but to transform challenges into opportunities for growth and innovation. They exhibit a remarkable capacity to inspire and motivate their teams, fostering a culture of determination and adaptability. Resilient leaders serve as beacons of stability in times of crisis, guiding their organizations through turbulent waters with grace and determination.

Furthermore, resilience is intricately linked to adaptability, another key leadership quality. Leaders who can adapt to changing circumstances, pivot when necessary, and learn from failures are often the ones who thrive in today's fast-paced, ever-evolving business world. Resilience, therefore, serves as the driving force behind adaptability, allowing leaders to bounce back from setbacks and continue their journey with newfound wisdom and determination.

Throughout our exploration of resilience, we will draw inspiration from leaders who have embodied this quality in its truest sense. Their stories of triumph over adversity, their ability to remain composed under pressure, and their unwavering commitment to their goals will serve as beacons of inspiration. We will delve into the strategies and practices that enable leaders to cultivate resilience within themselves and their teams, strengthening their capacity to lead effectively in the face of uncertainty.

J.K. Rowling's journey through adversity and her demonstration of resilience offer profound insights into the human capacity to overcome challenges and achieve greatness. Before the world came to know her as the creator of the beloved Harry Potter series, Rowling's life was marked by hardship and struggle. She was a single mother living on welfare benefits, facing financial instability while simultaneously battling clinical depression.

It was during these trying times that Rowling conceived the idea for the Harry Potter series. The concept of a young wizard attending a magical school emerged during a train delay, and it became the spark of her creative vision. Rowling poured her heart and soul into the story, often spending hours in coffee shops while her baby daughter slept in a pram. Her passion for storytelling and her unwavering belief in the significance of her work were the driving forces behind her resilience.

The rejection letters she received from multiple publishers could have been demoralizing, but Rowling's determination to see her vision through remained unshaken. It was Bloomsbury, a small publishing house in London, that finally recognized the potential of her manuscript. From there, the Harry Potter series took flight, captivating the hearts and imaginations of readers worldwide.

Rowling's story teaches us that resilience is not merely about bouncing back from setbacks; it is about using challenges as steppingstones to propel oneself forward. It is a testament to the power of passion and belief in one's vision, even when the odds seem overwhelmingly stacked against success. Rowling's journey reminds us that the path to greatness often traverses through adversity, but it is our resilience that determines the destination.

Oprah Winfrey's journey from a challenging and tumultuous childhood to becoming one of the most influential media moguls in the world exemplifies the essence of resilience. Born into poverty in rural Mississippi, she faced adversity from an early age. Raised by her grandmother in challenging circumstances, Oprah endured hardship and even abuse during her formative years. These early struggles could have easily stifled her aspirations, but they served as the crucible in which her resilience was forged.

Oprah's escape from her difficult upbringing came through education and a keen sense of ambition. She secured a scholarship to Tennessee State University, where she honed her skills in communication and broadcasting. This opportunity marked the beginning of her career in the media, but her journey was far from smooth.

In the competitive world of media, Oprah faced numerous setbacks and challenges. She worked her way up from local radio to television, enduring a string of disappointments and rejections along the way. Despite these obstacles, her unyielding spirit and belief in her ability to connect with people persevered.

It was in 1986 that Oprah embarked on what would become the iconic "The Oprah Winfrey Show." Over the course of 25 years, her show became a cultural phenomenon. Her unique ability to engage with her audience, address challenging topics with empathy and authenticity, and offer guidance on self-improvement resonated with millions of viewers worldwide. The show's success catapulted her to international stardom and established her as a trusted source of inspiration and empowerment.

What sets Oprah apart is not just her rise to success but her commitment to giving back and effecting positive change. Her philanthropic efforts have touched countless lives, from educational initiatives to supporting underprivileged communities. Her resilience not only propelled her personal success but also became a force for societal transformation.

Oprah's story is a testament to the profound impact of resilience, personal growth, and the unwavering belief in one is potential. It underscores that resilience is not a passive trait but an active choice to persevere in the face of adversity, grow through challenges, and use one's influence in order to uplift others. Oprah's journey serves as an enduring source of inspiration, reminding us of all that resilience is a beacon of hope, guiding us through the darkest moments toward a brighter, more empowered future.

Mary Barra's remarkable journey as the CEO of General Motors (GM) is a testament to the power of resilience in the face of corporate crises. When she assumed leadership, GM was mired in a deeply troubling situation—the ignition switch recalled scandal. This crisis was not only financially damaging but, more critically, linked to tragic fatalities. The weight of this challenge could have been insurmountable for many leaders, yet Barra's resilience became the guiding light during these tumultuous times.

What set Mary Barra apart was her unwavering commitment to addressing the crisis head-on with transparency and accountability. She recognized that the first step in rebuilding trust and integrity within the organization and among stakeholders was acknowledging past mistakes. This commitment was evident in her willingness to testify before Congress, where she faced tough questions about GM's actions and decisions.

Barra's leadership during this period highlighted her remarkable resilience and strategic acumen. She understood that resolving the crisis was not solely about financial restitution; it was about regaining the trust of the public, customers, and employees. Her approach involved a multifaceted strategy that encompassed not only rectifying past errors but also instilling a profound cultural shift within GM— one that prioritized safety, quality, and ethical conduct more than anything else.

Under her leadership, GM underwent significant structural and cultural transformations. Barra's resilience fueled her determination to ensure that the mistakes of the past would not be repeated. She implemented stringent safety protocols, restructured the company's leadership, and fostered an environment where employees were encouraged to speak up about safety concerns.

The impact of Mary Barra's resilience extended far beyond GM's boardrooms. It sent a powerful message to the corporate world about the importance of ethical leadership, accountability, and the unwavering commitment to righting wrongs. Her ability to navigate a crisis of such magnitude with resilience and integrity serves as a compelling case study for leaders in any industry, underlining the transformative power of resilience in the face of adversity.

Mary Barra's story serves as a profound reminder that resilience is not merely about weathering storms but also about emerging from them with renewed purpose and a commitment to fundamental values. It highlights how a leader's resilience can steer an organization through the darkest of times and lead to a brighter and more ethically grounded future.

These leaders' stories highlight the multifaceted nature of resilience in the face of adversity. Their ability to overcome personal struggles, navigate professional setbacks, and emerge stronger is a testament to their mindset and determination. Strategies such as unwavering belief in their mission, passion for their work, and a commitment to core values were pivotal in their journeys. Their resilience serves as a source of inspiration for individuals facing challenges in their own careers and lives, emphasizing the importance of perseverance and a positive mindset in the pursuit of success.

Effective leadership is not a monolithic concept; rather, it is a rich tapestry woven from various qualities, with vision, empathy, integrity, and resilience forming the threads that bind it together. These qualities are not isolated attributes but are intricately interconnected, each reinforcing and complementing the others.

Primarily, let us explore the connection between vision and the other three qualities. A visionary leader possesses a clear sense of purpose and direction, guiding their team or organization towards a compelling future. This vision is often rooted in empathy, as understanding the needs, aspirations, and concerns of others is essential to crafting a vision that resonates. Empathy allows leaders to connect with their team members on a profound level, aligning their vision with the collective goals and values of the group.

Integrity, too, plays a pivotal role in the visionary leader's journey. Upholding a strong moral compass and ethical principles is essential to maintaining the trust and credibility required to lead effectively. A leader's integrity is intrinsically tied to their vision; it is the glue that binds the vision's authenticity and ensures it aligns with the greater good.

Now, let us introduce resilience into the equation. Resilience is the bedrock upon which these qualities stand. A visionary leader may encounter numerous obstacles, setbacks, and challenges along the path to realizing their vision. It is resilience that enables them to bounce back from adversity, learn from failures, and adapt their strategies. Resilience reinforces empathy, as leaders who have faced challenges are often more attuned to the struggles of others and better equipped to offer support. Moreover, integrity is tested in times of adversity, and resilient leaders demonstrate unwavering commitment to their values.

These core qualities form a symbiotic relationship in effective leadership. A visionary leader with empathy, integrity, and resilience creates a powerful constructive collaboration that inspires trust, fosters collaboration, and paves the way for transformative change. It is the leader who listens empathetically, acts with integrity, perseveres through adversity, and paints a compelling vision that ignites the sparks of innovation and progress.

In the modern world of leadership, the integration of these qualities is key. A leader who embodies this comprehensive approach not only sets a clear direction but also builds a culture of empathy, trust, and integrity while weathering the storms of change. Thus, the interplay of vision, empathy, integrity, and resilience creates a leadership dynamic that is adaptable, inspirational, and sustainable—a dynamic that shapes a brighter future for organizations and society.

Let us explore how you, as a leader or aspiring leader, can assess your strengths and areas for development in these vital traits and embark on a path of continuous improvement.

Assessing Your Core Qualities:

1. Vision: Begin by reflecting on your long-term goals and aspirations. Do you have a clear vision for your leadership journey and the impact you want to make? Consider how well you communicate this vision to your team or organization. Seek feedback from colleagues or mentors to gain insights into the clarity and persuasiveness of your vision.

2. Empathy: Reflect on your interactions with team members or colleagues. Do you actively listen to their concerns and perspectives? Are you attuned to their emotions and needs? Assess your ability to put yourself in others' shoes and understand their experiences. Consider seeking feedback to gain a better understanding of how others perceive your empathetic qualities.

3. Integrity: Examine your adherence to ethical principles and values in your leadership role. Have you consistently demonstrated

honesty, transparency, and ethical decision-making? Reflect on challenging situations where your integrity was put to the test. Assess your ability to maintain your moral compass under pressure.

4. Resilience: Reflect on past setbacks or challenges you have encountered in your leadership journey. How did you respond to adversity? Consider your ability to bounce back from failures and adapt to changing circumstances. Think about the strategies you have used to build resilience and cope with stress.

Developing Your Core Qualities:

1. Vision: To enhance your visionary leadership, engage in strategic thinking and planning exercises. Set aside time for envisioning the future of your team or organization. Seek feedback from stakeholders to refine your vision. Share your vision with enthusiasm and clarity, inspiring others to join you on the journey.

2. Empathy: Practice active listening by giving your full attention to others during conversations. Empathize by acknowledging their emotions and concerns. Develop your emotional intelligence through self-awareness and self-regulation exercises. Cultivate a genuine interest in understanding the perspectives of team members.

3. Integrity: Strengthen your integrity by aligning your actions with your values consistently. Engage in ethical decision-making training and seek guidance from mentors or ethics experts. Build a culture of integrity within your team or organization by setting a positive example.

4. Resilience: Enhance your resilience through stress management techniques, such as mindfulness and meditation. Embrace failure as an opportunity for growth and learning. Seek support from mentors or coaches who can provide guidance during challenging times.

Remember that leadership development is an ongoing process. Continuously seek opportunities for self-assessment and improvement. Engage in leadership development programs, workshops, and reading to expand your knowledge and skills.

Surround yourself with mentors and a supportive network that can provide valuable insights and guidance on your leadership journey.

As you embark on this path of self-assessment and development, keep in mind that leadership is not about achieving perfection but about striving to become a more effective and impactful leader with each step of your journey.

In conclusion, the core qualities of effective leaders—vision, empathy, integrity, and resilience—form the foundation of exceptional leadership. Through real-life examples and analysis, we have seen how these qualities are not just theoretical concepts but actionable principles that can transform organizations and inspire teams. As we continue our exploration of leadership, keep these core qualities in mind, for they are the essence of leadership excellence in the modern business world

Chapter 4

Emotional Intelligence and Leadership

"Leaders who master emotional intelligence foster
environments where empathy, understanding, and
collaboration lead the way to unparalleled success."

- Joel R. Klemmer

Chapter 4
Emotional Intelligence and Leadership

In this chapter, we will delve into the critical relationship between emotional intelligence (EI) and effective leadership. Emotional intelligence, often referred to as EQ, is the ability to recognize, understand, manage, and effectively use emotions—both your own and those of others. We will explore why emotional intelligence is a cornerstone of successful leadership and provide strategies for leaders to develop and enhance their EI skills.

Emotional intelligence, often referred to as EI or EQ (Emotional Quotient), is a multifaceted and nuanced skill set that delves into the intricate realm of human emotions and their profound impact on various facets of our lives, particularly in leadership roles.

At its core, emotional intelligence is the profound ability to recognize, comprehend, manage, and utilize not only our own emotions but also the emotions of those around us. It is like having a finely tuned instrument that allows us to navigate the symphony of human feelings and interactions with finesse. To truly grasp the essence of EI, we need to break it down into its four fundamental components, each akin to a pillar supporting the foundation of emotional intelligence:

Self-Awareness: Picture this as the bedrock of emotional intelligence. It involves the capacity to not just notice but truly understand our own emotions as they surface. It is about being in tune with our feelings, having the wisdom to decipher why we feel a certain way, and appreciating how our emotions sway our thoughts and actions.

Self-Regulation: Once we have laid the groundwork for self-awareness, the next step is to build upon it with self-regulation. Think of it as the conductor of our emotional orchestra. Self-regulation is all about having the ability to steer our emotional responses, especially when the stakes are high, or the pressure is on. It is about maintaining our composure, showing resilience, and adapting gracefully, even when the tempest of emotions rages within.

Social Awareness: Beyond our internal emotional landscape, emotional intelligence extends its reach to our interpersonal domain. Social awareness is akin to having a finely tuned radar for the feelings and needs of those around us. It is the skill of being acutely aware of the emotional climate in various social settings, of empathizing with the experiences of others, and of deciphering the unspoken emotional cues in the room.

Relationship Management: The pinnacle of emotional intelligence is reflected in our capacity to foster and nurture positive and productive relationships. Relationship management is the art of effective communication, conflict resolution, inspirational leadership, and the facilitation of collaboration and teamwork. It is about being the glue that holds teams together, the beacon that guides them through the storm.

Now, let us draw a distinct line between emotional intelligence (EQ) and intellectual intelligence (IQ). While IQ is the engine that fuels our cognitive abilities—our knack for problem-solving, logical reasoning, and critical thinking—EQ is the rudder that steers the ship of human interactions. In the realm of leadership, both IQ and EQ are indispensable, but they serve different functions.

IQ might open doors, providing the analytical prowess to dissect complex issues and devise ingenious strategies. Yet, it is EQ that determines whether you can navigate the maze of human emotions, build trust, and lead with empathy once you are through that door.

EI weaves its magic into the tapestry of leadership effectiveness, team dynamics, and organizational culture. Envisioning a leader with a high level of emotional intelligence (EI) paints a compelling picture of leadership effectiveness. This leader's self-awareness acts as a powerful compass, guiding them through the labyrinth of their own strengths and weaknesses. It is akin to having a detailed map of their internal landscape, allowing them to navigate it with precision. When they encounter adversity, their emotional self-regulation ensures that they remain steady at the helm. They are the captain of their emotional ship, able to weather the roughest seas without capsizing.

This leader's social awareness is akin to having a pair of empathetic antennae, constantly attuned to the feelings and thoughts of their team members. They can step into their colleagues' shoes and see the world from their perspective. This empathetic vantage point is invaluable when it comes to communication and leadership style. Instead of employing a one-size-fits-all approach, they tailor their interactions to resonate with everyone. They inspire, motivate, and support their team members in ways uniquely suited to each person's needs and aspirations.

The culmination of these EI components equips leaders with a formidable toolkit for leadership excellence. They make well-informed decisions rooted in a deep understanding of themselves and others. Conflicts, when they arise, are transformed into opportunities for growth and strengthened relationships. Trust within their teams is not just a buzzword; it is a tangible asset that fuels collaboration, innovation, and productivity. It is as if these leaders possess a secret formula for success, one that is not hidden away in a vault but is accessible to anyone willing to invest in developing their emotional intelligence.

The influence of emotional intelligence (EI) extends far beyond the leader's individual capabilities; it is a dynamic force that can transform team dynamics. Imagine a team where each member possesses a profound understanding of their own emotions and can effortlessly navigate the emotional landscape of their colleagues. This is not just a group of individuals; it is a well-tuned orchestra, with each instrument playing in harmony to create a symphony of productivity and innovation.

In such a team, conflicts are not dreaded; they are seen as opportunities for growth and learning. When disagreements arise, team members draw upon their emotional intelligence to address the issues constructively. They communicate with empathy and active listening, seeking to understand one another's perspectives and needs. Feedback flows freely, and it is not a source of anxiety but a catalyst for improvement. The team's atmosphere is one of trust and camaraderie, where individuals feel safe expressing themselves honestly and authentically.

Leaders who recognize the importance of EI within their teams actively foster its development. They understand that emotional intelligence is not a solitary endeavor but a collective journey. Through their own example and guidance, they encourage team members to embark on this journey, equipping them with the tools to enhance their self-awareness, self-regulation, social awareness, and relationship management. The result is a team that does not merely function; it thrives. Collaboration becomes second nature, creativity flourishes, and constructive interaction emerges as the driving force behind their shared accomplishments.

The influence of emotional intelligence (EI) does not stop at the team level; it permeates the entire organizational culture. Picture an organization where EI is woven into its very fabric, like vibrant threads that create a tapestry of positivity and productivity. In such an organization, leaders and employees alike possess a profound understanding of their emotions and the emotions of others.

Leaders, with their high EI, set the tone. They model self-awareness by openly acknowledging their strengths and areas for improvement. They demonstrate self-regulation by remaining composed and focused, even during times of uncertainty. Social awareness is their compass, allowing them to navigate the diverse perspectives and needs of their employees. Relationship management is their forte, as they foster an environment of trust, collaboration, and open communication.

This culture does not merely tolerate feedback; it thrives on it. Feedback is not perceived as criticism but as a valuable tool for growth and improvement. Employees feel safe to voice their ideas and concerns, knowing that their contributions are genuinely heard and valued. Conflicts are seen as opportunities for constructive resolution, not as disruptive roadblocks. Empathy and active listening are embedded in the organization's DNA, leading to stronger connections among team members.

In such a culture, employees are not just cogs in a machine; they are integral parts of a collective journey toward success. They are more engaged, motivated, and committed to their work because they know their well-being and personal growth matter. This kind of organizational culture does not just attract top talent; it retains it. Employees thrive in environments where they feel heard, respected, and understood, and they are more likely to stay and contribute their best efforts.

Leaders who understand the profound impact of EI on organizational culture actively cultivate it. They prioritize EI development not just for themselves but for every member of their team. They invest in training and resources to enhance emotional intelligence at all levels of the organization. This investment pays off in the form of a vibrant, collaborative, and innovative culture that drives the organization's success.

Daniel Goleman's exploration of emotional intelligence transcends the boundaries of academia and theory, making it a compelling case study of EI's transformative potential in leadership. His impact goes beyond his scholarly contributions; it extends into his practical application of EI principles in various facets of his career.

What truly distinguishes Goleman is his exceptional skill in communication and connection. He does not simply deliver information; he crafts narratives that resonate with the emotional core of his audience. His talks and writings are vehicles for empathy, self-awareness, and a deeper comprehension of the intricacies of human emotions.

Goleman's unique strength lies in his ability to make complex psychological concepts accessible and relatable. He does not just discuss emotional intelligence; he embodies it. His self-awareness shines through in his profound self-reflection and his exploration of the intricate landscape of human emotions. Even when addressing sensitive or challenging subjects, he demonstrates adept self-regulation, maintaining a composed and collected demeanor.

Goleman's exceptional social awareness is a cornerstone of his leadership effectiveness. He possesses an innate understanding of his audience—their needs, concerns, and motivations. This keen awareness enables him to tailor his message in a way that deeply resonates with individuals from diverse backgrounds. His expertise in relationship management is evident as he forges connections and engages with his audience, leaving an enduring impact.

This example not only underscores the significance of emotional intelligence in professional environments but also highlights its pervasive influence across various facets of life. Whether in public speaking, education, or writing, Goleman's capacity to harness the power of emotional intelligence positions him as a thought leader whose work continues to inspire and influence countless individuals.

Sir Richard Branson's, the dynamic founder of the Virgin Group, leadership is marked by a unique blend of charisma, approachability, and authenticity. He embodies emotional intelligence by prioritizing open and effective communication with employees and customers alike. His approachability creates an environment where individuals feel comfortable sharing their ideas and concerns, fostering a culture of inclusivity and innovation.

One of Branson's standout traits is his active listening skills. He does not merely hear what others say, he genuinely listens, absorbing their perspectives and feedback. This active engagement makes employees and customers feel genuinely valued and understood. Branson's ability to connect on a personal level transcends hierarchical boundaries, strengthening both internal and external relationships.

Branson's commitment to emotional intelligence has had a ripple effect throughout the Virgin Group's organizational culture. His emphasis on open dialogue and mutual respect has created a workplace where collaboration, creativity, and engagement flourish. Employees feel empowered to contribute their ideas and take ownership of their work, resulting in a positive and innovative atmosphere.

Beyond the confines of the organization, Branson's emotional intelligence extends to Virgin's customers. By actively seeking feedback, addressing concerns, and constantly improving the customer experience, he fosters customer loyalty and trust. This customer-centric approach has been pivotal in Virgin's success across diverse industries, from music to airlines.

Sheryl Sandberg, the Chief Operating Officer of Facebook, and her exemplary display of emotional intelligence, has made her a standout leader in the tech industry. Sheryl Sandberg's leadership style is distinguished by her emotional intelligence, which plays a pivotal role in her effectiveness as a leader. She goes beyond the traditional boundaries of corporate leadership by openly sharing her individual experiences with grief and resilience. This vulnerability allows her to connect with audiences on a deep emotional level, transcending the typical corporate persona.

One of Sandberg's standout qualities is her capacity for empathy and understanding. She has a genuine knack for recognizing the challenges and hardships that individuals face, whether they are within or outside the Facebook organization. Her empathetic approach makes her not only a relatable figure but also an inspirational one.

Sandberg's openness about her experiences with grief and resilience serves as an inspiration to many. She demonstrates that even in the face of profound personal loss, it is possible to find strength, resilience, and a sense of purpose. Her ability to channel her experiences into meaningful conversations resonates with individuals grappling with their own challenges, fostering a sense of community and support.

Sandberg's emotional intelligence extends to her role at Facebook, where she has played a pivotal role in shaping the company's approach to employee well-being and support. Her emphasis on mental health, resilience, and work-life balance has had a positive impact on Facebook's organizational culture. She recognizes that employees are not just professionals but whole individuals with diverse needs.

Sheryl Sandberg's leadership embodies the idea that emotional intelligence can be a catalyst for change, both within and outside the workplace. By openly discussing topics like grief and resilience, she has helped break down stigmas and encouraged more open conversations about mental health. Her impact is not limited to Facebook but extends to the broader corporate world and society at large.

In our exploration of emotional intelligence and its profound impact on leadership, Sheryl Sandberg's example serves as a testament to the transformative power of empathy, openness, and understanding.

These examples highlight how leaders with high emotional intelligence can influence not only their own effectiveness but also the dynamics of their teams and the culture of their organizations. As we continue our exploration of EI, we will delve deeper into each component of emotional intelligence, providing you with valuable insights and practical strategies to enhance your EI and become a more effective and empathetic leader.

Strategic Synergy

The initial stride in elevating your emotional intelligence (EI) is to assess your current levels. To accomplish this, there are various methods at your disposal for gauging your EI. Self-assessment stands as an excellent starting point; it involves introspection and reflection on your emotions, behaviors, and reactions. Utilizing self-assessment tools and questionnaires can provide valuable insights into your EI strengths and areas that require improvement. Additionally, you can seek a comprehensive view of your emotional intelligence by soliciting feedback from colleagues, superiors, subordinates, and peers through 360-degree feedback mechanisms. This feedback can pinpoint blind spots and areas for development, offering a well-rounded perspective on your EI profile. Once you have gathered feedback and self-assessed, it is crucial to interpret the results. Look for patterns and common themes in the feedback, identifying both your strengths and growth areas.

Self-Assessment: Commencing self-assessment is an essential step in the journey to enhance your emotional intelligence (EI). This process entails introspection and thoughtful consideration of your emotions, behaviors, and responses to various situations. To aid in this endeavor, there are valuable self-assessment tools and questionnaires available. By dedicating time to self-assessment and employing such tools, you lay a solid foundation for understanding your emotional intelligence better, paving the way for growth and improvement in this crucial aspect of leadership and personal development.

360-Degree Feedback: Embracing a 360-degree feedback approach is another valuable method to gain a holistic understanding of your emotional intelligence (EI). This approach involves actively seeking feedback from a spectrum of sources within your professional sphere, including colleagues, superiors, subordinates, and peers. It provides a well-rounded perspective on your EI, as it captures observations and insights from those who interact with you regularly. Constructive feedback collected through this process can be especially illuminating, as it can pinpoint blind spots and areas that may require further development. By being open to feedback from diverse sources, you create an opportunity for substantial growth in your emotional intelligence, aligning it with your aspirations for effective leadership and personal advancement.

Once you have gathered feedback and self-assessed, it is crucial to interpret the results. Look for patterns and common themes in the feedback. Are there specific emotions or situations where you struggle to maintain composure? Are there aspects of social awareness or relationship management that need attention? Identify the areas where you excel and where you can grow.

Developing emotional intelligence is an ongoing journey, akin to sculpting a work of art. It requires dedication, practice, and a commitment to personal growth. Here, we delve into strategies for enhancing each facet of emotional intelligence:

Self-Awareness: Imagine self-awareness as a mirror reflecting your inner world. Engage in regular self-reflection, journaling, or mindfulness practices to delve deeper into your emotional landscape. Actively listen to your inner thoughts and feelings, becoming attuned to your emotional triggers and patterns. Self-awareness starts with understanding oneself.

Self-Regulation: Picture self-regulation as the steady hand of a conductor guiding an orchestra through tumultuous passages. Cultivate emotional self-regulation by introducing a pause before reacting to intense emotions. In moments of turmoil, take a deep breath and create space for rational thought. Learn techniques like deep breathing and meditation to maintain composure during challenging situations. Self-regulation empowers you to steer through the storm with grace.

Social Awareness: Social awareness is akin to a pair of finely tuned antennae, noticing the subtlest signals from those around you. Practice empathy by actively listening to others and attempting to understand their perspectives. Tune into non-verbal cues, such as body language and tone of voice, to decipher the emotions concealed beneath the surface. Social awareness is your window into the feelings and needs of others.

Relationship Management: Think of relationship management as the art of crafting harmonious melodies within a group. Cultivate positive relationships by prioritizing effective communication, adept conflict resolution, and collaborative teamwork. Seek opportunities for collaboration and feedback, as they are the building blocks of strong relationships. By nurturing relationships, you create a symphony of success.

Motivation: Motivation is the fuel that propels your emotional intelligence journey forward. Set SMART goals (Specific, Measurable, Achievable, Relevant, Time-bound) for your emotional intelligence development. For instance, you might aim to respond calmly to criticism or actively seek out diverse perspectives in decision-making. Motivation drives your quest to become a more emotionally intelligent leader, even in the face of adversity.

Remember that developing emotional intelligence is not a destination but a lifelong expedition. Each strategy you employ is a brushstroke on the canvas of your emotional intelligence masterpiece. With commitment and practice, you can refine your emotional intelligence, fostering richer relationships and more effective leadership.

Creating a nurturing environment for the growth of emotional intelligence (EI), particularly within organizational settings, is paramount to the development of emotionally intelligent leaders. Here are several strategies that organizations can implement to foster the cultivation of EI:

Training Programs: Organizations can offer comprehensive EI training programs and workshops designed to equip leaders with practical tools and techniques for enhancing their emotional intelligence. These programs may include self-assessment tools, immersive case studies, and role-playing exercises. By investing in structured training, organizations can provide leaders with a structured framework for EI growth.

Coaching and Mentoring: One-on-one coaching or mentoring opportunities can be instrumental in a leader's EI development journey. Personalized guidance from experienced coaches can assist leaders in setting clear EI development goals, tracking their progress, and effectively navigating the challenges they encounter. Coaching creates a supportive space for leaders to refine their emotional intelligence.

Cultivating a Feedback Culture: Organizations should actively foster a culture that values and encourages the giving and receiving of feedback. Constructive feedback should be perceived as an opportunity for personal and professional growth, rather than criticism. By normalizing feedback, organizations create an environment where leaders can learn from their experiences and continually refine their EI.

Embedding EI in Leadership Development: Integrating emotional intelligence into leadership development programs ensures that future leaders are well-prepared with these vital skills. EI should be a foundational component of leadership development, emphasizing its significance in effective leadership. By instilling EI at the core of leadership training, organizations can nurture emotionally intelligent leaders from the outset.

Leading by Example: Senior leaders within organizations should exemplify and champion emotional intelligence behaviors in their interactions. These leaders serve as role models, showcasing the organization's commitment to fostering EI. When senior leaders consistently exhibit high levels of EI, it sends a powerful message that emotional intelligence is a core value within the organization.

Enhancing emotional intelligence is a journey that requires self-awareness, consistent practice, and a supportive organizational environment. By adopting these strategies, organizations can play a pivotal role in nurturing emotionally intelligent leaders who contribute to a more harmonious, productive, and empathetic workplace. Through ongoing assessment, goal-setting, and active development efforts, leaders can continuously refine their emotional intelligence and, in turn, become more effective in their roles.

The Dalai Lama's remarkable journey as a global icon of compassion and emotional intelligence transcends mere leadership; it represents a profound embodiment of these qualities. His spiritual leadership within Tibetan Buddhism has organically evolved to become a beacon of hope and wisdom for people worldwide, regardless of their faith or cultural background. At its core, his leadership underscores the extraordinary potential of emotional intelligence in shaping not just personal growth but also international relations.

His unwavering commitment to peace and nonviolence, even in the face of adversity, exemplifies the power of emotional intelligence in fostering resilience and empathy. The Dalai Lama's approach to interfaith understanding is a testament to his ability to bridge divides and build bridges of compassion. His interactions with leaders from diverse cultural and religious backgrounds illustrate how emotional intelligence can break down barriers, fostering genuine connections rooted in empathy and understanding.

In the Dalai Lama, we witness a living testament to the transformative potential of emotional intelligence in leadership, serving as a guiding light for individuals and nations seeking paths of harmony, tolerance, and cooperation in an increasingly interconnected world. His legacy serves as a vivid reminder of the profound impact that leaders with high emotional intelligence can have on the global stage, transcending boundaries, and inspiring positive change.

Brene Brown's impactful work as a leading advocate for vulnerability and emotional intelligence brings a fresh perspective to the concept of leadership. Her research on shame, courage, and empathy has not only enriched our understanding of these emotions but has also underscored their significance in personal and professional development.

Brown's message encourages individuals and leaders to embrace vulnerability as a strength rather than a weakness. This counterintuitive approach challenges traditional notions of leadership, highlighting the importance of authenticity and open communication. In the realm of emotional intelligence, vulnerability is the gateway to self-awareness and genuine connection with others.

Moreover, Brown's emphasis on cultivating empathy resonates deeply with the principles of emotional intelligence. She reminds us that empathy is a cornerstone of meaningful relationships and effective leadership. By putting ourselves in others' shoes and understanding their emotions and perspectives, we can create a more inclusive and compassionate world.

Brown's teachings also highlight the role of emotional intelligence in developing resilience. In today's fast-paced and often unpredictable world, leaders must navigate challenges and setbacks with grace. Emotional intelligence equips them with the tools to regulate their emotions, adapt to changing circumstances, and bounce back from adversity.

In Brene Brown, we find a modern-day advocate for vulnerability and emotional intelligence, demonstrating how these qualities can not only transform individual lives but also redefine leadership paradigms. Her insights encourage leaders to embrace their authentic selves, foster empathy, and build resilience—a recipe for more meaningful connections and positive change in the world.

In the sphere of philanthropy and addressing global challenges, Melinda Gates, the co-chair of the Bill and Melinda Gates Foundation, emerges as a compelling example of a leader who effectively applies emotional intelligence to her leadership style. What sets her apart is her empathetic approach, a foundational element of emotional intelligence.

Melinda Gates' leadership is marked by a profound ability to actively listen and deeply understand the needs and experiences of the individuals and communities her foundation seeks to assist. She does not approach these complex global issues from a distant or detached standpoint; instead, she immerses herself in the realities of those affected. This empathetic orientation enables her to identify not only the surface-level symptoms but also the root causes of multifaceted problems.

Importantly, Melinda Gates illustrates how emotional intelligence can serve as a driving force behind the creation of impactful and sustainable solutions to some of the world's most pressing challenges. Her leadership demonstrates that emotional intelligence is not merely a soft skill but a transformative tool that can shape a better future for our global community.

As we delve into Melinda Gates' philanthropic vision and leadership journey, we gain valuable insights into how emotional intelligence, with its cornerstone of empathy, can be harnessed to effect positive change on a grand scale. Her work reminds us that understanding, compassion, and an unwavering commitment to addressing the needs of others are at the heart of impactful and sustainable leadership in the face of global challenges.

Google, one of the world's most renowned technology companies, has long been admired for its innovative culture and employee-centric approach. At the heart of this success is its commitment to fostering emotional intelligence within its leadership ranks.

Google's former CEO, Sundar Pichai, exemplifies emotional intelligence in leadership. His empathetic and inclusive leadership style has transformed Google's work environment. Through EI-focused initiatives like emotional intelligence workshops and training programs, Google's leaders have honed their ability to understand and connect with their teams on a deeper level.

The positive outcomes of Google's EI-focused leadership are evident in various ways. Employee satisfaction and engagement have soared, leading to increased productivity and innovation. Moreover, Google's reputation as an employer of choice has attracted top talent from diverse backgrounds, enhancing its competitive edge.

The Mayo Clinic, a globally renowned healthcare institution, has a long history of patient-centered care. This commitment to empathy and emotional intelligence has been a cornerstone of its success.

Dr. William Mayo, one of the clinic's founders, believed that understanding patients' emotional needs was as vital as addressing their physical ailments. This philosophy has permeated the Mayo Clinic's culture, fostering a sense of compassion and empathy among its staff.

The positive outcomes of the Mayo Clinic's emotionally intelligent approach are evident in its exceptional patient outcomes and high levels of patient satisfaction. By prioritizing emotional well-being alongside physical health, the clinic has become a beacon of compassionate healthcare.

IBM, a global technology, and consulting corporation faced significant challenges in the early 1990s as it navigated the shifting landscape of the tech industry. Under the leadership of then-CEO Louis Gerstner, the organization embarked on a transformational journey that emphasized emotional intelligence as a key driver of change.

Gerstner recognized that effectively leading IBM through turbulent times required more than just strategic acumen; it necessitated emotional intelligence. He fostered a culture of openness and empathy, encouraging employees at all levels to voice their concerns and ideas. This inclusive approach resulted in a collective sense of ownership and purpose.

The positive outcomes of IBM's EI-focused transformation were profound. The company not only survived but thrived, adapting to the changing tech landscape and reestablishing itself as an industry leader.

IBM's success story serves as a testament to the power of emotional intelligence in guiding organizations through complex transitions. These case studies vividly illustrate the transformative impact of emotionally intelligent leadership in diverse organizational settings.

Whether in the realm of technology, healthcare, or corporate transformation, emotional intelligence has consistently proven to be a catalyst for positive change, fostering a culture of empathy, collaboration, and innovation that drives organizations toward excellence. The journey of leadership is an ongoing evolution, and emotional intelligence is a dynamic skill that can be honed throughout one's career. By comprehending the nuances of emotional intelligence and proactively cultivating its various components, leaders can facilitate the growth of better relationships, make judicious decisions, and cultivate a workplace environment characterized by positivity and productivity. Emotional intelligence empowers leaders to navigate the complex terrain of human interactions with empathy, self-awareness, and adaptability. As you progress on your leadership path, always keep in mind that EI is not a static trait but a flexible tool that can be continuously refined and sharpened. It serves as a compass guiding leaders toward more effective and meaningful leadership, enhancing their capacity to inspire, connect, and lead with authenticity and purpose. In doing so, they not only become better leaders but also contribute to the development of healthier, more compassionate organizations and a more harmonious world.

Chapter 5

Communication: The Heart of Leadership

"In the realm of leadership, effective communication is
the heartbeat that sustains trust, connects vision to reality,
and fuels the journey toward shared goals."

- Joel R. Klemmer

Chapter 5
Communication: The Heart of Leadership

Communication is undeniably the lifeblood of effective leadership, serving as the conduit through which leaders convey their vision, establish and nurture relationships, and guide their teams towards success. In the dynamic landscape of leadership, the ability to communicate clearly and effectively stands as a foundational pillar. In this exploration, we will delve into the paramount importance of proficient communication in leadership, understanding that it goes beyond mere words, encompassing both verbal and nonverbal facets. We will also emphasize the crucial role of active listening, as it completes the loop of effective communication. Along the way, we will offer practical insights and tips to enhance these vital communication skills, equipping you with the tools necessary to excel in leadership roles. So, let us embark on this journey to unravel the intricacies of communication in leadership and discover how it can transform your effectiveness as a leader.

At the heart of effective leadership lies the bedrock of clear and efficient communication. It is the cornerstone upon which trust is built, collaboration is nurtured, and teams are aligned with a common purpose. In the intricate tapestry of leadership, communication serves as the guiding thread, weaving together the diverse elements that constitute a successful leader's journey.

Imagine a leader who can articulate their vision with clarity, express their expectations with precision, and actively listen to the concerns and ideas of their team members. This leader possesses the tools to inspire confidence, foster an environment of open dialogue, and rally their team behind a shared goal.

Clear communication transcends mere conveyance of information; it forges connections, establishes rapport, and empowers individuals to work together harmoniously. In the chapters ahead, we will unravel the multifaceted nature of effective communication in leadership, exploring its various dimensions, from verbal and nonverbal aspects to the art of listening. By delving into these realms, we aim to equip you with the knowledge and skills to become a more proficient and impactful communicator, enhancing your prowess as a leader. So, let us embark on this journey to unravel the intricacies of communication in leadership and discover how it can transform your effectiveness as a leader.

In the intricate dance of leadership, poor communication stands as a formidable adversary, capable of unraveling even the most well-intentioned efforts. Its consequences ripple through the organizational fabric, leaving behind misunderstandings, conflicts, and decreased productivity in its wake. Let us delve into the repercussions of inadequate communication and illustrate them with real-world examples of leadership failures stemming from communication breakdowns.

Misunderstandings, often born from unclear or insufficient communication, can sow the seeds of chaos within an organization. Imagine a scenario where a leader outlines a project's objectives vaguely, leaving team members to interpret the goals differently. The result? Disjointed efforts, wasted resources, and frustration—all products of miscommunication.

Conflicts, too, find fertile ground in the absence of effective communication. When leaders fail to address differences or provide a platform for resolving disputes, tensions can escalate, poisoning the work environment. A classic example is the breakdown of communication within management teams, leading to power struggles and infighting rather than collaborative decision-making.

Decreased productivity is one of the most palpable outcomes of poor communication. When instructions are unclear, feedback is nonexistent, or expectations remain unarticulated, employees are left in a state of confusion. This leads to inefficiency, missed deadlines, and a general sense of frustration.

One illustrative example of a leadership failure stemming from communication breakdown is the demise of Blockbuster, once a video rental giant. Blockbuster's leadership failed to adapt to changing consumer preferences in the digital age. They ignored the significance of clear communication and failed to convey a strategic vision that aligned with emerging technologies and market trends. This lack of communication foresight led to Blockbuster's downfall as they lost relevance in the face of streaming services like Netflix.

These examples underscore the pivotal role of communication in leadership and its far-reaching implications. In the chapters ahead, we will explore the facets of effective communication, equipping you with the tools to mitigate these consequences and harness the power of communication for successful leadership.

In the context of leadership, the adeptness to construct clear and succinct messages stands as a fundamental element of effective communication. It acts as the linchpin that connects leaders with their teams, guiding them toward shared objectives and a common vision. Let us delve into strategies that empower leaders to articulate their thoughts and ideas with precision, placing a significant emphasis on the use of plain language and the avoidance of jargon.

First and foremost, understanding one's audience is paramount before disseminating any message. It is essential to discern the needs, expectations, and levels of expertise of the audience. Tailoring the language and complexity of the message to align with the comprehension level of the audience is pivotal for ensuring clarity. Whether addressing a team of experts or a diverse group with varying levels of familiarity with the subject, adapting the language appropriately is a prudent practice.

Structuring the message logically is another facet of effective communication. A message should typically begin with a concise introduction outlining the primary points to be addressed. Subsequently, the body of the message should contain the requisite details or information, followed by a summarizing conclusion. This structured approach aids the audience in following the narrative and retaining the salient points.

The use of plain and straightforward language is a hallmark of effective communication. It is imperative to eschew unnecessary jargon, acronyms, or technical terminology that could alienate or perplex the audience. Instead, leaders should opt for language that is readily accessible and comprehensible by all members of the audience, irrespective of their prior knowledge on the subject.

Providing context is a fundamental component of effective messaging. Context elucidates the importance and relevance of the conveyed information. Leaders should elucidate why the message is significant, how it connects with broader organizational goals, and the potential implications it carries.

Conciseness is a virtue in communication. While context is essential, superfluous verbosity should be avoided. Succinctness ensures that the message is clear and easily remembered by the audience.

Leaders should actively encourage feedback from their audience. They should create an environment where questions are welcomed, and requests for clarification are encouraged. Soliciting feedback not only ensures the audience's comprehension of the message but also fosters an environment of open and candid communication.

In the practice of effective communication, active listening is just as pivotal as delivering clear messages. Leaders must attentively listen to the feedback, questions, and concerns of their team members. Acknowledging the input and responding thoughtfully enhances the quality of communication and augments the overall effectiveness of the interaction.

By integrating these strategies into their communication practices, leaders can enhance their verbal communication skills. The resultant clarity and comprehensibility of their messages contribute to the establishment of trust, transparency, and effective collaboration within their teams, thereby augmenting their leadership effectiveness.

Effective public speaking is a hallmark of influential leadership. Leaders who can engage, inspire, and connect with their audience through compelling speeches wield a potent tool in their leadership arsenal. We will explore essential tips and techniques for leaders to enhance their public speaking skills, encompassing voice modulation, pacing, body language, and the art of delivering impactful speeches.

Voice modulation is an invaluable aspect of captivating an audience. Leaders should strive to vary the pitch, tone, and volume of their voice to infuse energy and dynamism into their speeches. Monotony can lead to disinterest, while modulation keeps the audience engaged. A judicious use of pauses can also be instrumental in accentuating key points and allowing the audience to absorb the information effectively.

Pacing is another critical element of public speaking. Leaders should aim for a pace that is steady and conducive to comprehension. Speaking too quickly can leave the audience struggling to keep up, while speaking too slowly may lead to disengagement. A well-paced speech allows the audience to follow the narrative comfortably.

Body language is a potent nonverbal component of public speaking. Leaders should be mindful of their posture, gestures, and facial expressions. Maintaining an upright posture exudes confidence and authority. Purposeful gestures can accentuate key points and convey enthusiasm. Facial expressions should be congruent with the message being delivered, as they contribute to the overall emotional resonance of the speech.

Engaging the audience is a paramount goal of public speaking. Leaders should aim to establish a connection with their audience by creating relatable narratives, anecdotes, or real-life examples. Storytelling is a compelling technique that can captivate the audience's attention, making the message more memorable and relatable. By sharing personal experiences or narratives, leaders can create an emotional bond with their listeners.

An impactful speech should be well-structured, with a clear introduction, body, and conclusion. The introduction should grab the audience's attention and set the tone for the speech. The body should present the main points or ideas logically and coherently, using supporting evidence or examples. The conclusion should summarize the key takeaways and leave a lasting impression.

Effective use of visual aids, such as slides or props, can enhance the impact of a speech. Visual aids should be used sparingly and should complement, rather than overshadow, the speaker's message. They should be clear, uncluttered, and easy to understand.

Practice is the linchpin of public speaking mastery. Leaders should rehearse their speeches multiple times, focusing on clarity, pacing, and delivery. Recording and reviewing practice sessions can provide valuable insights for improvement. Additionally, seeking feedback from trusted colleagues or mentors can offer constructive guidance.

Overcoming nervousness is a common challenge in public speaking. Leaders can manage anxiety by adopting relaxation techniques, such as deep breathing or meditation, before taking the stage. Visualizing a successful presentation can boost confidence. Embracing nerves as a source of energy rather than a hindrance can also be transformative.

By mastering voice modulation, pacing, body language, and the art of delivering captivating speeches, leaders can not only engage and inspire their audiences but also enhance their leadership influence and effectiveness.

Nonverbal communication, often underestimated, wields significant influence in the realm of effective leadership. In order to understand nonverbal communication, we will delve into the power of body language and its paramount role in communication. Understanding the significance of nonverbal cues, such as facial expressions, gestures, and posture, is essential for leaders. Moreover, we will offer guidance on how leaders can strategically employ body language to convey confidence, openness, and alignment with their verbal messages.

Facial expressions, one of the most potent nonverbal cues, serve as windows to one's emotions and intentions. Leaders should recognize that their facial expressions can either reinforce or contradict their spoken words. For instance, a warm smile can convey approachability and enthusiasm, while a furrowed brow may signal concern or confusion. By aligning their facial expressions with the content of their communication, leaders can enhance the authenticity and credibility of their messages.

Gestures, encompassing hand movements and body gestures, play a pivotal role in nonverbal communication. Leaders can employ gestures to emphasize key points, convey enthusiasm, or add clarity to their spoken words. However, an excess of distracting gestures can dilute the impact of the message. Leaders should strive for purposeful and deliberate gestures that complement their verbal communication.

Posture is a subtle yet influential aspect of body language. Leaders who maintain an upright and open posture convey confidence and approachability. Slouching or closed postures can undermine one's authority and deter effective communication. Leaders should be mindful of their posture, particularly in high-stakes situations, as it can significantly affect how their message is received.

Openness and receptivity are qualities that leaders often seek to convey through body language. Maintaining open body language, such as facing the audience or maintaining eye contact, fosters trust and engagement. Leaders should be cautious of defensive postures, such as crossed arms or avoiding eye contact, which can signal defensiveness or disinterest. Instead, they should strive to create an atmosphere of attentiveness and approachability.

Consistency between verbal and nonverbal cues is pivotal. Leaders should aim for congruence between what they say and how they express it nonverbally. Misalignment between verbal and nonverbal communication can breed confusion and undermine trust. Leaders should periodically assess their body language to ensure it aligns with their intended message.

By recognizing the significance of facial expressions, gestures, and posture, leaders can strategically employ these cues to convey confidence, openness, and alignment with their verbal messages. Consistency and authenticity in nonverbal communication enhance a leader's ability to engage, inspire, and effectively communicate with their audience.

Active listening, an essential skill in leadership, serves as a cornerstone of effective communication. The importance of understanding active listening and providing leaders with techniques to enhance their listening capabilities will ultimately strengthen their leadership skills.

Active listening is more than just hearing words; it involves a deep and genuine focus on the speaker and their message. Leaders who actively listen demonstrate respect, empathy, and a genuine interest in what others have to say. This not only fosters trust but also promotes open and transparent communication within teams.

Maintaining eye contact is a fundamental aspect of active listening. It conveys attentiveness and engagement, signaling to the speaker that their words are valued. Leaders should strive to maintain appropriate eye contact without making the speaker uncomfortable. Additionally, nonverbal cues like nodding or leaning slightly can further convey interest and understanding.

Asking clarifying questions is another valuable technique for active listening. Leaders can seek clarification or additional information to ensure they fully grasp the speaker's perspective. This not only demonstrates a commitment to understanding but also helps prevent misunderstandings or misinterpretations.

Paraphrasing or summarizing the speaker's points can be an effective way to confirm comprehension and show that their words have been heard and understood. Leaders can say, "So, if I understand correctly, you're saying..." or "Let me summarize what you've shared to make sure I've got it right."

Reflective listening involves mirroring the speaker's emotions or feelings, demonstrating empathy and validation. Leaders can respond with statements like, "It sounds like you're feeling frustrated about this situation," or "I can sense that this is important to you."

Avoiding interruptions is crucial for active listening. Leaders should resist the urge to interject with their own thoughts or solutions prematurely. Instead, they should allow the speaker to express themselves fully before responding.

Silence can be a powerful tool in active listening. Leaders should not rush to fill every pause but should instead provide space for the speaker to gather their thoughts or express themselves fully. Silence can also encourage the speaker to share more, providing valuable insights.

Active listening is an indispensable skill for leaders, facilitating effective communication, trust-building, and empathetic leadership. By maintaining eye contact, asking clarifying questions, paraphrasing, and using reflective listening techniques, leaders can become better listeners and enhance their ability to connect with their teams and colleagues.

Empathy, a cornerstone of effective communication, plays a pivotal role in leadership by fostering meaningful connections and understanding among team members. Empathy is the ability to comprehend and share the feelings and perspectives of others. It involves actively stepping into another person's shoes, acknowledging their emotions, and responding with care and understanding. For leaders, empathy serves as a powerful tool for building trust, enhancing relationships, and promoting collaboration within their teams.

Empathy enables leaders to connect with their teams on a deeper level by demonstrating a genuine interest in the well-being and concerns of their team members. When leaders actively listen to their employees' thoughts, feelings, and ideas, they create an environment where team members feel heard and valued. This, in turn, fosters a sense of belonging and trust.

Moreover, empathetic leaders can better understand the motivations, needs, and challenges of their team members. This understanding allows leaders to tailor their communication and leadership approaches to meet the unique requirements of everyone. It empowers leaders to provide support, encouragement, and guidance that aligns with the specific circumstances of their team members.

Empathy also plays a vital role in conflict resolution and problem-solving. Leaders who can empathize with the perspectives and concerns of conflicting parties can facilitate constructive dialogues and find mutually agreeable solutions. By acknowledging the emotions and viewpoints of all involved, leaders can mitigate conflicts and foster a more harmonious work environment.

Empathy serves as a requirement in effective communication within leadership. It enables leaders to forge genuine connections, build trust, and understand the emotions and perspectives of their team members. By practicing empathy, leaders create an inclusive and supportive workplace where individuals thrive, collaborate, and contribute to the collective success of the team.

Empathetic communication is a powerful tool that leaders can use to navigate conflicts, build trust, and create a positive work environment. Incorporating empathetic communication into leadership requires practice and a genuine desire to connect with and understand others. By doing so, leaders can create an inclusive and supportive work environment where team members feel valued and empowered, contributing to the organization's success. Effective leadership is intricately tied to the ability to surmount communication barriers that frequently emerge within today's diverse and rapidly evolving workplaces. These challenges manifest in various forms, ranging from linguistic disparities and cultural intricacies to generational differences and technological hurdles. A prominent barrier is language diversity, as team members often possess varying levels of proficiency in a common language. To mitigate this challenge, leaders should prioritize plain and unambiguous communication, eschewing jargon and providing translation resources as needed.

Cultural nuances constitute another significant obstacle, as divergent customs and practices can give rise to misunderstandings. Leaders can address this by investing in cultural sensitivity training for themselves and their teams, promoting active listening, and fostering an environment where open dialogue and feedback regarding cultural differences are encouraged.

Furthermore, generational divides in communication preferences are commonplace in many organizations. Effective leaders recognize the need for flexibility, encouraging cross-generational collaboration and emphasizing shared objectives to bridge these gaps successfully.

In the modern digital landscape, technology barriers have also emerged as a communication challenge. This may involve disparities in technology literacy, access to communication tools, or navigating the nuances of virtual interactions. To overcome these hurdles, leaders can implement comprehensive technology training, establish clear boundaries for the use of digital tools, and conduct regular check-ins to ensure everyone is on the same page.

By acknowledging and proactively addressing these various communication barriers, leaders can cultivate an environment of effective communication within their teams and contribute significantly to the overall success and cohesion of their organizations.

Navigating challenging conversations represents a pivotal aspect of effective leadership. It entails addressing sensitive subjects or conflicts in a timely and constructive manner. Neglecting these issues can lead to festering problems, lowered team morale, and hindered organizational progress. Therefore, it is crucial for leaders to grasp the significance of addressing such matters promptly and empathetically.

To navigate these conversations effectively, leaders should employ a structured framework that amalgamates empathy with assertiveness. This framework typically consists of several key steps:

First, adequate preparation is essential. Leaders should clarify their objectives, gather relevant information, and consider the perspectives of all involved parties. This helps anticipate viewpoints and potential reactions.

Creating a safe space is the next step. Leaders should ensure privacy and minimal distractions and begin with a statement that underscores the importance of open, honest dialogue and a commitment to finding a resolution.

Active listening plays a crucial role. Leaders should permit the other party to express their thoughts and emotions fully. Active listening demonstrates empathy and understanding, employing nonverbal cues like maintaining eye contact and nodding to convey attentiveness.

Asking clarifying questions is vital to ensure a comprehensive understanding of the other person's perspective, reducing assumptions or judgments. Expressing one's viewpoint follows, sharing one's perspective honestly and assertively while maintaining a respectful and calm tone. "I" statements can be used to express feelings and thoughts without resorting to blame or accusation. Empathy remains key throughout the conversation, as leaders acknowledge the emotions expressed by the other party, even if they do not necessarily agree with their viewpoint.

Seeking common ground comes next, with a focus on exploring potential solutions together. The emphasis here is on shared goals and interests, striving for mutually beneficial resolutions, and demonstrating flexibility and adaptability. Agreeing on the next steps and summarizing agreed-upon solutions is crucial to conclude the conversation, with clarity regarding responsibilities and timelines.

Leaders should follow up as necessary to monitor progress and maintain open communication, underscoring their commitment to resolution and ongoing support. Employing this structured framework enables leaders to approach challenging conversations with empathy and assertiveness, fostering trust, problem-solving, and improved relationships within their teams and organizations. Effective communication serves as the vehicle through which leaders articulate their vision, build trust, and guide their teams toward achievement. Leaders who have a command over clear and impactful communication possess a powerful tool for inspiring and motivating their teams, resulting in extraordinary accomplishments.

It is important to recognize that communication is not a static skill but rather a dynamic and evolving practice. Leaders should view it as a continuous journey of improvement, where they can refine and enhance their communication abilities over time. This ongoing commitment to mastering the art of communication will not only elevate their leadership effectiveness but also contribute to the overall success and growth of their teams and organizations.

Chapter 6

Decision Making and Problem Solving

"Decision-making is the legacy of our leadership, it shapes
the course of actions, outcomes, and the very
future we envision."

— Joel R. Klemmer

Chapter 6
Decision Making and Problem Solving

The vital aspects of decision making and problem solving in the realm of leadership. Effective leaders are adept at making informed decisions and navigating complex problems. We will explore various techniques and strategies for honing these essential skills and provide illuminating case studies that highlight successful decision-making processes in diverse leadership scenarios.

In the realm of leadership, the decision-making process stands as a fundamental pillar, holding paramount significance. At its core, this process encompasses the series of steps and considerations that leaders undertake to select a course of action from among various alternatives. It serves as the compass guiding leaders through the multifaceted landscape of challenges and opportunities.

Decisions within leadership span a wide spectrum, ranging from routine choices that impact day-to-day operations to strategic determinations that chart the course of an entire organization. The weight of these decisions is palpable, for they not only influence the direction and success of a venture but also reverberate throughout the organizational structure, affecting stakeholders at various levels.

Understanding the intricacies of decision making is indispensable for leaders, as it empowers them to navigate the complexities of leadership effectively. In this journey of exploration, we will unravel the decision-making process's layers, from its theoretical underpinnings to its practical applications, in order to equip leaders with the tools and insights they need to make sound and impactful decisions. So, let us embark on this voyage through the seas of decision making in the context of leadership, where the compass of knowledge will be our guide.

In the intricate landscape of decision making, leaders encounter a diverse array of choices, each requiring a tailored approach. Two overarching categories that encapsulate these choices are programmed decisions and non-programmed decisions, each with its unique characteristics and considerations.

Programmed decisions are the well-trodden paths of decision making. They are routine, repetitive, and rule based. These decisions are often based on established procedures, guidelines, and policies within an organization. Leaders use programmed decisions for everyday matters, where the process is clear-cut and familiar. For instance, determining the weekly work schedule for a team based on predefined rules is a programmed decision.

In contrast, non-programmed decisions are the uncharted territories of leadership. They are complex, unique, and typically require a higher degree of judgment and analysis. Non-programmed decisions arise in situations where no predefined procedures or guidelines can provide clear answers. Leaders must rely on their expertise, creativity, and critical thinking skills to navigate these unstructured challenges. For example, making a strategic decision to enter a new market or addressing a crisis that the organization has never faced before involves non-programmed decision making.

Within the realm of non-programmed decisions, intuition and heuristics play a significant role. Intuition is the gut feeling or instinctual response that leaders may experience when faced with complex or ambiguous situations. It draws upon their accumulated knowledge and experiences, allowing them to make rapid judgments. Heuristics, on the other hand, are mental shortcuts or rules of thumb that leaders use to simplify complex decision-making processes. While these cognitive tools can be valuable in expediting decision making, they also introduce the potential for biases and errors.

Recognizing the distinctions between programmed and non-programmed decisions, as well as understanding the roles of intuition and heuristics, equips leaders with the necessary framework to approach decision making with discernment and agility. In the chapters to follow, we will delve deeper into the intricacies of these decision-making types and explore how leaders can navigate both routine and novel challenges effectively.

Making informed decisions is a fundamental skill, and one structured approach to achieving this is through the rational decision-making model. This systematic method guides leaders through a series of steps to ensure that decisions are based on a thorough analysis of the situation, data, and available alternatives.

The rational decision-making model typically comprises several key stages:

Problem Identification: The process begins with recognizing and defining the problem or decision that needs to be addressed. This step involves clarifying the issue at hand, understanding its scope, and identifying the objectives or outcomes desired.

Generating Alternatives: Once the problem is well-defined, leaders brainstorm and generate a range of possible solutions or alternatives. It is essential to encourage creativity and diverse perspectives during this phase to ensure a comprehensive set of options.

Evaluating Options: With a list of potential solutions in hand, leaders then systematically evaluate each alternative. This evaluation considers factors such as feasibility, cost, benefits, and potential risks. Data and analysis play a critical role in this stage, as leaders gather information to assess the viability and potential consequences of each option.

Selecting the Best Alternative: After a thorough evaluation, leaders choose the alternative that best aligns with the organization's goals, values, and constraints. This decision should be based on a logical and objective assessment of the available data.

Implementation: Once the decision is made, leaders move forward with the implementation phase. This involves developing a clear plan, assigning responsibilities, and setting a timeline for executing the chosen solution.

Monitoring and Feedback: Effective decision making does not end with implementation. Leaders should continuously monitor the outcomes and impacts of their decisions, seeking feedback and adjusting as necessary to ensure the desired results are achieved.

The rational decision-making model places a strong emphasis on logic, analysis, and the systematic consideration of available information. It is a structured approach that aims to minimize biases and subjectivity in decision making. However, it is important to recognize that not all decisions can be approached in a purely rational manner, especially in complex, dynamic, or uncertain environments.

While the rational model provides a valuable framework for many decisions, effective leaders also need to be adaptable and open to other decision-making approaches, such as intuitive decision making, which relies on judgment, experience, and situational awareness. In practice, leaders often blend various decision-making techniques to address the diversity of challenges they encounter in their roles.

Delving into the realm of decision-making, it is essential to explore the concept of intuition and its role in this process. Intuition is that gut feeling, that inner voice, which often guides us in decision-making even in the absence of concrete data or lengthy analysis. In leadership, where decisions can have far-reaching consequences, the ability to harness and trust one's intuition is an asset.

Developing intuition as a leader involves honing the skill of recognizing patterns, drawing from past experiences, and tapping into that innate sense of knowing. It is about cultivating a deep understanding of your field, industry, or team dynamics so that your subconscious mind can draw on this knowledge when needed. Trusting your intuition requires a degree of self-assuredness and confidence in your judgment. It is about listening to that inner voice while still being open to critical evaluation.

Leaders who can effectively develop and trust their intuition are often better equipped to make swift decisions in high-pressure situations. They have a knack for sensing opportunities and potential pitfalls, even when the path forward is unclear. While intuition should never replace a thorough analysis in strategic decision-making, it can complement it, providing an additional layer of insight and guidance. The journey of developing and trusting one's intuition is a continuous process of self-awareness, learning, and refinement, which can significantly enhance a leader's decision-making prowess.

Problem solving, often regarded as a cornerstone of effective leadership, is a multifaceted skill encompassing the ability to identify, analyze, and resolve challenges. In the intricate landscape of leadership, problems can manifest in various forms, from intricate logistical dilemmas to complex interpersonal conflicts. Leaders proficient in problem solving possess the acumen to dissect these challenges systematically.

At its core, problem solving begins with the identification of an issue or obstacle that hinders progress or goal attainment. This requires keen observation, active listening, and a knack for recognizing patterns or deviations from the norm. Once a problem is identified, leaders embark on the analytical phase, delving into the root causes and underlying factors contributing to the issue.

Effective analytical people employ a structured approach that involves breaking down the problem into manageable components. They gather data, conduct research, and collaborate with relevant stakeholders to gain a comprehensive understanding. Armed with this information, leaders can then generate a range of potential solutions, considering both short-term fixes and long-term strategies.

The final phase of problem-solving entails evaluating and selecting the most appropriate solution. Leaders weigh the pros and cons, considering potential risks and benefits. This step requires a discerning eye for assessing the feasibility and impact of each option.

Effective problem solving is more than just a skill—it is a mindset that fosters resilience and adaptability. Leaders who excel in this area not only resolve challenges but also leverage them as opportunities for growth and innovation. In the ever-evolving landscape of leadership, the art of problem solving remains a vital tool for navigating complexities and achieving enduring success. Problem-solving is an essential skill that leaders must possess to effectively navigate the challenges they encounter in their roles. It involves identifying, analyzing, and resolving complex issues to achieve specific goals or overcome obstacles.

Problem-solving encompasses a structured approach to addressing difficulties and making informed decisions.

There are several problem-solving techniques that leaders can employ to tackle issues methodically:

Brainstorming: This technique encourages creative thinking and idea generation within a group. Team members come together to generate a wide range of potential solutions to a problem, promoting diverse perspectives and innovative approaches.

Root Cause Analysis: To address issues at their core, leaders can use root cause analysis. This method involves identifying the underlying causes of a problem rather than just addressing its symptoms. By digging deep into the root causes, leaders can implement more effective and lasting solutions.

SWOT Analysis: SWOT stands for Strengths, Weaknesses, Opportunities, and Threats. It is a structured approach to assessing a situation or problem by evaluating internal strengths and weaknesses and external opportunities and threats. SWOT analysis helps leaders make informed decisions by considering both internal and external factors.

Creative thinking is a fundamental component of effective problem solving. It involves approaching challenges with an open mind and a willingness to explore unconventional solutions. Creative problem solving often requires breaking away from traditional thought patterns and embracing innovative ideas.

Leaders who encourage creative thinking within their teams foster an environment where new and inventive solutions can emerge. This approach not only enhances problem-solving capabilities but also promotes a culture of innovation and adaptability within the organization.

In the realm of leadership, problem solving is an ongoing and dynamic process. Leaders must continuously refine their problem-solving skills, adapt to changing circumstances, and remain open to novel approaches. By mastering problem-solving techniques and nurturing creative thinking, leaders can effectively address challenges and lead their teams toward success in an ever-evolving landscape.

Decision making is an essential part of effective leadership, but it is no simple task. Leaders often grapple with a unique set of challenges that arise from the multifaceted nature of their roles. As a leader, you will find yourself standing at the crossroads of diverse stakeholder interests, where you must navigate a complex web of relationships while charting the course for your organization.

One of the central dilemmas you will encounter is the need to strike a delicate balance among competing interests. This involves considering the viewpoints and needs of a plethora of stakeholders— employees, shareholders, customers, and more. The decisions you make can have far-reaching consequences, and the interests of one stakeholder group may sometimes clash with those of another.

To shed light on the complexity of leadership decision making, let us explore some high-stakes scenarios and their implications. For instance, during a financial crisis, you may grapple with the tough choice of implementing layoffs to reduce costs or prioritizing employee welfare by retaining staff. While layoffs may lead to immediate financial relief, they can also negatively impact employee morale and long-term productivity.

Moreover, you will often need to decide whether to invest in new ventures or technologies that promise growth but come with inherent risks. Balancing the potential for innovation with the need to safeguard your organization's stability is a critical leadership challenge.

Ethical dilemmas are another facet of leadership decision making. You may find yourself in situations where your decisions must align with your organization's values and ethical standards. For instance, you might need to decide whether to report unethical behavior within your company, even if it implicates high-ranking individuals.

These examples underscore the intricate nature of leadership decision making. You will need to navigate complex scenarios that demand a careful weighing of options, rigorous analysis, and a deep understanding of the consequences your choices may entail. Moreover, your decisions can profoundly shape your organization's culture and reputation, exerting a substantial influence on its long-term success.

In this dynamic landscape of leadership, effective decision making is a skill that you must continually refine and hone. It involves not only making sound choices but also effectively communicating those decisions, fostering transparency, and rallying stakeholders around a shared vision. By embracing the multifaceted challenges and responsibilities that come with decision making, you can guide your organization toward growth, resilience, and ethical excellence.

Picture yourself in the shoes of Tim Cook, the CEO of Apple Inc., in 2014 standing at the crossroads of innovation and market dynamics. In the ever-evolving tech landscape, Apple faced a pivotal moment. The challenge was clear—how could the company maintain its leadership position and continue to captivate consumers in a world of rapid technological change? Cook's strategic vision came to the forefront. It involved daring moves, including the introduction of larger iPhone models, the grand unveiling of the Apple Watch, and a strategic expansion into the realm of wearables and services.

To comprehend the significance of this decision, one must delve into the intricacies of consumer preferences, dissect market trends, and anticipate technological advancements. The success of Apple hinged on its ability to not merely respond to change but to proactively predict it. The stakes were high, and the world was watching.

Tim Cook's decision to diversify Apple's product line was nothing short of audacious. It was a bold stride into uncharted territory, yet firmly grounded in a meticulous analysis of market data and a visionary outlook. The magic lies in the fusion of innovative thinking with data-driven decision-making. The outcome? Apple did not just thrive; it flourished.

As a result of this strategic move, Apple experienced a seismic shift in its fortunes. The wearables segment emerged as a major revenue driver, reshaping the company's financial landscape. This case serves as a compelling testament to the transformative power of strategic leadership, backed by a robust foundation of data-driven insights.

Now imagine yourself in the year 2020, a time when the global automotive industry was undergoing a profound transformation. The winds of change were blowing, and the clarion call for sustainability and clean energy was resonating louder than ever. In the midst of this tectonic shift, Jim Farley, at the helm of Ford Motor Company, confronted a monumental decision that would chart the course for the company's future—the pivot toward electric vehicles.

Farley's leadership vision was clear: Ford's destiny was intrinsically linked to its ability to embrace the electric revolution. In a world where traditional combustion engines were facing scrutiny and where the environmental consciousness of consumers was on the rise, Farley recognized that the road ahead was electric. It was a strategic choice that carried immense implications and was poised to reshape the legacy of Ford.

The decision to pivot toward EVs was not a mere leap of faith; it was a calculated move grounded in an acute understanding of industry trends, market dynamics, and the evolving preferences of consumers. Farley and his team embarked on an arduous journey that involved rigorous research, innovation, and collaboration with a diverse spectrum of stakeholders.

The result of this audacious decision was nothing short of transformative. Ford positioned itself as a pioneering force in the EV market, symbolized by groundbreaking initiatives such as the Mustang Mach-E and the electrification of the iconic Ford F-150—the revered workhorse of America. These ventures underscored Ford's commitment to sustainable mobility and its unwavering dedication to meeting the growing demand for eco-conscious transportation solutions.

In a series of tragic events, several individuals lost their lives due to cyanide-laced Tylenol capsules, a popular over-the-counter medication. The nation was gripped by fear, and Johnson & Johnson, a household name, found itself entangled in a nightmare scenario. It was a pivotal moment that would test the mettle of both the company and its CEO, James E. Burke.

Burke faced a daunting dilemma that would have a profound impact not only on public health but also on the reputation and future of Johnson & Johnson. The decision before him was monumental: how to respond to a crisis of unprecedented magnitude. The path he chose would set a precedent for crisis management and ethical leadership for years to come.

In the face of this life-and-death situation, Burke's response was swift and resolute. Without hesitation, he made the extraordinary decision to recall a staggering thirty-one million bottles of Tylenol, a move that would cost the company millions of dollars. However, this decision was not an automatic reaction driven by financial considerations. It was grounded in an unwavering commitment to the safety and well-being of the customers who had placed their trust in Johnson & Johnson's products.

Burke's leadership during this crisis was characterized by transparency, cooperation with authorities, and an unyielding dedication to improving product safety. It was not merely about crisis management; it was a testament to the ethical principles that underpinned his leadership philosophy. The recall was not just a financial hit for the company; it was a moral stand, a declaration that no cost was too high when it came to safeguarding human lives.

The Tylenol crisis and Johnson & Johnson's response stand as a paragon of ethical leadership in times of adversity. It reminds us that true leaders are defined not only by their actions in moments of triumph but, perhaps more significantly, by their decisions in the crucible of crisis. It serves as an enduring case study on how transparency, integrity, and a steadfast commitment to values can not only navigate a company through the darkest of storms but also emerge as a beacon of trust and resilience in the eyes of the public.

So, what can we glean from this remarkable case studies? It underscores that effective leadership decision-making is a delicate dance between visionary thinking and analytical precision. It teaches us that embracing change is not merely an option but a necessity in a fast-paced world. Above all, it illustrates that leaders who dare to envision and execute audacious strategies, grounded in data and a clear vision, can lead their organizations to unprecedented heights. Resonating within us the importance of unwavering ethical principles in leadership and the profound impact that a principled decision can have on the fate of an organization and the trust of a nation.

At the heart of leadership lies the art of problem-solving. Leaders are entrusted with the responsibility of not only setting a vision and inspiring others but also with the crucial task of overcoming obstacles and achieving goals. Whether it is a minor hiccup or a major organizational challenge, problems are an inevitable part of leadership.

However, the terrain of leadership is often riddled with complexities. In the real world, problems rarely come with straightforward solutions neatly wrapped in a bow. Leaders must grapple with uncertainty, ambiguity, and multifaceted issues that require thoughtful consideration. These challenges are the crucible in which leadership is forged and tested.

Imagine a CEO faced with the task of navigating a rapidly changing market landscape, where technological disruptions, shifting consumer preferences, and global economic fluctuations converge. The path forward is anything but clear-cut. It is a landscape characterized by uncertainty, where the traditional rulebook no longer applies.

In such situations, leaders must possess the ability to navigate complexity and ambiguity. They need to see beyond the surface, analyze the interconnected web of factors at play, and devise innovative solutions. This is where problem-solving in leadership transcends mere technical proficiency; it becomes an art form.

Amazon's challenge was monumental: how to manage its vast network of fulfillment centers, ensuring swift and efficient deliveries to a customer base with ever-increasing demands. In the dynamic world of e-commerce, speed is paramount, and customers expect their orders to arrive at their doorstep almost as soon as they click "buy." Jeff Bezos understood that to meet these expectations and stay competitive, Amazon needed a cutting-edge strategy.

The key to Amazon's systematic problem-solving approach lies in data analytics, automation, and robotics. The company harnessed the power of big data to gain valuable insights into consumer behavior, demand patterns, and inventory management. By meticulously analyzing this data, Amazon could anticipate customer needs, optimize its product stocking strategies, and streamline the order fulfillment process. This data-driven approach allowed Amazon to efficiently manage a staggering array of products while minimizing storage costs and maximizing shipping efficiency.

Furthermore, automation became a pivotal element in Amazon's fulfillment strategy. The company introduced a fleet of robots in its fulfillment centers to work alongside human employees, significantly reducing the time it took to retrieve items from storage and prepare them for shipment. These robots collaborated seamlessly with their human counterparts, enhancing overall productivity and order accuracy. The automation of routine tasks liberated Amazon's workforce to focus on more complex and value-added activities, further contributing to efficiency gains.

Continuous refinement was another hallmark of Amazon's problem-solving strategy. Recognizing that the e-commerce landscape was in a constant state of evolution, Bezos and his team emphasized adaptability. They invested in research and development, seeking innovative technologies and methodologies to stay ahead of the competition. From drone delivery prototypes to predictive analytics algorithms, Amazon explored various avenues to refine its operations continually.

Amazon's commitment to meeting customer expectations for rapid delivery while maintaining cost-effectiveness was instrumental in its success. The company's ability to adapt and innovate within the intricate logistics landscape reshaped the e-commerce industry. As a leader, Jeff Bezos's visionary problem-solving approach in fulfillment center optimization serves as a remarkable example of how data, automation, and a relentless pursuit of excellence can transform complex challenges into opportunities for growth and leadership in the digital age.

Google, the search engine giant, confronted a colossal challenge: to continually improve its search algorithms in the face of the internet's exponential growth. As the volume of online information exploded, the demand for more relevant and precise search results became increasingly pressing. In a world where information is at our fingertips, the quality of search outcomes is paramount.

Larry Page and Sergey Brin recognized that the heart of Google's success lay in delivering search results that matched users' intent as closely as possible. Their strategic response was a testament to innovation and data-driven decision-making. Google systematically embarked on a journey of refining its search algorithms, employing an iterative problem-solving approach to tackle this monumental task.

Central to this evolution was the incorporation of cutting-edge technologies, notably machine learning. Google harnessed the power of machine learning to enhance its search quality continuously. By analyzing user behavior patterns, the search engine became adept at understanding the nuances of individual queries and delivering results that precisely met users' needs. Machine learning algorithms, underpinned by massive datasets, allowed Google to adapt and respond dynamically to the ever-changing landscape of online content.

The iterative nature of Google's problem-solving approach was a defining characteristic of its success. Rather than resting on past achievements, Page and Brin and their team pushed for continuous innovation. They recognized that the digital realm was in perpetual flux, with new webpages, content formats, and user behaviors emerging incessantly. Google embraced this dynamism, viewing it not as a challenge but as an opportunity to excel.

User feedback played a crucial role in this process. Google actively sought input from its vast user base, listening to their experiences and concerns. This user-centric approach facilitated adjustments and refinements to the search algorithms, ensuring that the search results remained highly relevant and useful.

Over the years, Google's search algorithms evolved from their humble beginnings into sophisticated, intelligent systems capable of understanding natural language and semantic context. This evolution enabled Google to maintain its position as the world's premier search engine, setting the gold standard for delivering information accurately and efficiently.

Toyota, one of the world's leading automakers, grappled with a monumental challenge: how to enhance manufacturing efficiency without compromising product quality. In a fiercely competitive industry, the pressure to produce vehicles faster and more cost-effectively was ever-present. However, Toyota's leaders recognized that efficiency gains should never come at the expense of quality. This marked the genesis of their groundbreaking approach to problem-solving and manufacturing: the Toyota Production System (TPS).

At the core of TPS were lean manufacturing principles, designed to eliminate waste in all its forms. Waste, in Toyota's perspective, included not only physical waste like excess inventory but also inefficiencies in processes, underutilized employee skills, and suboptimal resource allocation. Taiichi Ohno, a visionary leader at Toyota, played a pivotal role in formulating and implementing these principles.

The essence of lean manufacturing was to do more with less, a concept that resonated deeply with Toyota's commitment to continuous improvement. The TPS approach systematically identified inefficiencies and bottlenecks in the production process and sought to eliminate them. This involved empowering employees at all levels to actively engage in problem-solving and contribute their insights.

One of the cornerstones of TPS was the concept of "Just-in-Time" production, which aimed to produce and deliver components and finished vehicles precisely when needed, thereby reducing inventory and associated costs. This was a testament to Toyota's commitment to efficiency and resource optimization.

Another fundamental element of TPS was "Kaizen," the philosophy of continuous improvement. Toyota ingrained this ethos into its organizational culture, encouraging employees to seek incremental improvements in their work processes daily. The cumulative effect of these small improvements was profound, as they added up to significant gains in efficiency and quality over time.

What set Toyota apart was its holistic approach to problem-solving. TPS was not merely a set of techniques but a comprehensive philosophy that encompassed every aspect of the manufacturing process. It embraced employee involvement, supplier relationships, and a relentless pursuit of perfection.

Over the years, Toyota's commitment to lean manufacturing principles bore fruit. The company achieved remarkable improvements in production efficiency while upholding its reputation for top-notch quality. Toyota vehicles became synonymous with reliability and durability.

Moreover, Toyota's influence extended far beyond its own operations. TPS became a global benchmark for efficient production and inspired countless organizations to adopt lean manufacturing principles. The lessons learned from Toyota's approach to problem-solving, efficiency, and quality continue to shape industries worldwide.

Decision making and problem solving are indispensable skills for effective leadership. Leaders who can navigate the intricacies of decision making and tackle complex problems with confidence are better equipped to guide their organizations toward success. As you continue your leadership journey, remember that these skills can be refined through practice and continuous learning.

Chapter 7

Leading Teams: Dynamics and Management

"Leadership thrives when diverse hands come together
to confront challenges, forging a path to success."

– Joel R. Klemmer

Chapter 7
Leading Teams: Dynamics and Management

Effective leadership in the contemporary business world is synonymous with the adept orchestration of teams. Leaders must wear multiple hats, acting as visionaries, motivators, and facilitators, all while fostering a sense of camaraderie among team members. The importance of teamwork cannot be overstated; it is the backbone of many successful organizations.

The process begins with constructing teams that are not just a random amalgamation of individuals but a harmonious ensemble that complements each other's strengths and compensates for weaknesses. It involves a judicious selection of team members based on their skills, experiences, and cultural fit. A diverse team, in terms of perspectives, backgrounds, and skill sets, can often bring a wealth of ideas and innovation to the table.

Moreover, setting clear goals and expectations is paramount. Team members should have a crystal-clear understanding of their roles, responsibilities, and the collective objectives towards which they are working. Effective communication is essential in this phase, ensuring everyone is on the same page and aligned with the organization's mission.

Once a team is formed, the leader's role transforms into that of a mentor and coach. It is about empowering team members, providing them with the necessary resources and support, and instilling a sense of ownership and accountability. Leaders must also be adept at recognizing and appreciating the contributions of their team members. Recognizing and celebrating achievements, no matter how small, can significantly boost morale and motivation.

Conflicts are an inevitable part of any team dynamic, but effective leaders view them as opportunities for growth and improvement rather than roadblocks. Conflict resolution is a vital skill, and leaders must be adept at facilitating constructive dialogues and finding common ground. The goal is to transform conflicts into opportunities for creative problem-solving and innovation.

In parallel, fostering a collaborative environment is essential for harnessing the collective intelligence of the team. This entails creating a culture where ideas are freely shared, feedback is welcomed, and collaboration is actively encouraged. When team members feel that their contributions are valued and that they have a stake in the team's success, it can lead to enhanced creativity and productivity.

In the modern business landscape, remote and virtual teams are becoming increasingly prevalent. Leading such teams requires a unique skill set that includes effective communication across distances, trust-building in a virtual setting, and utilizing technology to facilitate collaboration. Leaders must adapt to these new challenges while ensuring that remote team members feel as connected and valued as their in-person counterparts.

Building high-performing teams is a cornerstone of effective leadership in the modern business landscape. Teams, often described as the building blocks of organizations, play a pivotal role in achieving organizational goals. They are the engines that drive projects, solve complex problems, and innovate solutions. Understanding the importance of team dynamics is essential for leaders looking to harness the full potential of their teams.

Strategic Synergy

Teams are not just a collection of individuals; they are a synergy of talents, expertise, and shared objectives. In today's complex and fast-paced business environment, the ability to collaborate effectively within teams can make or break an organization's success. Teams are the vehicles through which strategic initiatives are executed, and their performance directly impacts the achievement of organizational goals.

Consider a scenario where a company aims to launch a new product in a competitive market. The task is multifaceted, involving product design, marketing strategy, supply chain management, and more. Without effective teams, each of these components may operate in silos, resulting in inefficiencies and missed opportunities. However, when these teams work together cohesively, the organization can streamline its efforts, make agile decisions, and bring the product to market more efficiently.

One of the core strengths of teams lies in their diversity. Teams are often composed of individuals with varying backgrounds, experiences, and skill sets. This diversity can be a powerful catalyst for innovation and problem solving. When team members bring different perspectives to the table, they offer a broader range of ideas and approaches.

For example, in a software development team, a programmer, a user interface designer, and a quality assurance analyst each bring their unique expertise to the project. The programmer's focus may be on functionality, the designer's on user experience, and the analyst's on quality. When these individuals collaborate, their diverse viewpoints can lead to the creation of a more robust and user-friendly product.

In addition to diversity, effective team dynamics encompass trust, communication, and a shared sense of purpose. Teams that trust each other are more likely to take risks, share ideas openly, and support each other in overcoming challenges. Open and transparent communication within a team ensures that everyone is on the same page, reducing the chances of misunderstandings and conflicts. A shared sense of purpose, driven by a common set of goals and values, gives teams a cohesive identity and direction.

Building successful teams is a critical responsibility for leaders, and it requires a thoughtful approach.

Team formation and composition are intricate processes that require careful consideration and guidance from leaders. Understanding the stages of team formation and knowing how to assemble and structure effective teams are essential aspects of successful leadership.

Team formation typically follows a series of stages, which are commonly referred to as forming, storming, norming, performing, and adjourning. These stages, first introduced by psychologist Bruce Tuckman in 1965, describe the natural progression of a team's development:

Forming: In this initial stage, team members are introduced, and they get to know each other. They often feel polite and tentative, trying to understand the team's purpose and their roles within it. Team members may have questions about objectives and procedures, and they rely on the leader for guidance and direction.

Storming: As the team starts to work together, conflicts and differences in opinions may emerge. This stage can be challenging, as team members assert themselves and vie for leadership positions or influence. Effective leaders recognize that this phase is a necessary part of team development and help the team navigate through conflicts constructively.

Norming: During this stage, team members begin to resolve their differences, develop norms or rules for collaboration, and establish clearer roles and responsibilities. Trust starts to build, and team members become more cohesive. Leaders play a crucial role in facilitating this transition by encouraging open communication and setting expectations.

Performing: The performing stage is characterized by increased productivity and collaboration. Team members work together efficiently, leverage each other's strengths, and achieve their goals. Leaders should continue to support the team by providing resources and recognition for their efforts while allowing them a degree of autonomy.

Adjourning: In some team dynamics models, adjourning is considered an additional stage that occurs when the team's project is completed. During this phase, team members may experience a sense of loss as they disband. Leaders can help by acknowledging the team's achievements and providing closure.

There are essential aspects of assembling and structuring effective teams. Building successful teams is a critical responsibility for leaders, and it requires a thoughtful approach. Here, we can explore each factor that plays a pivotal role in this process.

Diversity: The importance of diversity in team composition cannot be overstated. Diverse teams bring together individuals with varying backgrounds, skills, and perspectives. This diversity fosters creativity, as team members approach problems from different angles and offer fresh insights. Leaders should actively seek to assemble teams with a mix of experiences, expertise, and cultural backgrounds. By doing so, they create an environment where innovation and problem-solving flourish.

Roles and Responsibilities: Clarity in roles and responsibilities is the bedrock of effective teamwork. When each team member understands their specific role and what is expected of them, it minimizes confusion and potential conflicts. Leaders should define roles and responsibilities clearly, considering the strengths and weaknesses of each team member. This approach ensures that tasks are allocated appropriately, and everyone can contribute effectively.

Communication: Effective communication lies at the heart of successful teams. Leaders should create an environment that encourages open and transparent communication. Team members should feel comfortable sharing their ideas, concerns, and feedback. Active listening is a skill that should be cultivated within the team. Leaders can foster this by setting an example of attentive listening and creating opportunities for team members to express themselves freely.

Goals and Objectives: Teams must have a clear sense of purpose. Leaders should establish well-defined goals and objectives that align with the organization's mission. When team members understand the "why" behind their work and the expected outcomes, they are more motivated and focused. It is essential to communicate these goals effectively and regularly revisit them to ensure alignment and progress tracking.

Support and Resources: To excel, teams need adequate support and resources. Leaders should provide the tools, training programs, and mentorship required for team members to perform at their best. This support may include access to specialized software, ongoing skill development opportunities, or access to subject matter experts. Leaders should regularly assess the needs of their teams and ensure they have the resources necessary for success.

Leadership: Finally, leadership within the team is crucial. Appointing a capable team leader or facilitator is essential for guiding the team through its various stages of development. This leader should not only provide direction but also serve as a mediator during conflicts and ensure that team members remain motivated and engaged. Leadership within the team can be rotational, where different members take on leadership roles in different projects or phases, fostering a sense of shared responsibility.

Effective team leadership is a multi-faceted skill that distinguishes exceptional leaders from the rest. It is not just about telling team members what to do but guiding them towards achieving collective goals. The art of team leadership and management is about key principles.

Assembling the Right Team: One of the foundational steps in effective team leadership is the strategic assembly of the right team members. We need to explore the selection process, offering insights on how to identify individuals whose diverse skills and perspectives can propel your team towards innovation and problem-solving. Research into the role of diversity can be the catalyst in sparking creativity within your team and enhance your ability to address complex challenges.

Fostering a Collaborative Environment: In addition to team composition, nurturing a collaborative environment is vital for effective team leadership. Look at key strategies and best practices for creating an atmosphere where open and transparent communication thrives. Active listening is emphasized, ensuring that team members feel heard and valued, leading to the uninhibited exchange of ideas and concerns.

Defining Roles and Responsibilities: Ambiguity within a team can lead to misunderstandings and conflicts. To mitigate this, we want to provide guidance on the clear definition of roles and responsibilities. By ensuring that every team member comprehends what is expected of them, we can minimize potential sources of discord and boost overall team efficiency.

Establishing Clear Goals and Objectives: Effective teams are those with a shared sense of purpose. The critical process of setting clear, actionable goals and objectives for your team will ensure that every member understands the collective mission and expected outcomes of their combined efforts are paramount for success.

Providing Support and Resources: No team can excel without the necessary support, resources, and training. The leadership role ensures that teams have access to the tools, training programs, or mentorship required for their success. By providing the appropriate support, you empower your team to perform at its best.

Leadership in Team Development: Effective team leadership does not stop at the formation stage; it extends throughout the team's journey. You want to place an importance on appointing a team leader or facilitator who can guide the team through its stages of development. This individual serves as a mediator during conflicts, provides direction when needed, and keeps the team on track toward its goals.

Leadership Styles in Team Management: Leadership is not a one-size-fits-all concept, and this is particularly evident in team management. Different situations and teams call for various leadership styles, each with its unique approach and benefits. Go beyond the basics to discuss leadership styles that have proven to be exceptionally effective in your team management.

Use transformational leadership, known for inspiring and motivating team members to reach new heights. Dive into the realm of servant leadership, where leaders prioritize the well-being and growth of their team members, and democratic leadership, which emphasizes collaboration and decision-making by the entire team.

Influence of Leadership Styles on Team Dynamics and Outcomes: As we explained, the leadership style you choose can significantly impact your team's dynamics and outcomes. Transformational leadership can ignite enthusiasm and innovation within your team, propelling them towards outstanding achievements. Servant leadership fosters trust and loyalty, resulting in a more committed and engaged team. Democratic leadership can empower team members, making them feel valued and respected in the decision-making process.

Whether you are leading a small, close-knit team or a large, diverse group, understanding and mastering these leadership styles can be a game-changer. Go the extra mile to equip yourself with the knowledge and tools you need to become an agile and effective team leader who can adapt their style to meet the ever-evolving needs of your team and organization. Continually improve to unlock the secrets of effective team leadership and management, which will in turn unlock the full potential of your teams and drive them towards unparalleled success.

In the realm of team leadership and management, the importance of clear and well-defined goals and expectations cannot be overstated. These elements serve as the rally point for your team, guiding their efforts, fostering collaboration, and ultimately driving success.

Clear goals serve as the foundation upon which your team's actions are built. They provide direction and purpose, answering the fundamental question of what your team aims to achieve. Goals create a shared vision, aligning team members towards a common objective.

When team members understand their roles and responsibilities within the context of defined goals, accountability naturally emerges. Everyone knows how their contributions contribute to the overall mission. This awareness encourages ownership of tasks and promotes a sense of responsibility within the team.

Clear goals encourage collaboration by creating a unified focus. When everyone knows what they are working towards, team members can pool their efforts effectively. This synergy enables the team to tackle complex challenges, draw on each other's strengths, and innovate collectively.

Well-defined goals serve as a source of motivation. They provide team members with a sense of purpose and accomplishment as milestones are reached. Additionally, transparent goals can increase engagement by showing individuals how their work directly contributes to the team's progress and the organization's success.

To set and communicate goals effectively, leaders can employ several strategies. Firstly, ensure that goals are specific, measurable, achievable, relevant, and time-bound (SMART). This framework provides clarity and structure to your objectives.

Effective communication is key to conveying goals and expectations. Engage in open and transparent dialogue with your team.

Discuss the overarching mission, individual roles, and how each team member's contributions tie into the larger goal.

Be open to feedback and encourage your team members to share their perspectives on the goals and expectations. Periodically assess progress and adapt goals as needed to address changing circumstances or emerging opportunities.

Setting clear and well-communicated goals and expectations is a cornerstone of effective team leadership. These goals provide a roadmap for your team's journey, fostering collaboration, accountability, motivation, and engagement. By employing strategies such as SMART goal setting, open communication, and adaptability, leaders can harness the power of clear objectives to guide their teams toward success in the modern business world.

In doing so you are nurturing healthy team dynamics in the delicate ecosystem. At the heart of these dynamics lies the cornerstone of trust, an essential element that binds team members together and enables seamless collaboration.

Trust is the glue that holds a team together, fostering an environment where individuals feel safe to express themselves, take risks, and work harmoniously towards common goals. Without trust, even the most talented team can falter, as doubts and insecurities undermine collaboration.

Trust-building is an ongoing process that begins with leaders setting the example. It is about being authentic, consistent, and reliable. Leaders can foster trust by delivering on promises, being transparent about decisions and actions, and admitting mistakes when they occur. When leaders trust their team members, it often leads to reciprocity.

Communication is a vital tool for building trust. Leaders should encourage open and honest dialogue, where team members feel comfortable sharing their thoughts, ideas, and concerns. Actively listen to your team members, acknowledge their contributions, and respond constructively to their feedback.

Align your team around shared goals and a compelling vision. When everyone understands and believes in the mission, it can enhance trust and motivation. Ensure that team members recognize how their individual roles contribute to the collective success.

Collaboration thrives in an environment of trust. Encourage your team to work together by providing opportunities for joint projects, brainstorming sessions, and cross-functional initiatives. Recognize and reward collaborative efforts to reinforce its importance.

Conflicts are a natural part of any team dynamic. Leaders should be adept at resolving conflicts promptly and fairly. Address issues directly, encourage open communication to understand different perspectives, and guide the team towards mutually beneficial solutions.

Organize team-building activities that promote trust and collaboration. These activities can be both fun and insightful, helping team members build rapport and understand each other's strengths and weaknesses.

Trust and collaboration are the bedrock of productive team dynamics. Leaders play a pivotal role in fostering trust by setting an example of transparency, effective communication, and accountability. By aligning the team around shared goals, resolving conflicts constructively, and providing opportunities for collaboration and team building, leaders can create an environment where their teams can thrive and achieve collective success.

Effective communication is the conduit through which ideas flow, conflicts are resolved, and goals are achieved. The profound significance of communication within teams and offer practical tips for fostering open and constructive communication among team members.

Communication is the lifeblood of teams. It serves as the vehicle for sharing information, clarifying expectations, and aligning efforts towards common objectives. Effective communication enhances transparency, trust, and collaboration, all of which are essential for team success.

Trust is the foundation of productive team communication. Team members must trust that their voices will be heard and respected. Leaders can foster trust by actively listening to their team members, valuing their input, and acknowledging their contributions. When trust is established, team members are more likely to communicate openly and honestly.

Leaders should create an environment where team members feel comfortable expressing their thoughts, ideas, and concerns. Encourage open dialogue by setting an example. Be approachable and willing to listen, even when the message might be challenging to hear. Foster a culture where questions and constructive feedback are welcome.

Active listening is a fundamental communication skill. Encourage team members to not only hear what others are saying but also understand their perspectives. This involves giving full attention, asking clarifying questions, and empathizing with their viewpoints. Active listening promotes deeper understanding and prevents misunderstandings.

Effective communication is clear and concise. Encourage team members to articulate their thoughts in a straightforward manner. Avoid jargon and unnecessary complexity. The goal is to ensure that messages are easily understood and interpreted correctly.

Keep team members informed about project progress, changes, and relevant developments. Regular updates help prevent surprises and keep everyone on the same page. Use a combination of team meetings, emails, and collaboration tools to share information effectively.

Conflict is natural within teams, but it must be managed constructively. Provide guidance on how conflicts should be addressed, emphasizing respectful and solution-focused discussions. Encourage team members to express their concerns and work together to find resolutions.

Establish a feedback loop where team members can provide input on processes, procedures, and team dynamics. Constructive feedback can lead to improvements and enhance communication over time.

Effective communication is the life force that powers successful teams. It builds trust, promotes openness, and facilitates collaboration. Leaders play a pivotal role in creating an environment where team members feel comfortable communicating their ideas and concerns. By actively listening, promoting clarity, resolving conflicts constructively, and fostering a culture of feedback, leaders can enhance communication within their teams, leading to improved performance and outcomes.

Conflict within teams is not inherently negative; in fact, it can be a catalyst for growth and innovation. However, effective leaders must be adept at managing conflicts constructively to prevent them from harming team productivity and cohesion.

Conflicts within teams often stem from differing opinions, perspectives, and personalities. These differences, while natural, can create tension and disrupt team dynamics. Leaders should recognize that not all conflicts are detrimental; some can lead to better decision-making and creative solutions. However, it is essential to manage conflicts when they become destructive.

Differing opinions are a common source of conflict in teams. These disagreements can arise from varying interpretations of data, differing priorities, or alternative approaches to a problem. Leaders should encourage team members to express their opinions openly while maintaining a respectful and constructive tone. Acknowledge that diversity of thought can lead to better decision-making when managed effectively.

Conflict is an inherent aspect of team dynamics and can arise from a variety of sources, each presenting its unique challenges. One common source of conflict stems from differing goals among team members. When individuals have conflicting objectives or prioritize different outcomes, it can lead to friction within the team. These clashes of interest may arise due to varying perspectives on what should be prioritized or achieved.

Personality clashes constitute another frequent cause of conflict within teams. Differences in personality traits, communication styles, or work habits can generate tension and disagreements. When team members' individual preferences and behaviors clash, it can disrupt the overall team dynamic.

Role ambiguity is another factor that can contribute to conflicts within teams. When roles and responsibilities are unclear or ill-defined, it may lead to overlaps, gaps, or misunderstandings about who should be responsible for specific tasks or decisions. Such ambiguity can result in disputes regarding accountability and authority.

Scarce resources, whether they involve limited budgets, recognition, or other valuable assets, can be a significant source of conflict. Competition for these resources within the team can spark disagreements, as members vie for their fair share or attempt to secure advantages for themselves or their projects.

Miscommunication or inadequate communication practices can also give rise to conflicts. Poorly articulated instructions, misunderstandings, or a lack of clarity in conveying information can lead to disagreements among team members. When individuals interpret messages differently or feel that they have been left in the dark, it can breed discord.

Performance issues and disparities in perceived effort can create conflicts as well. When some team members believe that others are not pulling their weight or contributing as expected, it can lead to accusations and disputes. Differences in performance standards or expectations can also contribute to these conflicts.

Lastly, change and uncertainty can generate resistance and conflicts within teams. When significant changes occur, such as organizational restructuring or shifts in project goals, team members may react with apprehension or resistance. The uncertainty surrounding these changes can lead to disputes about their implications and necessity.

Understanding these common sources of conflict is crucial for leaders and team members alike. By recognizing these potential triggers, teams can take proactive measures to address and mitigate conflicts, fostering a more harmonious and productive working environment.

Effective conflict resolution is an indispensable skill for leaders when fostering a harmonious team environment. Here, we explore proven conflict resolution strategies that leaders can employ to address and resolve conflicts within their teams.

First and foremost, open communication serves as a cornerstone for resolving conflicts. Leaders should actively encourage and facilitate open and honest communication among team members. Creating a safe space where concerns, grievances, and opinions can be freely expressed promotes understanding and lays the foundation for conflict resolution.

Active listening is another key strategy in conflict resolution. Leaders must ensure that team members not only hear but actively listen to one another. This involves giving full attention to what others are saying, asking clarifying questions to gain a deeper understanding, and empathizing with their perspectives. Active listening fosters empathy and helps prevent miscommunication.

In cases where conflicts escalate and direct communication may not suffice, mediation can be a valuable approach. Leaders may consider involving a neutral third party with expertise in conflict resolution to mediate and facilitate resolution discussions. This mediator can help guide the process toward a mutually acceptable solution.

To prevent conflicts stemming from role ambiguity, leaders should proactively define and clarify roles and responsibilities within the team. When everyone understands their respective duties and boundaries, it minimizes the potential for conflicts arising from overlapping or unclear responsibilities.

Establishing ground rules for team behavior and communication is another effective conflict prevention strategy. By setting clear team norms and expectations, leaders can prevent future conflicts by ensuring that all team members understand the acceptable standards of behavior and communication.

Encouraging team members to focus on underlying interests rather than fixed positions can lead to more productive conflict resolution. Leaders should promote a problem-solving approach that seeks solutions where all parties involved can benefit, thereby creating a win-win outcome.

Providing conflict resolution training to team members equips them with the necessary skills to manage conflicts constructively. These training programs can cover various aspects of conflict resolution, such as active listening, negotiation, and mediation techniques, empowering team members to handle conflicts more effectively.

Finally, leaders should ensure that any resolutions and agreements reached during conflict resolution discussions are well-documented. This documentation helps prevent misunderstandings in the future by providing a clear record of what was agreed upon. It also reinforces accountability and ensures that both parties uphold their commitments.

By incorporating these conflict resolution strategies into their leadership toolkit, leaders can effectively manage and resolve conflicts within their teams, promoting a more productive and harmonious work environment.

In addition to resolution strategies there are effective conflict resolution techniques that are essential tools in a leader's repertoire for maintaining team harmony and productivity. Here, are specific techniques that leaders can employ to navigate and resolve conflicts within their teams:

Maintain Neutrality: One of the cardinal rules in conflict resolution is to stay neutral. Leaders should avoid taking sides or showing favoritism when mediating conflicts. This impartial stance fosters trust and ensures that the resolution process is fair and unbiased.

Demonstrate Empathy: Empathy is a powerful tool in conflict resolution. Leaders should strive to understand and acknowledge the feelings and perspectives of those involved in the conflict. Demonstrating empathy validates individuals' emotions and encourages open dialogue.

Stay Calm: Emotions can run high during conflicts, and leaders must model composure and emotional control. By remaining calm and composed, leaders set a positive example for team members and create an environment where rational discussion can take place.

Use "I" Statements: Encouraging team members to use "I" statements is a valuable technique. This approach involves expressing feelings and concerns using phrases like "I feel" or "I think" instead of placing blame on others. "I" statements promote individual accountability and prevent finger-pointing.

Facilitate Brainstorming: To generate potential solutions to the conflict, leaders can facilitate brainstorming sessions. Encouraging team members to contribute ideas and solutions fosters a sense of collaboration and ownership in the resolution process. Brainstorming can uncover creative solutions that might not have been apparent otherwise.

Follow-Up: Conflict resolution does not end with an agreement. Leaders should follow up with the involved parties to ensure that the agreements reached are upheld. This step reinforces accountability and helps prevent conflicts from resurfacing in the future. Regular check-ins can also identify any lingering issues or concerns that need addressing.

By incorporating these conflict resolution techniques into their leadership approach, leaders can effectively navigate and resolve conflicts within their teams. These techniques promote fairness, empathy, and open communication, fostering a healthy and collaborative team environment. The benefits of fostering a collaborative team culture are multifaceted and extend to various aspects of team performance and organizational success.

Collaboration acts as a catalyst for innovation. When team members from diverse backgrounds and with different perspectives come together, they can generate fresh ideas and novel approaches to challenges. The synergy of collaboration often leads to innovative solutions and creative problem-solving that might not have been achievable by individuals working in isolation.

Teams that collaborate effectively tend to be more productive. Collaboration streamlines tasks and projects, as team members support each other's efforts and work collectively toward shared objectives. The division of labor, combined with cooperation, enhances efficiency, enabling teams to accomplish tasks in a more streamlined and timely manner.

Collaborative teams excel in making well-informed decisions. By leveraging the collective knowledge and expertise of team members, they can thoroughly evaluate options and alternatives. The diversity of perspectives allows for a more comprehensive consideration of factors, leading to more thoughtful and effective decision-making processes.

A collaborative environment fosters higher levels of employee engagement. When individuals feel that their contributions are valued and they witness the tangible impact of their work within a team, they are more likely to be motivated and committed to their roles. This heightened engagement leads to increased job satisfaction and a stronger sense of purpose among team members.

Collaboration encourages the sharing of knowledge and expertise among team members. Through collaboration, team members learn from each other, acquire new skills, and expand their areas of expertise. This knowledge sharing not only benefits individual development but also contributes to the overall competence and proficiency of the team.

Several prominent organizations serve as exemplars of fostering collaborative environments within their teams, and their success stories provide valuable insights into the benefits of such cultures.

Google is synonymous with innovation and collaboration. The company's renowned "20% time" policy allows employees to dedicate a portion of their work hours to personal projects. This approach nurtures creativity and encourages employees to explore new ideas and solutions, often leading to groundbreaking innovations. Google's commitment to fostering a culture of collaboration has contributed to its position as a global leader in technology and innovation.

Apple's success is built on the synergy between its design and engineering teams. Collaboration is deeply ingrained in the company's DNA, with these teams working closely together to develop iconic products like the iPhone and iPad. By bringing together creative visionaries and technical experts, Apple consistently produces innovative and aesthetically pleasing products that resonate with consumers worldwide.

The renowned animation studio Pixar places a strong emphasis on collaboration among its creative teams. From writers and animators to directors and producers, Pixar's culture encourages open communication and cross-disciplinary collaboration. This approach has yielded a remarkable track record of critically acclaimed and commercially successful films, showcasing the power of teamwork in creative endeavors.

Under the leadership of CEO Satya Nadella, Microsoft has undergone a significant transformation toward a more collaborative organizational culture. The company now prioritizes open communication and cross-functional collaboration among its teams. This shift has been instrumental in driving innovation and enabling Microsoft to adapt to rapidly changing markets. By embracing collaboration, Microsoft continues to thrive as a technology giant in the modern era.

Effective team development and performance evaluation are integral aspects of successful leadership. Leaders play a pivotal role in guiding their teams toward peak performance and growth.

Leaders are not just taskmasters; they are also coaches and mentors. Their ability to foster team development and guide performance is crucial in achieving organizational goals. By providing support, feedback, and a conducive work environment, leaders can inspire their teams to reach new heights.

Recognizing and nurturing the potential of team members is a fundamental responsibility of leaders. This involves identifying individual strengths, weaknesses, and areas for growth. Through effective communication and feedback, leaders can help team members discover their talents and unleash their full potential.

Coaching is an essential leadership skill that goes hand in hand with team development. Effective coaching empowers team members, helps them overcome challenges, and fosters continuous improvement. In this section, we will delve into the intricacies of coaching within the context of team development.

Leaders serve as coaches by guiding team members in setting and achieving their goals. Coaching involves active listening, providing constructive feedback, and offering support. It is about helping individuals grow both personally and professionally, ultimately benefiting the entire team.

Successful coaching requires specific strategies, such as setting clear objectives, tailoring coaching approaches to individual needs, and creating a safe space for open communication. Leaders can employ techniques like active questioning, goal setting, and regular check-ins to facilitate team members' growth.

Measuring team performance is a critical aspect of effective leadership. It involves assessing how well a team is achieving its goals and contributing to the organization's success.

Key Performance Indicators (KPIs) and metrics provide quantifiable measures of team performance. They serve as benchmarks against which progress, and success can be gauged. Leaders should identify relevant KPIs and metrics that align with the team's objectives and regularly track them to monitor performance.

Feedback is a cornerstone of performance evaluation. Leaders should provide timely and constructive feedback to team members. This feedback should be specific, highlighting both strengths and areas for improvement. Additionally, leaders should encourage team members to provide feedback to one another, fostering a culture of open communication and growth.

Teams should strive for continuous improvement. This involves regularly reviewing performance data, identifying areas where enhancements are needed, and taking action to implement positive changes. Leaders play a pivotal role in guiding this process, ensuring that teams remain adaptable and responsive to evolving challenges.

Leading teams effectively is a multifaceted skill that requires a deep understanding of team dynamics, communication, conflict resolution, and performance management. Leaders who can build and manage high-performing teams are better equipped to drive innovation and achieve organizational success. As you continue your leadership journey, remember that the strength of a leader lies not only in individual competence but also in the ability to inspire and guide teams towards excellence.

Chapter 8

Adaptive Leadership in a Changing World

"In the ever-evolving landscape of our world, adaptive
leadership stands as the guiding force, steering
us towards transformation and sustained achievement."

– Joel R. Klemmer

Chapter 8
Adaptive Leadership in a Changing World

The critical concept of adaptive leadership, which is essential in a world characterized by constant change and uncertainty. Leaders who can adapt to evolving circumstances and guide their organizations through challenges are the ones who thrive.

In today's dynamic and rapidly changing business landscape, adaptability has become a cornerstone of success for both leaders and organizations. The imperative of adaptability is a concept that underscores the crucial need to embrace change, respond to challenges, and continuously evolve to thrive in an ever-shifting environment.

The modern business world is characterized by unprecedented technological advancements, globalization, and evolving consumer preferences. These factors, among others, have accelerated the pace of change. Leaders and organizations that fail to adapt risk becoming obsolete.

Adaptability is not merely about reacting to change; it is about proactively embracing it. Leaders who champion adaptability create a culture where innovation and agility are prized attributes. They recognize that change presents opportunities for growth and improvement.

Adaptability goes hand in hand with resilience and effective problem-solving. When faced with adversity, adaptable leaders, and organizations pivot, learn from setbacks, and use challenges as steppingstones to success.

In a competitive landscape, staying ahead requires a commitment to adaptability. Leaders must encourage their teams to be open to new ideas, take calculated risks, and be willing to experiment and learn from failures.

The Imperative of Adaptability does not imply constant upheaval. It is about striking a balance between stability and change. Effective leaders can maintain core values and strategies while adapting and innovating in response to external shifts.

The Era of Constant Change represents a transformative period in which the world is characterized by unceasing and rapid shifts in various aspects of life, including technology, business, society, and culture. This era reflects the reality that change has become a constant, defining feature of our lives, demanding adaptability, innovation, and resilience from individuals, organizations, and societies.

One of the hallmark features of this era is the relentless pace of technological innovation. Breakthroughs in fields like artificial intelligence, automation, biotechnology, and communication have disrupted industries and transformed the way we live and work.

The world has become more interconnected than ever before, with globalization enabling the free flow of information, goods, and ideas across borders. This interconnectedness has led to increased competition, collaboration, and the exchange of diverse perspectives.

Societal norms, values, and demographics are evolving, leading to shifts in attitudes, expectations, and social structures. Issues like diversity, sustainability, and social justice have gained prominence and are driving change across various sectors.

Economic landscapes are characterized by uncertainty, marked by fluctuations in markets, business models, and employment patterns. Organizations must adapt to survive and thrive in these volatile conditions.

Climate change and environmental degradation are pressing issues in this era. Sustainability has become a focal point, driving changes in industry practices, regulations, and consumer behavior.

Effective leadership in the Era of Constant Change requires a unique skill set. Leaders must be visionary, agile, and capable of navigating ambiguity. They must foster cultures of innovation, encourage lifelong learning, and prioritize adaptability.

Individuals and organizations must embrace continuous learning and reskilling to remain relevant. Lifelong learning has become essential for personal and professional growth.

The rapid pace of change in the modern business world is nothing short of remarkable. It is characterized by an unprecedented rate of transformation across various dimensions, including technology, markets, consumer behavior, and organizational structures. This relentless pace of change has profound implications for businesses and leaders alike.

Technology is at the forefront of rapid change. Breakthroughs in artificial intelligence, automation, the internet of things (IoT), and other areas are revolutionizing industries. Businesses must continuously adapt to leverage these technologies for efficiency and competitiveness.

The global economy is more interconnected than ever. Supply chains span the globe, and businesses can instantly reach international markets. This level of globalization exposes companies to new opportunities and threats, requiring adaptability in market strategies and regulations.

Consumer behavior evolves rapidly due to changing preferences, demographics, and digitalization. Businesses need to stay attuned to these shifts to provide products and services that meet evolving demands.

New competitors can emerge seemingly overnight, disrupting established industries. Businesses must be vigilant and ready to pivot to address competitive threats swiftly.

Regulations and compliance requirements can change frequently and have a significant impact on business operations. Staying up to date and ensuring compliance is vital.

Economic conditions can be unpredictable, with recessions, market volatility, and global events affecting businesses' financial stability. Companies must build resilience and adaptability into their financial strategies.

The workforce is undergoing a transformation, with remote work, the gig economy, and changing skill requirements becoming the norm. Businesses must adapt their hiring, retention, and training practices accordingly.

Environmental and social concerns are shaping consumer preferences and regulatory environments. Sustainability is no longer an option but a business imperative.

The digital age brings increased risks of cyberattacks and data breaches. Companies need to continuously fortify their cybersecurity measures to protect sensitive information.

Innovation cycles are accelerating, with shorter timeframes to bring new products and services to market. Companies must foster cultures of innovation and rapid prototyping.

In today's fast-paced business world, change is the only constant. External factors like technology, globalization, and shifts in the market are driving the need for adaptability like never before.

Technology is advancing at an unprecedented rate, with innovations like automation and artificial intelligence transforming industries. This means that businesses must adapt by upskilling their workforce and embracing digital transformation to stay competitive.

Globalization has expanded market opportunities but also brought complexity. Companies must adapt to diverse cultures, regulations, and supply chain challenges. The global talent pool offers opportunities but requires adaptability in hiring and management practices.

Market shifts, often fueled by changing consumer preferences, force companies to adapt their products and strategies. New competitors leveraging innovative technologies can enter markets swiftly, demanding adaptability from established businesses. Additionally, regulatory changes necessitate adaptability to comply with evolving standards.

In this dynamic landscape, cultivating a culture of adaptability is essential. It involves proactively monitoring external trends, fostering innovation, providing ongoing training, and having the agility to pivot swiftly when needed. Ultimately, businesses that embrace adaptability are better equipped to thrive in a world where change is the norm.

Resistance to change can have significant consequences for individuals, teams, and organizations. Resistance to change often stems from fear, uncertainty, and a sense of loss. Individuals may be worried about their job security, unfamiliar processes, or the potential disruption of their routine. As a result, they may resist new initiatives, technologies, or organizational shifts.

On an individual level, resistance can lead to decreased job satisfaction, increased stress, and a decline in morale. Employees who resist change may feel disengaged and demotivated, which can negatively impact their performance and productivity. Over time, this can lead to talent attrition, as employees seek more accommodating work environments.

Within teams, resistance to change can disrupt collaboration and communication. Teams that are resistant to change may struggle to adapt to new ways of working or fail to align with the organization's goals and vision. This can hinder progress and impede the achievement of collective objectives.

For organizations, resistance to change can result in missed opportunities, decreased competitiveness, and even financial losses. Failing to adapt to changing market conditions or customer preferences can lead to a decline in market share. Additionally, resistance can hinder innovation, making it difficult for organizations to stay ahead in rapidly evolving industries.

Resistance to change can pose several risks that organizations should be mindful of. These risks encompass both short-term and long-term consequences and can impact various aspects of an organization's operations.

When employees resist change, organizations may find it challenging to introduce new processes, technologies, or strategies. This resistance can result in a stagnant status quo, where the organization fails to adapt to evolving market conditions, customer demands, or industry trends. As a result, the organization may fall behind competitors who embrace change more readily.

In today's fast-paced business environment, adaptability is crucial for staying competitive. Resistance to change can lead to missed opportunities for innovation and improvement. Organizations that are slow to respond to changing market dynamics risk losing their competitive edge and market share to more agile competitors.

Resistance to change can cause disruptions in workflow and hinder productivity. Employees who are resistant may spend more time and effort clinging to old processes or methods, which can lead to inefficiencies. This decreased productivity can result in missed deadlines, reduced output, and increased operational costs.

When employees resist change, they may become disengaged and demotivated. A lack of engagement can result in decreased job satisfaction and increased turnover rates. High turnover, in turn, can disrupt team dynamics and increase recruitment and training costs.

Resistance to change can stifle creativity and innovation within an organization. Employees who are resistant may be less willing to experiment with new ideas or approaches, limiting the organization's ability to adapt, grow, and innovate.

The presence of resistance can lead to a negative work environment characterized by tension, conflicts, and low morale. This can adversely affect team cohesion and employee well-being, which, in turn, can impact overall organizational culture.

Managing resistance to change can entail additional costs, such as providing training, support, or incentives to encourage adoption. Moreover, prolonged resistance can result in financial losses due to missed opportunities, decreased efficiency, and reduced revenue.

In some cases, resistance to change can become public knowledge and harm an organization's reputation. Stakeholders, including customers and investors, may view an organization's inability to adapt negatively, potentially affecting brand perception and trust.

If resistance is not effectively addressed, change initiatives may fail to achieve their intended objectives. The organization may invest resources in change efforts that ultimately do not yield the desired results, leading to frustration and disillusionment among stakeholders.

Organizations that are resistant to change may struggle to attract top talent. Highly skilled and innovative professionals often seek dynamic and forward-thinking workplaces, making it challenging for resistant organizations to recruit the best talent.

Kodak serves as a poignant example of a once-industry-leading company failing to adapt adequately to the digital revolution. Kodak, a long-standing giant in the photography industry, has a rich history of success with its film and camera products. However, several key factors contributed to its ultimate downfall.

One of the most striking aspects of Kodak's story is that the company's own engineers invented the digital camera in 1975. This early recognition of the potential of digital technology indicated that

Kodak was well aware of the changing landscape. Despite this invention, Kodak's leadership was reluctant to shift away from its highly profitable film-based business model. This hesitancy significantly delayed the company's entry into the digital camera market, providing a head start to competitors.

Another crucial aspect was Kodak's missed opportunities. The company had multiple chances to leverage its digital inventions and innovations effectively. However, rather than aggressively marketing its digital cameras and investing in digital imaging technology, Kodak remained heavily reliant on film sales. This passive approach allowed rivals like Canon, Nikon, and later, smartphone manufacturers, to dominate the digital camera market.

Furthermore, Kodak struggled to adapt as digital photography surged in popularity. The traditional film business, which had been a primary source of revenue, faced a rapid decline as consumers embraced digital cameras and smartphones for photography. Kodak's film sales plummeted, and its traditional revenue streams eroded.

The culmination of these challenges led to a significant turning point for Kodak. In 2012, the company filed for Chapter 11 bankruptcy protection. This action symbolized its inability to cope with the digital revolution and its changing market dynamics. As a result, Kodak was forced to sell various assets and underwent a substantial downsizing process.

Nokia, renowned as the world's leading mobile phone manufacturer, enjoyed a dominant position for many years. Yet, its downfall can be attributed to a series of critical missteps.

One of Nokia's major misjudgments was underestimating the transformative impact of smartphones. While competitors like Apple and Samsung recognized the potential of touch-screen devices, Nokia remained steadfast in its commitment to traditional cell phone designs and operating systems. This decision proved to be a grave miscalculation as the global consumer base began to shift towards smartphones, driven by the allure of versatile functionalities and app ecosystems.

Nokia's reluctance to pivot towards smartphones and adapt to evolving consumer preferences caused its market share to dwindle rapidly. Competing with rivals who had already embraced the smartphone era became increasingly challenging for Nokia. The company's lack of innovation in this critical segment further eroded its position.

The consequences of these strategic missteps were severe. Nokia, once synonymous with mobile phones, saw its market dominance slip away. In a move that symbolized its decline, Nokia eventually sold its phone business to Microsoft in 2014. This marked the end of an era for the Finnish giant, as it could no longer compete effectively in the evolving mobile phone landscape.

The decline of Sears, once a prominent retail giant in the United States, serves as a stark example of the consequences of failing to adapt to the evolving retail landscape. For decades, Sears had been a fixture in American households, offering a wide range of products through its vast network of physical stores and catalogs. However, a series of strategic missteps led to its downfall.

One of the primary reasons behind Sears' decline was its failure to invest adequately in both its brick-and-mortar stores and its e-commerce operations. As the retail industry underwent a significant transformation, driven by the rise of online shopping and changing consumer preferences, Sears lagged behind. While competitors like Amazon and Walmart embraced digital innovation and improved their online shopping experiences, Sears struggled to keep pace.

This failure to adapt left Sears at a severe disadvantage. As more consumers turned to e-commerce for convenience and a broader selection of goods, the company's outdated stores and limited online presence deterred customers. The result was a decline in foot traffic and sales, ultimately pushing Sears into a financial crisis.

In 2018, Sears was forced to file for bankruptcy, marking a significant turning point in its history. The company had to close hundreds of stores, and its once-dominant position in the retail industry eroded. What was once a symbol of American retail success had succumbed to the challenges posed by a rapidly changing retail landscape.

Adaptive leaders play a pivotal role in the success of organizations operating in today's dynamic and rapidly changing business landscape. These leaders possess a distinctive set of characteristics that enable them to navigate uncertainty, drive innovation, and guide their teams toward success. One key trait of adaptive leaders is their remarkable flexibility and openness to change. They understand that rigidity and resistance to change can hinder progress, so they embrace change as an opportunity for growth and adaptation. Alongside their adaptability, adaptive leaders have a clear and inspiring vision for the future, which they communicate effectively to their teams. This vision provides a sense of direction and purpose, particularly in times of uncertainty.

Resilience is another crucial characteristic of adaptive leaders. They can bounce back from adversity and maintain a positive outlook, which often serves as an inspiration for their teams. Furthermore, these leaders foster a culture of innovation within their organizations. They encourage creativity, experimentation, and the generation of new ideas as a means to adapt to changing circumstances and stay ahead in the market.

Empathy is another hallmark of adaptive leaders. They understand and connect with team members on a personal level, recognizing that different individuals may react differently to change. This empathy allows them to address concerns and perspectives effectively, maintaining trust and cohesion within their teams. Effective communication is a fundamental skill for adaptive leaders. They keep their teams well-informed about changes and updates, actively listen to feedback, and maintain transparency in their dealings. These communication practices build trust and ensure that their teams stay engaged and committed.

Adaptive leaders are also willing to take calculated risks. They acknowledge that some degree of risk is necessary for innovation and growth, so they encourage their teams to take thoughtful risks and learn from both successes and failures. Moreover, they are committed to ongoing learning and self-improvement. In an environment where change is constant, adaptive leaders continuously seek new knowledge and skills to remain at the forefront of evolving challenges and trends.

Collaboration is another cornerstone of adaptive leadership. These leaders not only foster collaboration within their teams but also promote it across departments and with external partners. They understand the value of diverse perspectives and resources in navigating change and uncertainty effectively. While they value input and collaboration, adaptive leaders can also make tough decisions when necessary. They do not shy away from choices that align with their vision and goals, even when these choices may be challenging.

Adaptive leaders possess agility in their decision-making and problem-solving. They can quickly adjust their strategies and tactics as circumstances change, ensuring that their organizations remain responsive and competitive in an ever-evolving business landscape. In today's fast-paced and dynamic business environment, adaptive leaders are indispensable. They guide their organizations through uncertainty and change, inspiring their teams to embrace challenges as opportunities for growth. Their commitment to innovation, learning, and collaboration ensures that their organizations remain resilient and prepared for the challenges of the future.

Adaptive leaders are distinguished by their unique ability to uphold a clear vision for their organizations while remaining flexible in their approach. This exceptional balancing act enables them to navigate through periods of change and uncertainty with remarkable effectiveness. At the core of their leadership lies a vision deeply rooted in the organization's core values and purpose. This vision serves as the ultimate destination, unwavering and constant, providing a moral compass for decision-making. It is this steadfast commitment to their organization's fundamental beliefs that ensures continuity even as the external landscape evolves.

However, the strength of adaptive leaders lies in their adaptability in strategy and tactics. They recognize that the path to achieving their vision must often adjust to changing circumstances, emerging opportunities, and evolving market dynamics. They actively promote innovation and experimentation within their teams, allowing for the exploration of new avenues and the ability to pivot when required. In doing so, they avoid becoming ensnared by outdated approaches and maintain a responsiveness to the ever-shifting business environment.

Adaptive leaders are acutely receptive to feedback from multiple sources, including team members, customers, and industry experts. They understand that constructive feedback illuminates areas where their strategies may require adjustment. By welcoming diverse perspectives, they can fine-tune their approach while staying aligned with their overarching vision. Moreover, these leaders engage in regular review and adjustment processes, evaluating progress toward their vision and swiftly making changes when necessary. This iterative approach ensures that their organizations remain agile and responsive, capable of adapting to evolving circumstances.

Scenario planning is another key tool in the arsenal of adaptive leaders. They engage in forward-thinking by envisioning multiple potential futures and crafting contingency plans for each scenario. This strategic foresight equips them to maintain a clear vision while remaining prepared to adapt based on the unfolding circumstances. Effective communication serves as a linchpin in their leadership style. They ensure that their teams comprehend both the overarching vision and the rationale behind strategic shifts, providing clarity and transparency that instill confidence in team members.

Balancing stability with flexibility is a hallmark of adaptive leaders. While they embrace change, they simultaneously provide a stable foundation for their teams. This stability often stems from the organization's core values and shared purpose, offering a sense of security and continuity even amidst turbulence. These leaders lead by example, serving as role models for their teams by showcasing a willingness to learn, grow, and adapt. Their actions set the tone for the entire organization, inspiring team members to embrace change with the same enthusiasm.

In essence, adaptive leaders preserve a clear vision by anchoring it in enduring values and purpose. This vision serves as an unwavering guiding star, directing their decisions and actions. Simultaneously, they exhibit flexibility in their strategies, recognizing that the path to realizing the vision may evolve. This dual approach empowers them to remain resilient and responsive in the face of change, motivating their teams to navigate uncertainty with unwavering confidence.

Balancing core values with an openness to new ideas represents a pivotal aspect of leadership, particularly for adaptive leaders. Core values serve as the bedrock of an organization's identity and purpose, offering stability and a sense of belonging. These principles provide a framework for decision-making and behavior within the organization. Core values act as a moral compass, ensuring continuity even during turbulent times. They inspire employees, fostering a connection to the organization's mission and a profound sense of pride and purpose.

Conversely, embracing new ideas and change is imperative for growth and adaptability in today's rapidly evolving business environment. The world constantly witnesses the emergence of new technologies, market trends, and consumer preferences. An organization resisting change risks stagnation and obsolescence. Openness to novel ideas nurtures innovation, encourages creative problem-solving, and allows an organization to remain competitive and agile.

Adaptive leaders discern the symbiotic relationship between these two dimensions. They comprehend that core values should not be unbending or dogmatic but rather serve as guiding principles. These values should inform the organization's response to change and novel concepts. Leaders cultivate an environment in which change is perceived as an opportunity for advancement, not a threat.

Navigating this equilibrium necessitates reflective and strategic decision-making on the part of leaders. Adaptive leaders ensure that any new idea or alteration aligns with the organization's core values and purpose. They communicate transparently, explaining why specific core values are unwavering and how new ideas can coexist harmoniously. Inclusivity characterizes their decision-making process, as they seek diverse perspectives, fostering both innovation and a sense of ownership among team members.

These leaders cultivate a growth mindset, viewing failures as learning opportunities, setting an example that encourages their teams to do the same. They engage in scenario planning, envisioning various potential futures and assessing how core values can persist while adapting to evolving circumstances. Moreover, adaptive leaders remain flexible, recognizing that the balance between core values and novel ideas may necessitate adjustments as the organization evolves. In essence, they use core values as guiding principles that inform their openness to new ideas and change, creating a culture where innovation and tradition can harmoniously coexist.

Resilience is a critical attribute in both individual development and leadership, particularly in the context of handling setbacks and adversity. It encompasses a range of aspects that contribute to one's ability to rebound and adapt effectively in challenging situations.

Emotional resilience stands at the core, allowing leaders to manage their emotions, even under high-pressure circumstances. Leaders who possess emotional resilience can maintain composure and make rational decisions amidst adversity. They understand their emotional responses, acknowledge them, and find constructive ways to express and process their feelings.

Resilience also hinges on adaptability, the capacity to modify strategies, perspectives, and plans in response to unforeseen challenges. Leaders with adaptability readily embrace change as an opportunity for growth, rather than resisting it. This flexibility empowers them to pivot when necessary, discover new solutions, and confront setbacks with versatility.

Effective problem-solving is another integral facet of resilience. Resilient leaders view setbacks as puzzles to be unraveled rather than insurmountable barriers. They disassemble complex issues into manageable components, identify root causes, and fashion actionable remedies. This problem-solving approach infuses them with the confidence and determination to confront adversity head-on.

Resilience dovetails with optimism and positive thinking, as leaders possessing this trait focus on opportunities rather than fixating on failures. They maintain an affirmative outlook and possess unwavering belief in their ability to surmount challenges, bolstering their own spirits while inspiring and motivating their teams.

Support networks also play a pivotal role in resilience. Resilient leaders benefit from robust support systems, encompassing both personal and professional spheres. They can lean on trusted mentors, colleagues, friends, and family members for guidance, encouragement, and diverse perspectives during tumultuous times.

Moreover, resilience is intertwined with continuous learning and growth. Leaders who exhibit resilience treat setbacks as invaluable learning experiences. They meticulously dissect what went wrong, distill lessons, and apply those insights to future endeavors. This adaptive learning process ensures that they become increasingly capable and resilient over time.

Prioritizing well-being is a fundamental tenet of resilience. Leaders who are resilient comprehend that both physical and mental health are vital for tackling adversity. Thus, they engage in self-care practices, including exercise, mindfulness, and stress management, to fortify their resilience. They recognize that a sound mind and body constitute a sturdy foundation for surmounting setbacks.

During crises – whether organizational or unforeseen emergencies – resilient leaders shine. They adeptly navigate ambiguity, make tough decisions, and provide steadfast guidance to their teams. Their resilience instills confidence and trust among team members, imparting the assurance that they are under capable leadership.

In sum, resilience is an indispensable quality for leaders facing setbacks and adversity. It encompasses emotional regulation, adaptability, problem-solving, optimism, support systems, learning, well-being, and crisis leadership. Cultivating resilience enables leaders not only to withstand challenges but to flourish in adversity, serving as exemplars for their teams and organizations.

Adaptive leaders exhibit a distinct willingness to engage in calculated risk-taking, a quality that sets them apart in the constantly shifting landscape of leadership. They do not approach risks recklessly but rather employ a thoughtful and informed decision-making process. This involves a thorough assessment of available information, an evaluation of potential outcomes, and a consideration of the consequences of their choices. In doing so, they align their decisions with their overarching goals and vision.

One of the key attributes of adaptive leaders is their capacity to strike a delicate balance between risk and reward. They comprehend that avoiding risks entirely can result in stagnation and missed opportunities, while taking uncalculated risks can lead to detrimental outcomes. Thus, they identify risks that offer the potential for substantial rewards while working diligently to minimize potential downsides.

Moreover, adaptive leaders perceive failure as an invaluable source of learning and growth rather than as a devastating setback. They acknowledge that not every risk they undertake will yield favorable results. However, they view these setbacks as opportunities to refine their strategies and enhance their decision-making processes. This resilience in the face of adversity enables them to emerge from failures stronger and more resourceful.

These leaders are instrumental in fostering a culture of innovation within their teams and organizations. They recognize that innovation often entails taking risks, such as investing in new technologies, exploring uncharted markets, or launching innovative products. By championing calculated risk-taking among their teams, they nurture creativity and progress.

Agility is another central characteristic of adaptive leaders. They remain prepared to swiftly adjust their strategies and tactics if circumstances change or if a risk does not unfold as anticipated. This adaptability allows them to navigate evolving situations deftly and mitigate the consequences of adverse outcomes.

Furthermore, adaptive leaders inspire confidence in their teams and stakeholders. Their readiness to engage in calculated risks, coupled with their competence and transparency, instills trust. Team members are more inclined to follow leaders who exhibit the courage to venture into the unknown when they perceive these leaders as having done their due diligence and maintaining a clear vision.

Adaptive leaders possess a comfort with ambiguity and uncertainty, attributes essential for navigating the contemporary business environment. They understand that risk-taking invariably involves venturing into uncharted territories and are poised to navigate these complex, unpredictable waters with composure and adaptability.

Additionally, these leaders employ strategic risk management practices. They proactively identify potential risks, assess both their impact and likelihood, and develop contingency plans. This structured risk management approach minimizes the adverse effects of unforeseen events and bolsters their capacity to lead effectively in an unpredictable world.

Adaptive leaders exhibit a calculated risk-taking mindset that distinguishes them as prominent figures in dynamic and ever-evolving leadership contexts. They approach risk with prudence, utilize failures as steppingstones to success, foster innovation, and remain nimble in response to change. Their ability to balance risk and reward fosters trust, fuels growth, and equips them to flourish as leaders in an uncertain and rapidly changing landscape.

Embracing change as an opportunity rather than a threat is a fundamental mindset that distinguishes adaptive leaders. This perspective is pivotal in navigating the complex and unpredictable terrain of the modern business world. Several key factors underscore the significance of this approach.

Firstly, it is important to recognize that innovation and growth often stem from change. Leaders and organizations that view change as an opportunity tend to be more open to exploring new ideas, technologies, and processes. This mindset fosters creativity and can lead to breakthroughs that fuel growth and enhance competitiveness in the market.

Secondly, adaptation to market dynamics is critical for staying relevant and competitive. Markets evolve, consumer preferences shift, and technologies advance. Leaders who resist change and cling to outdated practices risk falling behind. In contrast, those who embrace change proactively adapt to meet evolving market demands, positioning themselves for success.

Additionally, the ability to embrace change as an opportunity is closely tied to resilience and agility. Change is inevitable, and adversity is a part of any journey. Leaders with this mindset tend to be more resilient, bouncing back from setbacks with greater resolve and adaptability. They maintain their effectiveness even in the face of challenges, inspiring their teams to do the same.

Furthermore, a competitive advantage often arises from embracing change. Organizations that innovate and adapt more swiftly than their competitors position themselves as industry leaders. This can translate into increased market share and profitability, reinforcing the value of embracing change.

Moreover, attracting and retaining talent is easier for organizations that embrace change and offer opportunities for growth and development. Talented individuals are drawn to forward-thinking organizations, and existing employees are more likely to remain engaged when they see their organization as open to change.

A customer-centric approach is also facilitated by embracing change. Leaders who view changes in customer expectations and behaviors as opportunities to better serve their customers enhance satisfaction and loyalty, ultimately benefiting the organization.

Additionally, embracing change necessitates a commitment to continuous learning and improvement. Leaders who model this behavior inspire their teams to do the same, fostering a culture of ongoing enhancements in performance and productivity.

Moreover, this approach prepares organizations for uncertainty, a hallmark of the modern business environment. Leaders and organizations adept at embracing change are more equipped to respond effectively to unexpected events and crises.

Furthermore, embracing change enhances problem-solving skills. Change often brings about new challenges, and leaders who embrace change become adept problem solvers, analyzing complex situations, making informed decisions, and devising innovative solutions.

Lastly, embracing change positions organizations for the future. They are better equipped to anticipate trends, adapt to emerging technologies, and seize new opportunities, ensuring their long-term relevance and sustainability.

In essence, embracing change as an opportunity is a strategic and forward-thinking approach to leadership. It empowers leaders to harness the transformative potential of change, foster innovation, and maintain relevance in an ever-evolving world. Rather than viewing change as a threat to the status quo, adaptive leaders see it as a means to shape a brighter and more promising future for themselves and their organizations.

Reframing challenges as learning experiences involves adopting a growth mindset, where setbacks are seen as opportunities for personal and professional development. This mindset shift is underpinned by the belief that abilities and intelligence can be cultivated through effort and learning. When individuals encounter challenges, they are more inclined to approach them with a positive attitude, recognizing them as chances to learn and improve. By focusing on finding solutions and encouraging creativity in addressing problems, challenges become avenues for empowerment and engagement. Seeking feedback from mentors or colleagues can provide valuable insights, helping individuals view challenges as opportunities for skill refinement and knowledge enhancement.

Reflection and journaling are effective tools for processing challenging experiences. They offer the opportunity to navigate emotions, identify lessons learned, and set objectives for growth. Additionally, celebrating small achievements and milestones, no matter how incremental, reinforces the idea that challenges contribute to personal and professional development. Understanding that failure is a natural part of the learning process is essential. Instead of fearing failure, individuals can embrace it as a teacher that imparts valuable lessons. Analyzing what went wrong, extracting insights, and applying them to future endeavors is a key aspect of this perspective.

Building resilience is integral to reframing challenges as learning experiences. Resilience involves developing coping mechanisms, maintaining a positive outlook, and adapting to change. By viewing challenges as opportunities to enhance resilience, individuals can emerge stronger in the face of adversity. Setting learning goals is another critical step. Clear objectives for learning help individuals align their experiences with growth opportunities, providing direction and motivation during challenging times. Learning from role models who have overcome adversity and turned challenges into successes can serve as a wellspring of inspiration and practical insights.

Creating a workplace culture that encourages continuous learning and regards challenges as opportunities for development is vital for leaders. Team members should be motivated to share their experiences and insights, fostering an environment of mutual growth. Additionally, practicing self-compassion is essential. Treating oneself with kindness and understanding during challenging periods helps counteract self-criticism and negative self-talk, promoting a supportive and constructive mindset for personal growth. Cultivating curiosity as a habit is also beneficial. Approaching challenges with curiosity leads to a sense of wonder and excitement, even in difficult circumstances. Overall, these techniques facilitate a profound shift in perspective, enabling individuals and organizations to see challenges as valuable opportunities for learning, growth, and personal development, ultimately leading to greater resilience, innovation, and long-term success.

Scenario planning is a strategic approach used by organizations to prepare for an uncertain future. It involves a structured process of creating multiple possible scenarios or narratives about what the future might hold. The aim is not to predict a single future but to develop a range of scenarios that encompass various possibilities. The process begins with identifying key drivers, such as economic, technological, regulatory, and market factors, which could significantly impact the organization. These drivers serve as the building blocks for constructing scenarios.

Each scenario is a detailed description of a potential future, considering how these drivers might interact and influence each other. These scenarios are designed to be internally consistent and plausible, even if they represent extreme or unlikely outcomes. After developing scenarios, organizations assess their potential impacts, including risks, opportunities, and challenges. This analysis helps organizations understand the implications of each scenario for their business.

The real value of scenario planning lies in its role in anticipating future challenges. It enables organizations to be proactive in identifying risks and vulnerabilities, thus allowing them to take measures to mitigate potential negative impacts. Moreover, scenario planning fosters creativity and innovation by encouraging out-of-the-box thinking. It prompts organizations to consider unconventional solutions that may be relevant in different future contexts.

Another significant benefit is that scenario planning promotes strategic agility. Organizations that engage in this process are better prepared to adapt to changing circumstances. They have a clearer understanding of the actions they should take in response to specific developments, ensuring that they remain on course even when the future is uncertain. Additionally, scenario planning encourages a long-term perspective, shifting the focus from short-term decision-making to long-term strategies that are robust and sustainable over time.

Ultimately, scenario planning leads to improved decision-making. When organizations have a more comprehensive view of potential future landscapes, they can make more informed decisions and allocate resources more effectively. This, in turn, provides a competitive advantage, as agile and well-prepared organizations are often better positioned to thrive in volatile or uncertain environments. In summary, scenario planning is a valuable tool for organizations navigating a complex and unpredictable business landscape, enhancing their resilience and competitiveness by anticipating and preparing for future challenges.

Scenario planning is a strategic approach that organizations can use to anticipate future challenges and make informed decisions. To effectively develop and utilize scenarios, a structured process is required. It begins by identifying the key drivers or factors that will likely shape the future, encompassing economic, technological, political, social, and environmental aspects. These drivers must be carefully analyzed to determine their impact and level of uncertainty.

Once the key drivers are understood, organizations can create plausible scenarios, each telling a compelling story about a possible future. These scenarios should encompass a range of outcomes, including optimistic, pessimistic, and moderate possibilities. To make scenarios more actionable, they should be detailed and supported by quantitative values when possible. This involves assigning numerical values or ranges to critical variables within each scenario and developing models or simulations for deeper analysis.

Engaging stakeholders is essential in scenario planning. Key internal stakeholders should participate in discussions, workshops, or brainstorming sessions to gather diverse perspectives. External experts and industry thought leaders can also provide valuable insights.

Scenarios can help assess risks and opportunities more precisely. They should be used to identify the strategic and operational challenges that might arise in different future contexts and how the organization can position itself to seize opportunities and mitigate risks. This assessment becomes the basis for informed decision-making.

Regularly monitoring the external environment for signals and changes is vital. Scenario planners must adapt to evolving circumstances by updating scenarios and strategies accordingly.

Effective communication is crucial in ensuring that the entire organization understands the rationale behind strategic decisions. Using scenario narratives and visual aids can make complex information more accessible.

To enhance readiness, organizations can conduct scenario-based exercises or war games to simulate decision-making in uncertain conditions, testing the robustness of their strategies. Additionally, scenario planning should be viewed as an ongoing learning process. Organizations should assess the accuracy of past scenarios and learn from deviations between scenarios and actual developments, using this feedback to continually refine their approach to scenario planning. Ultimately, scenario planning equips organizations with the tools needed to navigate an uncertain future, fostering adaptability and resilience.

Leadership is a cornerstone in crafting and nurturing the culture of an organization. The term "organizational culture" refers to the collective beliefs, values, behaviors, and norms that guide how members of an organization interact and work together. This culture defines the identity of the organization and significantly influences how employees perceive their roles and responsibilities within it. In this context, the role of leadership in shaping and cultivating organizational culture is of paramount importance.

First and foremost, leaders set the tone for the entire organization, and this tone profoundly affects the culture. Particularly, senior executives play a pivotal role in creating an environment where certain behaviors, values, and attitudes are encouraged and embraced. Consistency in leaders' actions and behaviors is key, as it sends strong signals about what is valued and acceptable within the company.

Additionally, leaders are responsible for defining and effectively communicating the core values of the organization. These values serve as guiding principles that inform decision-making and behavior. By emphasizing values such as integrity, innovation, or customer focus, leaders establish a solid foundation upon which the desired culture can be built.

Moreover, leaders act as role models for employees. When leaders consistently exhibit behaviors and attitudes that align with the desired culture, they become exemplars for others to emulate. This modeling effect is a powerful tool for cultural reinforcement and adoption throughout the organization.

Effective leaders also excel in communication, especially when it comes to the organization's mission, vision, and cultural expectations. Through clear and consistent communication, leaders ensure that every member of the organization understands what the culture entails and comprehends why it is crucial.

Furthermore, leaders have a responsibility to ensure that organizational systems, practices, and policies are aligned with the desired culture. This includes aspects like performance management, rewards systems, and decision-making processes. When these elements harmonize with the culture, it reinforces the cultural norms and expectations.

In the recruitment and development of employees, leaders have a substantial influence. They can shape hiring practices to seek individuals who are not only skilled but also culturally aligned. Moreover, leaders invest in training and development programs that help employees understand and embrace the culture.

Accountability is another critical aspect where leaders demonstrate their commitment to culture. They hold themselves and others accountable for upholding the culture's standards. When deviations from cultural norms occur, leaders take appropriate action, underscoring that cultural expectations are non-negotiable.

Effective leaders remain open to feedback from employees about the culture. They use this feedback as a tool to assess the culture's effectiveness and make adjustments when necessary. This adaptability ensures that the culture remains relevant and aligned with the organization's goals.

Lastly, leaders take the initiative in recognizing and celebrating individuals and teams that exemplify the desired cultural behaviors. Through this recognition and celebration, leaders reinforce the importance of living the culture.

Leadership is a pivotal force in shaping organizational culture. Leaders do so through their actions, values, and communication, and they play a central role in ensuring that the culture remains vibrant and aligned with the organization's objectives and values. Effective leaders understand that cultivating a healthy culture is an ongoing commitment that requires continuous attention, modeling, and consistent reinforcement.

Creating a workplace culture that values and encourages adaptability among employees is crucial in today's dynamic business landscape. To cultivate such a culture, leaders need to lead by example, showcasing their own adaptability in actions and decisions. Effective communication plays a pivotal role; leaders should clearly articulate the necessity of adaptability and its alignment with the organization's goals, helping employees grasp the broader context and benefits. Offering training and development programs that enhance adaptability-related skills, such as problem-solving and resilience, is essential. Continuous learning and skill development should be actively promoted.

Additionally, leaders can foster adaptability by encouraging calculated risk-taking. Employees should be made aware that mistakes are viewed as opportunities for learning and growth rather than failures. Innovation and adaptive behaviors should be recognized and rewarded. Empowering employees in decision-making processes when appropriate allows them to take ownership and adapt as needed. Cross-functional collaboration and diverse teams should be encouraged, as different perspectives and skill sets can lead to more creative and adaptable solutions.

A feedback culture should be nurtured, where employees feel comfortable providing input on processes and procedures. Leadership should be responsive to their suggestions for improvement. Celebrating adaptability by recognizing and rewarding employees who demonstrate resilience in the face of change or adversity can inspire others. Clear expectations regarding adaptability in job roles should be set, with specific examples provided to guide employees. A healthy work-life balance should be promoted to prevent burnout, as well-rested and mentally refreshed employees are more likely to exhibit adaptability and resilience.

Continuous improvement processes should be implemented, allowing teams to regularly assess their work and identify ways to adapt and enhance their processes. Flexibility in work arrangements, such as remote work or flexible hours, can accommodate employees' changing needs and preferences, enhancing their sense of control and adaptability. Crisis preparedness plans and protocols should be developed and communicated, ensuring that employees are prepared for unexpected events and can respond with adaptability and resilience.

Leaders should measure and track the organization's adaptability using key performance indicators (KPIs) and metrics, sharing these insights with employees to demonstrate the value of adaptability. Furthermore, leaders can consider implementing awards or recognition programs that specifically acknowledge and celebrate adaptability, fostering healthy competition and motivating employees to embrace change. Through these comprehensive strategies, leaders can create a workplace culture that not only survives but thrives in an ever-evolving business landscape, enhancing employee satisfaction and engagement along the way.

Empowering teams to take ownership of adaptive initiatives plays a pivotal role in shaping the culture of an organization and fostering adaptability. This transformative approach signifies a significant departure from traditional top-down leadership styles, placing a premium on autonomy and accountability among team members. The significance of this empowerment becomes evident across several crucial dimensions.

Firstly, when teams are entrusted with the autonomy to make decisions and take ownership of adaptive initiatives, they naturally develop a deeper sense of commitment. This commitment arises from the recognition that the success or failure of the initiative rests squarely on their shoulders. This heightened level of dedication and responsibility translates into a more motivated and engaged workforce.

Secondly, empowerment unleashes innovation and creativity within teams. Freed from rigid constraints, team members are encouraged to explore uncharted territory, experiment with novel ideas, and propose innovative solutions to navigate the challenges posed by changing circumstances. This creative freedom nurtures a culture of innovation and agility within the organization, enabling it to adapt proactively.

Moreover, empowered teams exhibit a remarkable ability to respond swiftly to changes. They do not have to wait for directives from higher-ups; instead, they can adapt in real-time to emerging opportunities or threats. This agility in responding to dynamic business environments can confer a significant competitive advantage.

Empowerment also contributes to skill diversification among team members. While they excel in their primary roles, they also develop a broader skill set encompassing problem-solving, decision-making, and leadership skills. This multifaceted skill development makes teams more adaptable and versatile in addressing complex challenges.

Enhanced employee engagement is another tangible benefit of empowerment. When team members take ownership of their work, they experience a greater sense of purpose. They recognize that their contributions directly influence the organization's success, leading to increased job satisfaction and higher retention rates.

Furthermore, empowered teams are adept at identifying and managing risks associated with adaptive initiatives. They proactively assess potential challenges, formulate mitigation strategies, and pivot when necessary. This proactive risk management approach minimizes the likelihood of costly setbacks.

Empowerment often goes hand-in-hand with leadership development. Team members may assume leadership roles within their teams, honing their leadership skills and contributing to leadership succession planning. This distributed leadership model further strengthens the organization's adaptability.

Lastly, empowerment fosters a culture of trust. Leaders who empower their teams demonstrate trust in their abilities and judgment. Conversely, teams trust that leaders will provide the necessary support and resources, creating a reciprocal and reinforcing atmosphere of trust within the organization.

Empowering teams to take ownership of adaptive initiatives transcends mere leadership style; it represents a strategic imperative for organizations navigating today's rapidly changing landscape. This approach enhances commitment, innovation, responsiveness, and employee engagement while minimizing risks and nurturing a culture of trust and leadership development. As organizations confront evolving challenges, empowering teams emerges as a cornerstone of their adaptability and long-term success.

Spotify, a leading music streaming company, has gained recognition for its innovative organizational structure. Within Spotify, the concept of "squads" plays a pivotal role in fostering adaptability. These squads are composed of small cross-functional teams with significant autonomy, allowing them to take charge of decision-making and project execution. Empowered to experiment and adapt swiftly, these squads have been instrumental in keeping Spotify at the forefront of the highly dynamic music streaming industry. This agile approach has enabled Spotify to respond effectively to shifts in consumer preferences and technology advancements, maintaining its competitive edge.

Zappos, a prominent online retailer specializing in shoes and clothing, stands out for its strong emphasis on employee empowerment. Within the company, a distinctive culture encourages employees to assume responsibility for customer service interactions and grants them the authority to make decisions aimed at enhancing customer satisfaction. This empowering environment has played a pivotal role in Zappos' achievements, enabling it to navigate the ever-changing e-commerce terrain effectively. By fostering a sense of ownership among its employees, Zappos has remained adaptable and responsive to the evolving demands and trends in the online retail industry, solidifying its position as a successful player in the market.

Netflix, a prominent player in the streaming industry, has cultivated a distinctive culture characterized by "freedom and responsibility." Within the organization, there exists a high degree of trust in employees' abilities to make decisions that are in alignment with the overarching goals and vision of the company. This empowerment is not limited to specific areas but extends across various aspects, including content creation, marketing strategies, and customer service. Netflix's capacity to swiftly adapt its content offerings and technology solutions has proven instrumental in navigating the ever-evolving landscape of the entertainment industry. By granting its employees the autonomy to drive decisions and innovations, Netflix has maintained its competitive edge and established itself as a dynamic and influential force in the streaming market.

Leading through ambiguity and uncertainty poses unique challenges for leaders in today's dynamic business landscape. One of the primary difficulties lies in the lack of a clear roadmap or precedent to follow. In such situations, leaders often find themselves navigating uncharted territory, which can be unsettling. Making decisions becomes more complex as the usual data and historical patterns may not provide reliable guidance. Leaders must rely on their judgment, intuition, and the available information to chart a course forward.

Moreover, leading through ambiguity demands effective communication. Leaders must provide a sense of direction and purpose to their teams, even when they themselves may not have all the answers. This requires transparent and open communication to keep employees informed and engaged. It also means acknowledging uncertainty and being honest about the challenges ahead.

Another challenge is managing the potential stress and anxiety that can arise in uncertain times. Leaders must be aware of their own emotional state and model resilience and adaptability for their teams. Maintaining morale and motivation becomes crucial, as uncertainty can lead to insecurity and decreased productivity.

Furthermore, leaders may face resistance to change and ambiguity from team members who are more risk-averse or uncomfortable with uncertainty. Managing and mitigating this resistance while maintaining team cohesion can be challenging.

Leading through ambiguity and uncertainty involves making decisions without clear guidance, effective communication, managing stress, and addressing resistance to change. While challenging, it is also an opportunity for leaders to demonstrate their adaptability and resilience, fostering a culture of learning and growth within their organizations.

Navigating ambiguity and uncertainty is a complex challenge for leaders in the modern business landscape. To excel in this endeavor, several strategies and guidance can be employed. Firstly, leaders must maintain a constant flow of information to stay informed about the situation. By keeping abreast of the latest developments, industry trends, and market conditions, leaders are better equipped to make informed decisions and provide pertinent guidance to their teams.

Additionally, adopting a growth mindset is crucial. Leaders should embrace uncertainty as an opportunity for growth and learning. This mindset encourages viewing challenges as chances to develop new skills and adapt to changing circumstances. Communicating this mindset to the team fosters a culture of resilience and encourages a positive response to ambiguity.

Clear communication is paramount. Leaders must be transparent and open in their communication, sharing both what they know and what they do not. Addressing any concerns or questions promptly is essential, as effective communication builds trust and reduces anxiety within the team.

Setting priorities is another vital aspect of guiding a team through uncertainty. Leaders should determine the most critical priorities and focus the team's efforts on them. Clear short-term and long-term goals must be defined to provide a sense of direction, ensuring that every team member comprehends their role in achieving these objectives.

Flexibility and adaptability are key attributes for leaders. Being flexible in approach and open to adjusting strategies as needed allows leaders to respond quickly to new information and emerging opportunities. This nimbleness is a valuable asset in uncertain times.

Maintaining composure under pressure is an indispensable leadership quality. Leaders set the tone for their teams, and their demeanor significantly impacts the team's response to ambiguity. Practicing self-regulation, staying calm under pressure, taking breaks, managing stress through techniques like mindfulness or exercise, and maintaining a positive attitude are all vital elements of this composure.

Empowering team members to make decisions within their areas of expertise is crucial. Encouraging ownership of their work and decision-making helps distribute the burden of decision-making and fosters a sense of responsibility and engagement.

Scenario planning is a proactive approach to uncertainty. Leaders should anticipate various scenarios and create contingency plans. Being prepared with multiple options can significantly reduce anxiety and enhance readiness to respond to unforeseen events.

Seeking advice is a sign of wise leadership. Leaders should not hesitate to consult mentors, colleagues, or experts in their field for fresh perspectives and valuable insights.

Leading by example is an essential aspect of guiding a team through uncertainty. Leaders should demonstrate the behavior and attitudes they expect from their team members, as their actions and responses serve as a model for how others should navigate uncertainty.

Providing support is a crucial leadership role during uncertain times. Leaders should make themselves available to listen to their team's concerns and provide emotional support. Acknowledging the challenges team members may be facing and offering assistance where possible is vital for team morale and resilience.

Finally, learning from experience is integral to leadership growth. After navigating through uncertain times, leaders should conduct a post-mortem analysis to identify strengths and areas for improvement. These insights can be invaluable for enhancing leadership and crisis management skills, ensuring greater preparedness for future uncertainties.

In the dynamic landscape of modern business, adaptive leaders must prioritize continuous learning and personal growth. This commitment is rooted in several profound reasons. Firstly, as the business environment constantly evolves due to technological advancements and shifting market dynamics, leaders need to expand their knowledge to make informed decisions. Additionally, learning fuels innovation and creativity, empowering leaders to devise groundbreaking solutions. Adaptability, a hallmark of effective leadership, is closely linked to ongoing learning, allowing leaders to flexibly adjust their strategies in response to change.

Furthermore, continuous learning equips leaders with an extensive problem-solving toolkit, enhancing their ability to tackle challenges. By fostering a culture of continuous improvement, adaptive leaders inspire their teams to excel and innovate. Moreover, in times of uncertainty, resilient leaders who have invested in personal growth are better equipped to navigate setbacks and emerge stronger. Continuous learning also facilitates networking, offering leaders access to valuable resources, mentors, and collaborative opportunities. As role models, leaders who prioritize learning set the stage for leadership development within their organizations.

In our interconnected world, understanding global dynamics and cultural nuances is essential for effective leadership. Continuous learning may involve cross-cultural training, international business courses, or global market analysis, enabling leaders to navigate the complexities of a globalized economy. Lastly, learning contributes to personal fulfillment, enhancing job satisfaction and the overall sense of purpose. Therefore, adaptive leaders recognize that continuous learning is not merely a professional obligation but a lifelong commitment, positioning them for success in an ever-changing landscape where adaptability and innovation are key to effective leadership.

Enhancing adaptability is a critical pursuit for leaders navigating today's rapidly evolving landscape. To fortify this essential skill, leaders have a range of resources and practices at their disposal. A commitment to lifelong learning is paramount, and leaders can achieve this through various avenues such as books, online courses, workshops, and seminars. E-learning platforms offer a plethora of courses focusing on leadership, adaptability, and related subjects.

In addition to formal learning, mentorship is a valuable resource for leaders seeking guidance and insights from experienced mentors. Building a professional network by attending industry events, conferences, and seminars is another way to access diverse perspectives and potential collaboration opportunities.

Executive coaching is a personalized option for leaders looking to enhance specific skills, including adaptability. Peer learning groups can provide a supportive environment for sharing challenges and best practices among colleagues and fellow leaders.

Effective self-assessment is a cornerstone of personal growth, with tools like 360-degree feedback assessments offering valuable insights into leadership styles and areas for improvement. Participation in cross-functional projects within the organization exposes leaders to different viewpoints and approaches.

Scenario planning exercises can help leaders anticipate and prepare for potential challenges, fostering proactive adaptability. Mindfulness techniques and stress management practices, available through apps like Headspace and Calm, contribute to maintaining composure and clarity during uncertain times.

Cultural awareness and diversity training are essential for leaders in global contexts, equipping them to work effectively in diverse environments. Leadership development programs, often offered by reputable institutions and organizations, provide comprehensive training on leadership skills, including adaptability.

Reflective practice, involving self-assessment and critical reflection on leadership decisions and outcomes, is a valuable habit. Finally, leaders can leverage professional associations, industry-specific groups, and technology tools to stay updated on trends, collaborate effectively, and undergo leadership assessments. By embracing these resources and practices, leaders can cultivate adaptability as a central pillar of their leadership approach, thriving amid the challenges of a dynamic business landscape.

Adaptive leadership is not only a response to change but an initiative-taking approach to navigating the ever-evolving landscape of the business world. Leaders who embrace adaptability are better equipped to lead their organizations through uncertainty and thrive in dynamic environments. As you continue your leadership journey, remember that adaptability is a skill that can be cultivated and refined over time.

Chapter 9

Mentorship and Developing Future Leaders

"Guiding the next generation of leaders is more than a journey, it ignites brighter futures and cultivates legacies."

— Joel R. Klemmer

Chapter 9
Mentorship and Developing Future Leaders

Mentorship and leadership development play a pivotal role in shaping the future of leadership within an organization. Effective leaders understand that their legacy is not solely based on their own accomplishments but also on their ability to cultivate the potential of those who will follow in their footsteps.

Mentorship, at its core, involves experienced and knowledgeable leaders guiding and supporting less experienced individuals, often referred to as mentees or protégés. It serves as a bridge between the wisdom of seasoned leaders and the potential of emerging leaders. Through mentorship, seasoned leaders impart not only their knowledge but also their insights, values, and leadership philosophies.

One of the central aspects of mentorship is the transfer of tacit knowledge—the practical wisdom that is often gained through years of experience. While formal education and training provide essential skills and knowledge, mentorship fills the gap by offering real-world context, decision-making strategies, and the nuances of effective leadership.

Effective mentorship relationships often include ongoing coaching, feedback, and opportunities for the mentee to apply what they have learned in real-world situations. This process accelerates the development of leadership skills and allows emerging leaders to gain confidence and competence.

Identifying potential leaders within an organization is a crucial step in the leadership development process. It involves recognizing individuals who demonstrate not only competence in their current roles but also the potential and desire to take on greater responsibilities. Potential leaders exhibit qualities such as adaptability, problem-solving skills, effective communication, and the ability to inspire and motivate others.

Once potential leaders are identified, organizations can create structured leadership development programs that include mentorship components. These programs may involve matching mentees with suitable mentors, providing formal leadership training, and offering opportunities for mentees to take on leadership roles or projects.

In addition to formal mentorship programs, organizations can encourage informal mentoring relationships to flourish. This can happen naturally when leaders within an organization take an active interest in the growth of their team members and offer guidance and support on an ongoing basis.

Effective mentorship and leadership development benefit both individuals and organizations. For mentees, it accelerates their growth as leaders and provides a roadmap for their career advancement. For mentors, it offers a sense of fulfillment and the opportunity to leave a lasting impact on the organization's culture and success.

Mentorship and leadership development are integral components of nurturing the next generation of leaders. They bridge the gap between theory and practice, imparting valuable insights and fostering leadership qualities. Identifying and nurturing potential leaders within your organization not only secures its future but also creates a culture of continuous growth and development.

The relationship between mentorship and leadership is a mutually beneficial and symbiotic one, characterized by the exchange of knowledge, experience, and personal growth. This partnership is at the core of developing effective leaders and ensuring the ongoing legacy of leadership within organizations.

At the heart of mentorship lies the transfer of knowledge and expertise from experienced leaders, mentors, to emerging leaders, mentees. This knowledge encompasses not only technical skills and industry-specific insights but also the soft skills and wisdom accumulated through years of leadership experience. Through mentorship, mentees gain access to a wealth of practical information that often eludes formal education or training programs.

Effective leadership demands a diverse skill set, including communication, problem-solving, decision-making, and emotional intelligence. Mentors play a pivotal role in helping mentees refine these skills. They provide guidance, share personal experiences, and offer constructive feedback, thereby accelerating the development of leadership competencies.

Mentorship frequently serves as a gateway to career advancement for mentees. Mentors can offer counsel on navigating organizational politics, identifying growth opportunities, and positioning oneself for promotions. They also act as advocates and sponsors, endorsing their mentees' abilities and aiding them in ascending the corporate hierarchy.

Leadership is not a solitary journey; it thrives on collaboration and networking. Mentors often introduce mentees to their professional networks, forging valuable connections that facilitate career growth. These networks extend beyond the organization and into the industry, expanding the horizons of mentees.

In addition to practical guidance, mentors provide emotional support and encouragement. Leadership can be daunting, and having a mentor who believes in a mentee's potential can bolster confidence and resilience. Knowing that an experienced mentor has their back can help emerging leaders navigate challenging situations with greater assurance.

Joel R. Klemmer

For organizations, mentorship ensures leadership continuity by identifying and preparing future leaders who can assume key roles as senior leaders retire or transition. This seamless leadership transition is crucial for maintaining organizational stability and success.

The mentorship relationship is not one-sided. While mentors share their wisdom with mentees, they also benefit from the partnership. Teaching and mentoring can provide mentors with fresh perspectives, keep them informed about industry trends, and reinforce their own knowledge and expertise.

Moreover, mentorship serves as a vehicle for transmitting an organization's culture, values, and mission. Mentors instill these critical elements into their mentees, guaranteeing alignment with the organization's overarching vision.

Mentorship is a dynamic and mutually beneficial process that plays a pivotal role in personal and organizational growth. It creates a symbiotic relationship where both mentors and mentees stand to gain significantly, ultimately contributing to the success of the organization.

For mentees, mentorship serves as a powerful catalyst for personal and professional development. It provides a unique opportunity to acquire specialized knowledge, skills, and insights from experienced mentors. Mentees benefit from career guidance, goal setting, and valuable industry insights that can significantly accelerate their progress. Moreover, mentorship boosts self-confidence, as mentees gain assurance from knowing they have a trusted ally to navigate challenges. The mentor-mentee relationship also extends their professional network, opening doors to new opportunities.

On the mentor's side, participating in mentorship offers numerous advantages. It reinforces the mentor's own knowledge and expertise, as they revisit and share their experiences with mentees. Exposure to fresh perspectives and innovative ideas from mentees keeps mentors sharp and informed about emerging trends. Furthermore, mentorship enhances the mentor's leadership and coaching skills, allowing them to become more effective leaders within the organization. Witnessing the growth and success of mentees is immensely satisfying for mentors.

For organizations, mentorship is a strategic investment with a host of benefits. It ensures a continuous pipeline of talent prepared to take on leadership roles as senior members retire or move on, ensuring leadership continuity. Mentorship also significantly boosts employee engagement and job satisfaction, as mentees feel valued and supported in their career journeys. It fosters knowledge transfer within the organization, preserving critical knowledge, best practices, and organizational culture. Additionally, it contributes to talent development, reducing the need for external recruitment and onboarding costs. Ultimately, mentorship helps shape a positive organizational culture that values growth, collaboration, and shared success.

In essence, mentorship is a triple-win scenario where mentees, mentors, and organizations all reap substantial rewards. It propels mentees toward success, enhances mentors' personal and professional growth, and equips organizations with capable leaders and an enriched culture. This symbiotic relationship is a cornerstone of individual and collective achievement.

Mentorship has a profound and enduring impact on leadership skills and career growth, transcending the immediate mentor-mentee relationship. These enduring effects are transformative for both mentees and mentors, shaping their professional journeys in significant ways. Firstly, mentorship serves as a crucible for developing leadership skills, laying a sturdy foundation that mentees continue to refine and apply throughout their careers. As they face diverse challenges and complexities with the guidance of their mentors, their efficacy as leaders progressively improves.

Furthermore, mentorship significantly enhances mentees' confidence and self-efficacy. This boost in self-assuredness empowers them to confront and conquer obstacles, fostering a belief in their ability to handle intricate leadership roles and responsibilities as they progress in their careers. Moreover, mentorship cultivates expansive professional networks. Over time, these networks evolve into invaluable assets, opening doors to an array of opportunities, from job offers to strategic partnerships, thus enhancing leadership and career growth.

Mentees frequently find that mentorship expedites their career advancement. The skills, knowledge, and insights gleaned from their mentors set them apart in their respective fields, positioning them as strong contenders for promotions and leadership positions. Additionally, mentorship equips mentees with adaptability, a vital leadership attribute. As they navigate diverse challenges and transitions in their careers, they can draw upon the adaptability skills instilled during mentorship to thrive in dynamic environments.

Mentorship instills a perpetual thirst for knowledge and growth, fostering a lifelong learning mindset among mentees. This continual quest for improvement ensures their enduring relevance and adaptability in leadership roles. Additionally, as mentees progress, they often assume mentorship roles themselves, perpetuating a culture of guidance and support within organizations—a crucial element of effective succession planning.

The far-reaching influence of mentorship extends to the organizations that invest in these programs. Companies benefit from a well-prepared and skilled leadership pipeline, reduced turnover, and a positive workplace culture that values professional development. In essence, mentorship sets in motion a cascade of effects, enriching the leadership capabilities and career trajectories of individuals while concurrently enhancing the success and resilience of the organizations they serve.

Warren Buffett's relationship with his mentor, Benjamin Graham, is a testament to the profound impact mentorship can have on one's life and career. Benjamin Graham, a highly respected economist and investor, became a guiding light for Buffett during his formative years in the world of finance.

Buffett often speaks reverently of Graham, describing him as the most influential person in his life, apart from his family. What made Graham's mentorship particularly significant was his role in teaching Buffett the principles of value investing. Graham's approach to investing emphasized the careful analysis of stocks, seeking those that were undervalued in the market. This method not only became the cornerstone of Buffett's investment philosophy but also the key to his immense wealth.

Graham's magnum opus, "The Intelligent Investor," became a seminal work that profoundly influenced Buffett's investment strategies. Buffett has repeatedly referred to the book as his "investment bible." He studied it meticulously and adopted many of its principles, such as the concept of the "margin of safety" and the importance of long-term investing.

One of the most significant lessons Buffett learned from Graham was the value of patience and discipline in investing. Graham's teachings instilled in Buffett the idea that successful investing required a steady and rational approach, unswayed by market emotions or short-term fluctuations. This wisdom has guided Buffett throughout his career, allowing him to weather financial storms and capitalize on long-term opportunities.

Moreover, Graham's mentorship extended beyond the technical aspects of investing. He imparted a fundamental belief in the importance of ethics and integrity in the financial world. Graham's principled approach to finance left an indelible mark on Buffett, shaping his character as an investor and as a person.

Warren Buffett's relationship with Benjamin Graham was more than just a mentorship; it was a profound and enduring influence that laid the foundation for one of the most successful investment careers in history. Graham's teachings on value investing, patience, and ethics continue to resonate through Buffett's actions and philosophy, serving as a testament to the enduring power of mentorship in the world of finance.

Maynard Webb's relationship with Reid Hoffman exemplifies the transformative power of mentorship in the tech industry. Maynard Webb, a seasoned executive with a successful career, found in Reid Hoffman not just a mentor but also a catalyst for personal and professional growth.

Webb's career trajectory was already impressive, with key roles at IBM, Gateway, and as the COO of eBay. However, his encounter with Reid Hoffman, co-founder of LinkedIn and a visionary entrepreneur, added a new dimension to his journey. Hoffman's mentorship went beyond typical career advice; it encouraged Webb to think innovatively and explore uncharted territories.

One of the most significant impacts of this mentorship was the book "Rebooting Work," authored by Maynard Webb. Under Hoffman's guidance and encouragement, Webb delved into the world of literature, sharing insights from his extensive career experiences. "Rebooting Work" became a valuable resource for professionals seeking guidance on adapting to the evolving workplace landscape.

Hoffman's mentorship extended beyond the confines of eBay and LinkedIn, fostering a relationship built on trust, shared visions, and a passion for innovation. Webb's appreciation for Hoffman's mentorship goes beyond the realm of career success; it reflects the profound influence a mentor can have on one's sense of purpose, creativity, and ability to inspire change.

In this story of mentorship, Maynard Webb's journey from a seasoned executive to an author and advocate for workplace transformation showcases the enduring impact of mentorship on personal and professional development. Hoffman's guidance not only enriched Webb's career but also ignited his passion for reinventing work in the digital age.

The mentorship relationship between Mark Zuckerberg and Steve Jobs is a remarkable tale of two tech titans connecting across generations to share insights, wisdom, and vision. While Mark

Zuckerberg was the young and ambitious co-founder and CEO of Facebook, Steve Jobs was the seasoned and iconic co-founder of Apple, Inc. Their bond transcended the competitive tech landscape, and Jobs became a mentor and source of inspiration for Zuckerberg.

One of the most profound lessons Zuckerberg learned from Jobs was the significance of user experience and product design. Steve Jobs was legendary for his obsession with creating products that were not only functional but also aesthetically pleasing and user-friendly. Under his mentorship, Zuckerberg gained a deeper understanding of the pivotal role design plays in shaping a product's success. This influence is evident in Facebook's continuous efforts to enhance user interfaces and provide an engaging platform.

Beyond product design, Jobs imparted his wisdom on navigating the complexities of the tech industry. He shared insights on strategy, innovation, and the importance of staying focused on a few key priorities. Zuckerberg often speaks about how Jobs' mentorship influenced his leadership style, emphasizing the value of simplicity, clarity of purpose, and relentless pursuit of excellence.

The mentorship between these two tech luminaries extended beyond business and design; it touched on life philosophies and personal growth. Jobs' ability to challenge conventional thinking and encourage Zuckerberg to think differently played a significant role in shaping Facebook's trajectory.

The tragic passing of Steve Jobs in 2011 marked the end of a unique mentorship journey, but his influence continues to resonate in Mark Zuckerberg's approach to leadership, innovation, and user-centric design. The Zuckerberg-Jobs mentorship stands as a testament to the enduring impact of mentorship in the tech world, where knowledge and inspiration are passed down from one generation of visionaries to the next.

Leadership potential is often discerned through a blend of inherent qualities and observable characteristics that individuals exhibit in various facets of their lives. These indicators collectively serve as reliable markers of a person's capability to assume leadership roles effectively. Among the key qualities and characteristics that signify leadership potential, one notable trait is initiative. True leaders tend to display a proactive approach to problem-solving and taking action, actively seeking opportunities and addressing challenges without waiting for directives. Demonstrating a willingness to go beyond assigned tasks and show self-motivation are pivotal elements that showcase leadership potential.

Another pivotal trait is effective communication skills, which serve as a cornerstone of leadership. Individuals with leadership potential typically possess the ability to express their thoughts with clarity, engage in active listening, and persuasively convey their ideas. The capacity to inspire and motivate others through communication stands as a strong indicator of their potential as leaders.

In our fast-paced and ever-changing world, adaptability is increasingly recognized as a valuable trait. Leaders must skillfully navigate uncertainty and embrace change. Those who can adeptly adapt to new circumstances, draw lessons from failures, and exhibit resilience when confronted with challenges are more likely to demonstrate leadership potential.

Furthermore, emotional intelligence plays a crucial role in leadership potential. Leaders need to comprehend and manage not only their emotions but also the emotions of those they lead. A high degree of emotional intelligence empowers individuals to foster robust relationships, empathize with team members, and make decisions that consider the well-being of all involved.

Leaders are frequently faced with the responsibility of making decisions that impact their teams and organizations. Consequently, strong decision-making skills are a hallmark of effective leadership. Those with leadership potential often exhibit the capability to make informed choices, even in high-pressure situations or complex scenarios.

Collaboration and teamwork are also vital attributes associated with leadership. Leaders frequently find themselves at the helm of teams, necessitating the ability to collaborate effectively, delegate tasks judiciously, and inspire collective effort. A readiness to acknowledge team contributions and celebrate shared accomplishments further underscores leadership potential.

Leadership often entails leading and working within teams, necessitating the ability to collaborate effectively, delegate tasks judiciously, and inspire collective effort. Individuals who willingly share credit and celebrate team accomplishments often demonstrate leadership potential. Additionally, leaders are often at the forefront of change and innovation. Therefore, a capacity for creative problem-solving and the generation of fresh ideas, along with an inclination to explore novel approaches to processes or products, is often observed in those with leadership potential.

Resilience is another critical quality associated with leadership potential. Leaders must confront setbacks and adversities with unwavering resolve. The ability to bounce back from adversity, maintain a positive outlook, and persist in the face of challenges reflects a sense of responsibility and integrity, both of which are integral to effective leadership.

Leaders are known for their vision and goal-oriented approach. They possess a clear and compelling vision of the future and set well-defined goals to guide their teams toward that vision. Those with leadership potential typically display a strong sense of purpose and the ability to inspire others with their vision, thereby propelling them toward leadership roles.

While these qualities and characteristics serve as reliable indicators of leadership potential, it is essential to acknowledge that leadership potential is not static. It can be cultivated and refined over time through experiences, mentorship, and personal development efforts. Organizations and individuals alike stand to benefit significantly by recognizing, nurturing, and fostering individuals with the potential to become effective leaders.

Identifying emerging leaders within your organization is a multifaceted endeavor that demands a nuanced approach. To pinpoint individuals with the potential for leadership roles, you must rely on a comprehensive evaluation process. Begin by scrutinizing employees' performance records and achievements, seeking those who consistently go above and beyond, take on extra responsibilities, and contribute positively to team and organizational objectives. Simultaneously, pay heed to proactive and initiative-taking employees who willingly embrace challenges, suggest process improvements, and showcase a genuine passion for their work.

In addition to performance, evaluate the communication skills of your team members. Effective leaders are adept communicators, capable of clearly articulating their ideas, actively listening to others, and fostering constructive discussions. Individuals who stand out in this regard often exhibit the ability to inspire and influence through their words. Moreover, consider adaptability and a learning-oriented mindset as crucial indicators of leadership potential. Given the ever-evolving nature of the business landscape, emerging leaders must demonstrate an eagerness to adapt to change, acquire new skills, and navigate uncertainties with resilience.

Problem-solving capabilities are another essential trait to observe. Emerging leaders excel in approaching challenges methodically, seeking innovative solutions, and displaying resilience in the face of setbacks. Their aptitude for making sound decisions in complex situations sets them apart. It is equally vital to gauge leadership potential, even if an employee's current role does not inherently demand it. Assess whether individuals inspire trust, confidence, and respect among their colleagues. The ability to function as a team player, motivator, or influencer can be indicative of latent leadership qualities.

Additionally, the consideration of feedback and recommendations from peers and supervisors can provide invaluable insights into leadership potential. Conducting 360-degree feedback assessments allows for a comprehensive understanding of an employee's skills, behaviors, and areas for improvement. Encourage employees to engage in self-assessment and reflection regarding their career aspirations and leadership objectives, fostering an environment that values personal growth and development.

The establishment of mentorship programs and succession planning initiatives can be instrumental in identifying emerging leaders and nurturing their growth. Mentors play a vital role in recognizing potential leaders and guiding them on their leadership journey. Simultaneously, succession planning ensures that individuals are identified and prepared for leadership roles well in advance. Leadership training and development programs are equally essential, providing employees with opportunities to hone their skills and prepare for leadership positions through workshops, seminars, and courses that focus on leadership competencies.

Furthermore, keenly observe how employees handle challenging situations and navigate pressure. Emerging leaders often exhibit emotional intelligence and the ability to manage difficult conversations effectively. Finally, track the career progression of employees, noting those who consistently ascend to roles of greater responsibility and influence. Identifying emerging leaders is an ongoing process that necessitates a supportive organizational culture promoting leadership growth. Offering feedback, mentorship, and tailored developmental opportunities is pivotal to their advancement and the overall success of your organization's leadership pipeline.

Promoting diversity and inclusion in leadership development is essential for organizations, as it goes beyond ethics and brings about strategic advantages. Diversity encompasses a wide range of differences, such as race, gender, age, ethnicity, and more, while inclusion is about creating an environment where every individual feels valued and empowered to contribute fully. These principles, when integrated into leadership development, yield several significant benefits.

Firstly, diverse leadership teams offer broader perspectives that enhance decision-making. Different backgrounds and experiences lead to a wider variety of viewpoints, enabling organizations to consider various angles and potential outcomes more effectively.

Secondly, inclusivity encourages innovation and creativity. Inclusive leadership environments foster collaboration among people from diverse backgrounds, resulting in unique insights and ideas. This diversity of thought can lead to creative solutions and innovative problem-solving approaches.

Furthermore, promoting diversity and inclusion boosts employee engagement. When individuals feel that their contributions are valued, it enhances morale, job satisfaction, and overall engagement levels within the organization.

Moreover, it contributes to improved talent acquisition and retention. Organizations that prioritize diversity and inclusion tend to attract a more diverse talent pool. Prospective employees seek out inclusive cultures, and once onboard, they are more likely to stay in environments where they feel respected and valued.

Additionally, inclusive leadership teams are often more attuned to diverse customer bases, which enhances market responsiveness. Their ability to understand and cater to a wide range of customer needs can lead to more effective marketing and product development efforts.

Lastly, diverse leadership teams are better equipped to identify potential risks and opportunities, contributing to effective risk management and adaptability.

To actively promote diversity and inclusion in leadership development, organizations should implement a range of measures. These include making leadership programs accessible to individuals from diverse backgrounds, offering training on unconscious bias and inclusive leadership behaviors, regularly assessing diversity metrics, using diverse interview panels, and promoting open communication and feedback channels.

Furthermore, organizations should support and encourage Employee Resource Groups (ERGs) that provide a platform for employees to connect and share their experiences related to diversity, fostering a sense of belonging. Continuous learning and ongoing cultural initiatives should also be integral to an organization's strategy.

Prioritizing diversity and inclusion in leadership development not only aligns with ethical principles but also yields strategic advantages. Such organizations benefit from improved decision-making, increased innovation, higher employee engagement, better talent acquisition and retention, enhanced market responsiveness, and effective risk management. These factors provide a competitive edge in today's ever-evolving business landscape.

One significant benefit of having a diverse leadership team is the wealth of varied perspectives and ideas it brings to the table. Leaders with different backgrounds, experiences, and viewpoints can engage in in-depth discussions that lead to more comprehensive and creative solutions to complex problems. This diversity of thought fosters an environment where innovative approaches to challenges can emerge, contributing to improved decision-making and problem-solving.

Furthermore, diverse leadership teams tend to make more informed decisions. They consider a broader array of viewpoints, leading to a thorough analysis of potential risks and benefits. This holistic approach results in better-informed choices and a higher likelihood of making balanced and effective decisions that account for a range of stakeholder perspectives.

Effective problem-solving is another area where diversity in leadership shines. A diverse leadership team offers a wide range of problem-solving approaches and strategies. This diversity allows for the identification of problems from multiple angles and the development of innovative solutions that may remain hidden in a homogenous group's discussions.

In a rapidly changing business environment, adaptability is key to success. Diverse leadership teams excel in this regard because they can draw from a broader range of experiences and perspectives. They are better equipped to anticipate and adapt to new challenges, leveraging their collective insights and considering multiple scenarios when strategizing for the future.

Moreover, diversity in leadership positively impacts employee engagement and retention. When employees see leaders who reflect the diversity of the workforce, they are more likely to feel valued and included. This sense of belonging leads to higher job satisfaction and greater loyalty, ultimately benefiting the organization's stability and performance.

Diverse leadership also extends its positive influence to market reach. Understanding and connecting with diverse customer bases is crucial in many industries. Leaders who can relate to and comprehend the needs and preferences of diverse customers are more likely to capture market share and thrive in competitive markets.

Additionally, diverse leadership teams can play a pivotal role in mitigating bias and discrimination within the organization. Their heightened awareness of such issues allows them to create and implement policies and practices that promote fairness and equity, reducing the risk of legal and reputational problems.

Lastly, organizations with diverse leadership teams tend to enjoy a more positive reputation and brand image. In today's socially conscious climate, consumers and investors value diversity and inclusion. Companies that prioritize diversity at all levels of leadership enhance their public image and attract a broader range of stakeholders, contributing to long-term sustainability and success.

In sum, the impact of a diverse talent pool on leadership perspectives and outcomes is profound. It permeates various facets of an organization's functioning, fostering creativity, improving decision-making, and creating a more inclusive and innovative workplace culture. Embracing diversity is not only a strategic advantage but also a reflection of an organization's commitment to a brighter and more equitable future.

For mentors, it is crucial to set clear expectations right from the start. This includes discussing not only the goals of the mentoring relationship but also the time commitment involved and the preferred mode of communication. Transparency is key. Creating an open and inviting environment is equally important. Mentors should actively listen without judgment, making mentees feel at ease sharing their needs, challenges, and aspirations.

Rather than providing quick answers, mentors should aim to guide their mentees in finding solutions to their own questions and challenges. Encouraging critical thinking and problem-solving skills through thought-provoking questions is essential. When giving feedback, mentors should ensure it is specific, actionable, and constructive, always delivered with empathy. It is important to highlight the strengths of mentees while addressing areas for improvement.

Sharing personal experiences, both successes, and failures, can be incredibly valuable. These anecdotes offer real-world insights that mentees can learn from. Reliability, punctuality, and respect for mentees' boundaries help build trust. Mentors should empower mentees to take ownership of their development and celebrate their achievements, no matter how small.

Staying informed about industry trends and resources ensures that mentors can provide up-to-date guidance. Lastly, maintaining confidentiality and respecting the privacy of mentees is paramount to building trust in the relationship.

For mentees, defining clear goals and objectives for the mentoring relationship is essential. This clarity not only helps in aligning expectations but also guides the direction of the mentorship. Taking the initiative is a sign of commitment to personal growth. Mentees should proactively schedule meetings, ask questions, and seek guidance.

Feedback should be embraced with an open mind, viewed as an opportunity for learning and improvement. Effective communication is the bedrock of a successful mentoring relationship, and mentees should articulate their needs, concerns, and expectations clearly to their mentors.

Respecting the mentor's time through punctuality and preparedness is a sign of respect. Curiosity should be cultivated through thoughtful and relevant questions that deepen understanding. Taking ownership of the guidance received and applying it actively to one's work and personal development is crucial.

Exploring diverse perspectives by engaging with mentors from various backgrounds can broaden horizons. Expressing gratitude for a mentor's time and support fosters a positive and respectful relationship. Periodic self-assessment and evaluation of progress should be conducted, and mentees should engage in open discussions with their mentors about potential adjustments or changes to enhance the mentorship experience.

In essence, a successful mentoring relationship thrives on a collaborative effort built on trust, respect, and a shared commitment to growth and learning. Both mentors and mentees play pivotal roles in ensuring a mutually beneficial experience that fosters personal and professional development.

Trust is the bedrock upon which successful mentoring relationships are built. It is a fundamental element that fosters a sense of security and reliability between mentors and mentees. When trust is present, mentees feel comfortable sharing their challenges, seeking guidance, and admitting their shortcomings. In turn, mentors can offer candid feedback and share valuable insights without the fear of misunderstanding or judgment. Trust establishes an environment of dependability, where both parties can confidently rely on each other's support and guidance throughout the mentoring journey.

Communication is the lifeblood of any mentoring relationship. Effective and consistent communication is essential for mentors and mentees to understand each other's needs, expectations, and progress. It ensures that goals and objectives are not only well-defined but also mutually agreed upon. Mentors should actively listen to their mentees' concerns, questions, and feedback, while mentees must express themselves clearly and seek clarification when necessary. Clear communication prevents misunderstandings, mitigates conflicts, and fosters a more productive and harmonious mentoring experience.

Mutual respect forms the foundation of a respectful and supportive mentoring dynamic. It involves recognizing and appreciating each other's expertise, experiences, and perspectives. This respect encourages mentees to value the guidance and feedback provided by their mentors. Simultaneously, it motivates mentors to honor their mentees' individuality and autonomy in their decision-making processes. Without mutual respect, the mentoring relationship can become strained, leading to conflicts and a decreased willingness to collaborate effectively, which can hinder the achievement of mentoring goals.

In essence, the triad of trust, communication, and mutual respect is the essence of a thriving mentoring relationship. It not only creates an environment where mentors and mentees can engage openly, learn from each other, and work collaboratively toward shared objectives but also strengthens the emotional connection between them, making the mentoring relationship more fulfilling, enduring, and ultimately successful.

Personalizing mentorship to cater to the specific needs and goals of each mentee is not merely a recommended practice; it is a fundamental principle that enhances the effectiveness of mentoring relationships. Every mentee possesses a distinct set of attributes, experiences, and ambitions. Tailoring mentorship to these unique characteristics respects the individuality of each mentee, acknowledging that a one-size-fits-all approach is insufficient. By adapting the mentoring approach to align with each mentee's style, objectives, and challenges, mentors create a more engaging, relevant, and impactful experience.

One of the primary advantages of personalized mentorship lies in its ability to precisely align with the goals of the mentee. Whether the focus is on career advancement, skill development, or personal growth, customization ensures that the mentorship guidance directly addresses the mentee's specific objectives, making the relationship more meaningful and goal-oriented. Moreover, it allows mentors to address specific challenges or hurdles that each mentee encounters on their unique journey. Tailored advice and support can be provided to help mentees overcome these obstacles effectively, whether they relate to workplace dynamics, skill enhancement, or work-life balance.

Furthermore, personalization enhances motivation and engagement within the mentoring relationship. When mentors tailor their guidance to the mentee's interests and passions, the experience becomes more captivating and motivating. Mentees are more likely to be proactive and committed when they perceive a direct connection between the mentor's guidance and their personal aspirations. Cultural backgrounds and diversity also play a pivotal role in a mentee's experience. Customized mentorship accounts for these factors, ensuring that mentors are sensitive to cultural differences and able to provide guidance that respects and leverages the unique aspects of a mentee's background.

Personalized mentorship is adaptable and flexible, recognizing that mentees' needs may evolve over time. Mentors can adjust their approach, resources, and guidance to accommodate changing goals and circumstances, ensuring that the mentoring relationship remains pertinent and valuable. Moreover, it contributes to the development of trust and rapport between mentors and mentees. When mentees feel that their mentor comprehends their individual needs and cares about their unique growth journey, it strengthens the emotional connection and mutual trust within the relationship. Lastly, personalization allows for more precise measurement of progress and outcomes. By tailoring goals and milestones to each mentee, mentors can better track their development and offer targeted feedback and adjustments as needed, thereby optimizing the mentoring experience. In essence, personalizing mentorship is a dynamic and essential approach that honors individuality, drives engagement, and maximizes the positive impact of mentoring relationships.

IBM's Mentorship Program is widely recognized as a standout model for mentorship due to its unwavering emphasis on customization. This program takes a highly individualized approach, meticulously pairing mentees with mentors who not only possess relevant expertise but also share similar career interests and objectives. What truly distinguishes IBM's program is its resolute commitment to tailoring the mentorship experience to the unique needs of each participant.

One of the key facets of IBM's program is its proactive encouragement of participants to define their own goals and aspirations. Rather than imposing a predetermined set of objectives, mentees are empowered to articulate their personal and professional ambitions. This step is foundational, as it ensures that the mentorship journey is firmly rooted in the mentee's individual aspirations, creating a sense of ownership and relevance that is unparalleled.

Mentors within IBM's program play a pivotal role in the customization process. They are not just mentors but also active guides who craft their guidance to cater specifically to each mentee's distinct needs and objectives. Whether a mentee's primary focus is on advancing their career, honing specific skills, or achieving a more balanced work-life integration, mentors adapt their approach and insights accordingly. This adaptability ensures that the mentorship experience remains highly relevant and responsive, addressing the precise aspirations and challenges faced by each mentee.

In essence, IBM's Mentorship Program sets a remarkable example of mentorship customization by prioritizing the individuality of its participants. By facilitating mentees' active involvement in defining their goals and providing mentors who are committed to tailoring their guidance, the program creates a mentoring experience that is both highly personalized and impactful. Whether mentees seek career growth, skill refinement, or work-life balance, IBM's program showcases how customization can lead to more meaningful and effective mentorship outcomes.

Deloitte's Career Connections Program serves as a beacon of support for professionals who are in the process of re-entering the workforce after career breaks. What sets this program apart is its exceptional commitment to customization, recognizing the unique challenges and aspirations of returning professionals. Deloitte has established a mentorship system within the program that is finely tuned to cater to individual circumstances and career goals.

A standout feature of the Career Connections Program is its cadre of mentors who possess an intimate understanding of the specific challenges faced by individuals returning to the workforce. These mentors are not only experienced professionals within Deloitte but are also well-versed in the intricacies of career breaks and reintegration into the corporate world. This specialized knowledge equips them to offer guidance that is finely attuned to the needs of returning professionals, setting the program apart as an exemplar of tailored support.

Mentors within the Career Connections Program provide highly personalized advice and guidance. They actively collaborate with mentees to navigate the often-complex process of transitioning back into the workforce. This guidance encompasses a wide spectrum of topics, including skill reacquisition, industry updates, confidence-building strategies, and work-life balance. The mentorship experience is meticulously designed to ensure that returning professionals receive support that directly addresses their unique circumstances and aspirations, thereby boosting their chances of a successful career relaunch.

Deloitte's Career Connections Program shines as a model of mentorship customization, specifically tailored to the needs of professionals re-entering the workforce. Through its roster of mentors who understand the nuances of career breaks and its dedication to providing personalized guidance, the program stands out as a beacon of support for individuals seeking to transition back into their careers with confidence and success.

TechWomen is an exemplary international mentorship program renowned for its focus on empowering emerging women leaders in STEM (Science, Technology, Engineering, and Mathematics) fields. What truly sets this program apart is its unwavering commitment to a highly personalized approach, which ensures that the mentorship experience is finely tuned to address the unique circumstances, aspirations, and challenges encountered by women in STEM.

One of the standout features of TechWomen is the close collaboration that occurs between mentors and mentees. This collaboration extends beyond general guidance and enters into the realm of strategic planning. Mentors and mentees work in tandem to establish specific, measurable, and actionable goals, as well as comprehensive action plans to achieve those goals. This meticulous approach ensures that the mentorship experience is not a one-size-fits-all endeavor but rather a highly tailored journey designed to meet the individual needs and ambitions of each participant.

What makes TechWomen exceptionally effective is its ability to address the intricate career challenges and opportunities faced by women in STEM fields. These challenges often include issues related to gender diversity, workplace dynamics, and career advancement. The program's personalized approach enables mentors to offer guidance that is finely calibrated to address these specific challenges. Whether it

Joel R. Klemmer

involves breaking through gender barriers, expanding professional networks, or navigating the complexities of STEM industries, the mentorship provided by TechWomen equips mentees with the skills and strategies needed to overcome obstacles and seize opportunities.

TechWomen stands as a paragon of mentorship customization, particularly tailored to meet the needs of emerging women leaders in STEM. Through its emphasis on collaborative goal setting and action planning, the program empowers women to navigate the unique landscape of STEM fields with confidence. By providing guidance that is finely tuned to individual aspirations and challenges, TechWomen ensures that each mentee receives the support and insights necessary to excel in their STEM careers and contribute significantly to their respective fields.

Coaching serves as a cornerstone in leadership development by offering highly personalized guidance, feedback, and support to individuals aspiring to enhance their leadership skills and capabilities. It goes beyond generic leadership training programs by focusing on the unique needs and objectives of each leader. Coaches work closely with individuals to assess their specific strengths, weaknesses, and leadership styles, tailoring their guidance to address individual development areas effectively.

Leadership coaching extends to skill enhancement, encompassing a broad spectrum of leadership competencies. This can encompass communication, conflict resolution, decision-making, time management, emotional intelligence, and more. Coaches provide leaders with strategies and techniques to improve these skills, often offering opportunities for leaders to practice and apply them in real-world contexts.

One of the fundamental outcomes of leadership coaching is the cultivation of self-awareness. Coaches guide leaders in exploring their values, beliefs, motivations, and behaviors. This self-awareness not only deepens their understanding of themselves but also enhances their ability to comprehend their impact on others. Armed with this insight, leaders can make conscious choices about their leadership approach.

Coaching also entails feedback and assessment. Coaches offer constructive feedback and evaluation based on keen observations and assessments, providing an external perspective that highlights potential blind spots or areas requiring improvement. This external viewpoint acts as a catalyst for growth and self-improvement.

Goal setting is another pivotal aspect of leadership coaching. Coaches collaborate with leaders to establish clear, measurable, and achievable development objectives. These goals align with the leader's career aspirations and organizational goals, serving as a roadmap for their growth. Regularly tracking progress toward these objectives is an integral part of the coaching process.

Coaches play a critical role in maintaining accountability. They ensure that leaders adhere to their commitments and action plans. This accountability fosters a sense of ownership and responsibility for their own development, sustaining momentum and driving ongoing improvement.

Furthermore, coaching provides valuable support and encouragement for leaders. The leadership role can be challenging and, at times, isolating. Coaches offer a confidential and supportive environment where leaders can openly discuss their concerns, seek guidance, and receive motivation. This support equips leaders to navigate difficult situations with resilience and maintain their enthusiasm for development.

Leadership presence is another key focus area in coaching. Coaches assist leaders in enhancing their leadership presence, which encompasses attributes like confidence, authenticity, and the ability to inspire and influence others. Developing a strong and positive leadership image is central to effective coaching.

Coaches also address conflict resolution and interpersonal dynamics. Leaders gain guidance on how to handle disagreements, foster collaboration, and build productive working relationships with team members, colleagues, and stakeholders. These skills are pivotal for effective leadership.

Lastly, coaching is not a one-time event but a continuous process. Coaches help leaders develop the skills and habits required for sustained growth and improvement. By embedding leadership development into their ongoing professional journey, leaders can continually refine their leadership skills and adapt to the evolving challenges of their roles.

Coaching is characterized by its structured and goal-oriented nature. It involves a process where coaches collaborate with leaders to set specific, measurable, and time-bound objectives. The primary focus of coaching is to achieve these objectives through a series of targeted sessions. Coaches typically provide an external perspective, offering fresh insights and avoiding potential biases. They emphasize skill development, equipping leaders with techniques, strategies, and exercises tailored to address specific challenges. Coaches also play a crucial role in holding leaders accountable for their progress, ensuring that they actively work on their development. Coaching is often more short-term in nature, ideal for leaders with well-defined goals or immediate challenges to address.

In contrast, mentoring revolves around a relationship-based approach. It entails an experienced mentor providing guidance, advice, and support to a less-experienced mentee. Mentoring is often characterized by a longer-term and more informal relationship, where knowledge transfer takes center stage. Mentors draw upon their own experiences and expertise, offering insights deeply rooted in their industry or organizational backgrounds. This approach extends beyond skill development, encompassing broader aspects of career development, such as career planning, networking, and professional growth. Mentors also serve as role models, demonstrating leadership qualities and behaviors through their own experiences. Mentorship relationships can endure throughout a mentee's career, providing ongoing support and guidance across various career stages.

When it comes to the benefits of coaching in refining leadership skills, several key advantages emerge. Firstly, coaching offers objective and unbiased feedback, helping leaders identify areas for improvement without the influence of organizational or personal biases. Secondly, it places a strong emphasis on skill development, enabling leaders to address immediate challenges and enhance their competencies effectively. The structured nature of coaching ensures that leaders remain accountable for their development, sustaining motivation and commitment. Furthermore, coaches provide a fresh perspective, injecting external insights and strategies into leadership development, particularly valuable for leaders facing complex or novel situations. Lastly, coaching is particularly well-suited for addressing short-term goals and immediate leadership challenges, making it a powerful tool for targeted skill enhancement.

A robust leadership development plan begins with thorough self-assessment. Leaders must take the time to identify their existing leadership strengths and acknowledge areas that require further refinement. Moreover, they should deeply reflect on their core values and long-term career objectives, exploring how these align with their aspirations in leadership. This introspective phase serves as the cornerstone, offering clarity and self-awareness that will guide the creation of meaningful development goals.

Setting these goals involves a meticulous approach, encompassing both short-term and long-term objectives. Short-term goals should be crafted to be specific, measurable, and attainable within a defined timeframe, often spanning several months to a year. In parallel, long-term goals should seamlessly integrate with broader career ambitions, projecting beyond a one-year horizon. The authenticity of these goals, reflecting the leader's unwavering commitment to growth and development, is paramount.

Subsequently, leaders embark on a skill gap analysis, a critical step informed by their self-assessment. This analysis entails pinpointing with precision the specific leadership skills or competencies requiring development or enhancement. It also involves considering the behavioral changes or shifts in mindset that will be instrumental in effectively addressing the identified development areas.

Transforming these objectives into actionable steps and strategies is the next crucial phase. Leaders must break down their development areas into practical actions that can be executed on a daily, weekly, or monthly basis. The identification of necessary resources, be it books, courses, workshops, mentors, or coaches, is imperative. Equally important is establishing a well-defined timeline for each action step to ensure effective progress tracking.

Diversified development activities come into play. Leaders actively seek relevant training programs, workshops, or courses that are tailored to bolster their leadership skills. They tap into networking opportunities, forging connections with fellow leaders within their industry or organization, thereby gaining invaluable insights and learning from shared experiences. Exploring mentorship or coaching relationships can provide personalized guidance and feedback. Additionally, leaders proactively solicit feedback from colleagues and team members, obtaining nuanced insights into their leadership performance.

Setting clear key performance indicators (KPIs) is paramount for gauging progress toward leadership development goals. Regular assessments of the development plan must be conducted, allowing leaders to ascertain whether they are on track. Flexibility to make adjustments in response to evolving goals ensures that the plan remains adaptive and effective.

Leaders must embrace personal ownership and accountability for their development plan, maintaining unwavering commitment to their goals and action steps. They may consider sharing the plan with a trusted colleague or supervisor to provide a support system that reinforces accountability and offers valuable guidance.

The journey includes periodic reflective practices to evaluate the leadership journey. Leaders contemplate what they have learned, which strategies have proven effective, and areas where refinement is necessary. This reflective process guides adjustments to the leadership development plan, ensuring that it remains relevant and impactful.

Recognizing and celebrating achievements and milestones are pivotal aspects of the journey. These celebrations serve as powerful motivators, reinforcing the leader's commitment to the ongoing development journey.

Leaders should embrace a lifelong learning mindset, acknowledging that leadership development is an enduring journey. Opportunities for growth and improvement should be actively sought throughout their career. Remaining open to new experiences and challenges further enriches leadership skills and capabilities, ensuring ongoing growth and adaptability. This comprehensive framework equips leaders with a structured, adaptable, and deeply introspective approach to crafting individualized leadership development plans that resonate with their unique needs, values, and aspirations.

A comprehensive leadership development plan commences with a thorough self-assessment, a cornerstone that demands introspection into one's existing strengths and areas necessitating improvement. Concurrently, leaders should deeply reflect on their core values and career aspirations, seeking alignment with their leadership goals. With this self-awareness as a compass, the process proceeds to goal setting. It encompasses crafting specific, measurable, and time-bound objectives, spanning short-term milestones achievable within months to year, and long-term ambitions harmonizing with broader career trajectories. The authenticity of these goals mirrors the leader's unwavering commitment to growth and development.

Subsequently, leaders engage in a meticulous skill gap analysis, pinpointing the specific leadership competencies in need of refinement. Simultaneously, they delve into the behavioral shifts and mindset alterations necessary for addressing these development areas effectively. Transitioning from objectives to actionable strategies, leaders delineate practical steps to be undertaken daily, weekly, or monthly, coupled with resource identification - be it literature, courses, mentorship, or coaching. Setting well-defined timelines for each action step ensures robust progress tracking.

A multifaceted approach to development follows, encompassing diverse activities. Leaders actively seek relevant training programs, workshops, or courses tailored to bolster their leadership skills. Networking becomes an avenue for learning from peers and industry experts. Exploring mentorship or coaching relationships provides personalized guidance and feedback. Additionally, leaders proactively solicit feedback from colleagues and team members, augmenting self-awareness, and performance insights.

To gauge progress effectively, leaders establish key performance indicators (KPIs) for tracking their development journey. Regular assessments of the development plan ensure that they remain on course, with flexibility to make adjustments as goals evolve. Personal ownership and accountability are paramount, with the option of sharing the plan with a trusted colleague or supervisor to reinforce accountability and receive support.

Reflective practices punctuate the journey, allowing leaders to evaluate their progress. It is an opportunity to assess learning, effective strategies, and areas in need of refinement. Recognizing achievements and milestones serves as a motivational anchor. Furthermore, the framework emphasizes a lifelong learning mindset, acknowledging that leadership development is a continuous journey. Leaders remain receptive to new experiences and challenges, enriching their skills and adaptability. This holistic framework integrates key components, fostering goal-oriented progress, skill-building, and robust feedback mechanisms, ultimately shaping leaders into their aspirational roles.

One effective method for evaluating the impact of mentorship and leadership development programs involves the use of surveys and feedback forms. These tools can be designed to gather valuable insights from both mentors and mentees about their experiences within the program. Questions may cover the quality of the mentoring relationship, the specific skills or knowledge gained, and the overall influence on career growth. By carefully analyzing the responses provided, organizations can gain qualitative data that sheds light on the program's effectiveness.

Another crucial approach is the use of pre-and post-assessments. These assessments are administered to participants before they enter the program and again upon completion. The objective is to measure changes in leadership skills, knowledge, or behaviors over the course of the program. By comparing the results of these assessments before and after participation, organizations can quantitatively gauge the program's impact on its participants.

Furthermore, organizations can track performance metrics to assess program impact. By examining job performance, project outcomes, or leadership effectiveness before and after program participation, organizations can derive concrete data regarding the influence of mentorship and leadership development initiatives. This objective data allows for a clearer understanding of how the program has influenced participants' performance within the organization.

For a more comprehensive view, consider implementing 360-degree feedback. This involves collecting feedback from a variety of sources, including supervisors, peers, and subordinates, to evaluate changes in leadership behavior. Such feedback offers a well-rounded perspective on how participants' leadership styles have evolved as a result of mentorship and development initiatives.

Retention rates are another useful metric for assessing the impact of these programs. By monitoring whether individuals who have gone through the program are more likely to stay with the organization, organizations can gauge the program's effectiveness in boosting employee engagement and commitment.

Promotions and advancements within the organization can also be tracked as a measure of impact. By keeping tabs on the number of program participants who receive promotions or take on higher-level leadership roles, organizations can assess the program's success in preparing individuals for leadership positions.

Furthermore, organizations can gather qualitative insights through case studies and success stories. These anecdotal accounts offer a glimpse into the real-world impact of mentorship and leadership development initiatives, highlighting the personal and professional growth experienced by participants.

In-depth interviews with both mentors and mentees can provide a deeper understanding of their experiences. Such interviews can uncover nuances that may not be captured through surveys and assessments, offering a richer perspective on the impact of mentorship and leadership development.

Benchmarking against industry standards and best practices can provide context for evaluating program outcomes. By comparing your program's results to industry benchmarks, you can assess whether your initiatives are meeting or surpassing industry standards.

To justify program investments, consider conducting a cost-benefit analysis. Evaluate the costs associated with running the mentorship and leadership development programs against the benefits, such as increased employee retention, improved performance, and leadership pipeline development.

Long-term tracking is also crucial. Assess the lasting impact of mentorship and leadership development initiatives by monitoring participants' progress and development over several years. This longitudinal approach provides insights into whether the benefits are sustained over time.

Lastly, organizations can organize focus groups or feedback sessions with program participants. These interactive sessions can yield valuable input on program strengths and weaknesses, enabling organizations to refine and optimize future iterations of the initiative.

Incorporating these multifaceted assessment methods provides organizations with a comprehensive understanding of the impact of their mentorship and leadership development initiatives. Such a data-driven approach facilitates continuous improvement, ensuring that these programs effectively contribute to leadership development and organizational success.

Metrics and indicators play a pivotal role in evaluating the effectiveness of mentorship and leadership development programs. For mentorship programs, several key metrics can offer insights into their impact. These include the participation rate, which reveals the percentage of eligible employees engaging in the program. A high participation rate often signifies strong interest and engagement. Additionally, monitoring the mentorship completion rate provides an understanding of how many mentorship relationships successfully reach their intended conclusion. Regular satisfaction surveys with both mentors and mentees can help gauge overall program satisfaction. Assessing the mentee promotion rate can showcase the program's ability to influence career advancement.

When it comes to leadership development programs, a variety of metrics come into play. Collecting participant feedback through surveys and post-program evaluations is essential to understand the program's relevance, quality, and effectiveness. Measuring skill development is crucial, and this can be achieved through pre-and post-assessments that track improvements in specific leadership skills like communication, decision-making, and conflict resolution. The program's success can also be reflected in the leadership pipeline, as organizations monitor how many participants progress into higher-level leadership roles. Assessing employee retention rates among program participants is another key metric, as a successful program should contribute to retaining top talent. Furthermore, analyzing changes in job performance, project outcomes, and leadership effectiveness for program participants provides insight into the program's impact on organizational success.

Diversity and inclusion metrics are also significant considerations. These encompass evaluating the diversity of participants in terms of gender, race, ethnicity, and other demographic factors. Inclusion surveys can provide insight into the program's influence on creating an inclusive and equitable environment, assessing whether participants feel a sense of belonging and equal opportunity.

Conducting a cost-benefit analysis is crucial. Organizations should calculate the total program costs, encompassing resources, materials, and personnel expenses. Comparing these costs to the tangible benefits, such as increased employee retention, improved performance, and reduced turnover costs, can provide insights into the program's return on investment (ROI). A positive ROI indicates program success and demonstrates its value to the organization.

Other valuable metrics involve assessing promotions and advancements. This includes tracking the number of program participants who receive promotions or move into higher-level leadership roles within a specified time frame. The time-to-leadership metric measures the average time it takes for program participants to reach leadership positions within the organization.

In addition to these quantitative measures, it is essential to consider qualitative factors, such as the impact on employee engagement and satisfaction. Employee engagement surveys can help assess the program's influence on overall employee engagement levels and job satisfaction. Additionally, evaluating the long-term impact involves tracking the career progression and success of program alumni over several years, providing insights into the program's lasting influence.

Lastly, skill transfer is a critical consideration. Organizations should assess whether participants are successfully applying the skills and knowledge gained from mentorship and leadership development programs in their day-to-day work. Establishing a feedback loop that allows for continuous improvement based on participant feedback and program outcomes ensures that these initiatives can adapt and evolve to meet changing needs and goals effectively.

Indra Nooyi's journey to becoming the former CEO of PepsiCo is a testament to the profound impact of mentorship and her exceptional leadership abilities. Nooyi has consistently acknowledged the pivotal role that mentors played in shaping her career trajectory.

Throughout her career, Nooyi worked with senior leaders and mentors who not only provided guidance but also served as sources of inspiration and support. These mentors played a crucial role in helping her navigate the complexities of the corporate world. Their mentorship was instrumental in honing her leadership skills and strategic thinking.

Under Nooyi's visionary leadership, PepsiCo experienced remarkable growth and innovation. During her tenure as CEO from 2006 to 2018, she led the company through a transformative period. She recognized the shifting consumer preferences towards healthier options and sustainability, and she initiated strategic moves to align PepsiCo with these trends.

One of her notable achievements was the "Performance with Purpose" initiative, which emphasized sustainable and responsible business practices. Under her guidance, PepsiCo made significant strides in reducing its environmental footprint and promoting healthier product offerings.

Nooyi's commitment to diversity and inclusion was also a hallmark of her leadership. She not only championed diversity within PepsiCo but also used her influence to advocate for gender equality and diversity in corporate leadership roles globally.

Beyond her professional accomplishments, Indra Nooyi's leadership style and approach continue to inspire aspiring leaders. Her ability to balance financial performance with social responsibility showcases the potential for businesses to make a positive impact on society while remaining profitable.

The influence of Jeff Bezos's grandfather on his leadership journey and the foundation of Amazon is a fascinating narrative that delves deep into the shaping of one of the world's most influential entrepreneurs.

Jeff Bezos often cites the profound impact of his maternal grandfather, Lawrence Preston Gise, on his early years and subsequent leadership philosophy. During his formative years, Bezos spent summers at his grandfather's ranch in Texas. It was in this rustic environment that he was exposed to the values and lessons that would shape his future endeavors.

Lawrence Gise, a hardworking and resourceful individual, instilled in Bezos the virtues of hard work, resourcefulness, and self-reliance. Bezos witnessed firsthand the dedication required to maintain a ranch and manage its operations. This experience left an indelible mark on his work ethic, emphasizing the importance of diligence, perseverance, and attention to detail.

Gise's influence extended beyond physical labor; he fostered Bezos's intellectual curiosity. Bezos often recalls how his grandfather, a former rancher, and a civil engineer, encouraged his love for tinkering and problem-solving. Gise's guidance in fixing machinery and devising practical solutions instilled in Bezos a deep appreciation for innovation and a willingness to experiment.

Perhaps the most enduring lesson Bezos learned from his grandfather was the idea that taking calculated risks was an essential part of progress. Gise's background as an engineer and his propensity for calculated risk-taking underscored the importance of boldness and venturing into uncharted territory—a principle that Bezos would apply throughout his entrepreneurial journey with Amazon.

These formative experiences with his grandfather laid the groundwork for Bezos's leadership approach when he founded Amazon in 1994. Bezos combined his grandfather's values of hard work, innovation, and calculated risk-taking with a forward-thinking vision for the future of commerce.

Under Bezos's leadership, Amazon rapidly expanded its product offerings and transformed from an online bookseller into the global e-commerce and technology giant we know today. Bezos's relentless pursuit of customer-centricity, innovation, and long-term thinking became the cornerstones of Amazon's corporate culture.

The lessons Bezos imbibed from his grandfather also manifested in Amazon's commitment to experimentation and its willingness to invest in groundbreaking technologies like Amazon Web Services (AWS) and the development of the Kindle e-reader.

In addition to his grandfather's influence, Bezos has continued to seek mentorship and guidance throughout his career. He famously sought advice from former Walmart executive David Glass, whose insights played a role in shaping Amazon's logistics and distribution strategies.

Jeff Weiner's tenure as the former CEO of LinkedIn is a remarkable story shaped by mentorship, visionary leadership, and an unwavering commitment to creating a global platform that redefined professional networking. Central to his success is the mentorship relationship he shared with Reid Hoffman, one of LinkedIn's co-founders and an esteemed figure in Silicon Valley. This mentorship dynamic profoundly influenced Weiner's approach to leadership and the strategic direction he charted for LinkedIn.

Reid Hoffman, with his deep insights into the tech industry and entrepreneurship, served as a guiding force in Weiner's career. Under Hoffman's mentorship, Weiner honed his leadership skills, gaining a unique perspective on how to navigate the dynamic and rapidly evolving world of technology and social networking. This mentorship relationship instilled several key principles in Weiner's leadership philosophy.

Firstly, visionary thinking became a cornerstone of Weiner's approach, encouraged by Hoffman. He learned to think beyond the present and envision the long-term potential of LinkedIn. This visionary thinking drove LinkedIn's expansion into diverse areas, such as content sharing, talent solutions, and online learning, transforming it into a multifaceted platform.

Secondly, customer-centricity was paramount, influenced by Hoffman's emphasis on user experience and feedback. Weiner led LinkedIn with an unwavering commitment to serving its members and providing value to professionals worldwide. This dedication fueled the platform's growth and engagement.

Furthermore, a global perspective, nurtured by Hoffman's mentorship, shaped Weiner's leadership. LinkedIn expanded its reach across borders, connecting professionals from diverse cultures and industries. The platform's international growth mirrored Weiner's commitment to fostering global professional connections.

Innovation also played a pivotal role, with Weiner continually evolving LinkedIn's offerings to meet changing user needs. This commitment to innovation led to the introduction of features like the news feed, online courses through LinkedIn Learning, and strategic acquisitions.

Weiner adopted Hoffman's data-driven approach to decision-making, leveraging user data and analytics to inform strategic choices and enhance the user experience. This data-driven mindset contributed to LinkedIn's ability to adapt and evolve.

Under Weiner's leadership, LinkedIn experienced exponential growth, expanding its user base, and evolving into a multifaceted platform that encompasses professional networking, content sharing, job search, and skills development. His compassionate leadership approach, rooted in the belief that people should genuinely care about each other's success, fostered a culture of compassion and empathy within LinkedIn, reinforcing the enduring influence of his mentorship.

Mentorship and leadership development programs yield a host of positive outcomes that reverberate through both individuals and organizations. For individuals, these initiatives serve as fertile grounds for skill enhancement and knowledge expansion, empowering participants to refine their professional expertise. Such programs often become catalysts for career advancement, propelling individuals into higher roles and positions of greater responsibility. Furthermore, mentorship and coaching instill a profound sense of confidence and self-assurance, enabling individuals to approach challenges with poise and determination. The benefits extend to networking opportunities, as participants connect with experienced professionals and peers, expanding their professional circles. Importantly, mentorship and coaching are inherently personalized, offering tailored guidance that aligns with the unique aspirations and challenges of each individual. As a result, participants acquire essential leadership skills, including effective communication, decision-making process, conflict resolution abilities, and adept team management capabilities. This holistic development leads to heightened job satisfaction and fulfillment, as individuals witness tangible personal growth, backed by their organization's commitment to their advancement.

On the organizational front, the advantages of mentorship and leadership development programs are equally profound. These initiatives contribute to talent retention by fostering higher levels of employee engagement and job satisfaction, ultimately reducing turnover rates and the associated recruitment and training costs. Moreover, they play a pivotal role in succession planning, identifying, and preparing a steady stream of high-potential individuals to fill leadership positions, thereby ensuring organizational continuity and minimizing leadership gaps. The positive impact extends to productivity enhancements, with well-trained and confident leaders effectively steering teams toward heightened performance. Organizations benefit from a culture of innovation, as leaders equipped with diverse perspectives and robust critical thinking skills drive forward-thinking initiatives. Mentorship programs that prioritize diversity and inclusion further enrich organizational dynamics, promoting equitable workforces that make sounder collective decisions and nurture a more inclusive corporate culture. As a result, organizations with strong mentorship and leadership development programs gain a competitive edge, displaying the agility and adaptability necessary to thrive amidst industry changes. This commitment to employee growth and development fosters a constructive organizational culture where individuals feel valued and supported, leading to a more engaged and dedicated workforce. Ultimately, these initiatives fortify an organization's long-term success, cultivating capable leaders who can adeptly guide the company through challenges and seize emerging opportunities.

In conclusion, mentorship and leadership development are not only essential for individual growth but also crucial for the long-term success of organizations. Leaders who invest in nurturing future leaders contribute to a sustainable legacy of leadership excellence. As you continue your leadership journey, remember that mentorship and coaching are powerful tools for building a thriving leadership pipeline within your organization.

Chapter 10

Ethics

&

Social Responsibility in Leadership

"Leadership of the highest caliber is grounded in
unwavering ethics and a profound commitment
to social responsibility."

−Joel R. Klemmer

Chapter 10
Ethics and Social Responsibility in Leadership

E thical leadership constitutes a cornerstone of organizational integrity, extending far beyond the realm of merely achieving business objectives. It encompasses a profound commitment to principled conduct and social responsibility in guiding organizations towards success. Ethical leaders prioritize moral values, transparency, and the welfare of all stakeholders, not just profit margins. This holistic approach to leadership calls upon individuals to uphold high ethical standards, fostering a culture of accountability and ethical decision-making within their organizations. Leaders must recognize their ethical responsibilities, which encompass maintaining honesty, fairness, and integrity in all their interactions.

Ethical leadership is a foundational approach to guiding organizations, prioritizing moral values, responsible decision-making, and the welfare of all stakeholders. Beyond the pursuit of organizational objectives and profitability, ethical leadership centers on the ethical and socially responsible conduct of leaders. It encompasses several core principles that form the bedrock of this leadership philosophy.

Integrity stands as the cornerstone of ethical leadership, requiring leaders to uphold a steadfast commitment to moral and ethical principles, even in the face of challenging circumstances or temptations to compromise these principles. Ethical leaders consistently act with honesty and transparency, thereby earning the trust and respect of their teams and stakeholders.

Honesty is a fundamental aspect of ethical leadership, entailing truthful and transparent communication. Ethical leaders maintain candor regarding their organization's challenges, successes, and goals, fostering an atmosphere of trust and openness that is pivotal for ethical leadership.

Transparency goes hand in hand with honesty, necessitating openness and the ready accessibility of relevant information. Ethical leaders ensure stakeholders have access to necessary information, enabling informed decision-making. Transparency not only encourages accountability but also serves as a safeguard against unethical behavior or hidden agendas.

Accountability is another vital principle, with ethical leaders willingly accepting responsibility for their actions and decisions. They hold themselves and others accountable for upholding ethical standards and achieving organizational goals. This accountability ensures consistent adherence to ethical principles and enforces consequences for ethical breaches.

Fairness and justice are paramount, as ethical leaders treat all individuals equitably and respectfully, regardless of their background, position, or characteristics. They cultivate a workplace culture that values diversity and inclusivity while actively addressing discrimination or bias.

Empathy and compassion play a crucial role, with ethical leaders demonstrating understanding and care toward their team members and stakeholders. They remain attuned to others' needs and concerns, actively supporting their well-being and nurturing a sense of belonging within the organization.

Respect for others is integral to ethical leadership, involving the acknowledgment of individuals' dignity, autonomy, and rights. Ethical leaders create an environment where diverse perspectives are esteemed, and any form of harassment, discrimination, or mistreatment is unequivocally rejected.

Ethical leaders also adopt a long-term perspective, carefully considering the enduring consequences of their actions and decisions. They prioritize the sustainability and ethical reputation of the organization over short-term gains, recognizing the broader societal and environmental impacts that stem from their choices.

Moreover, ethical leaders embrace their organization's role in the wider community and society, actively engaging in socially responsible initiatives and contributing positively to their communities. They aspire to address societal challenges through ethical means, understanding their interconnectedness with the broader societal fabric.

Ethical leaders are environmentally conscious, valuing environmental stewardship and responsible resource management. They implement practices aimed at minimizing environmental harm, actively support efforts to combat climate change, and take measures to address ecological concerns.

Ethical leadership embodies a commitment to principles such as integrity, honesty, transparency, accountability, fairness, empathy, and social and environmental responsibility. Leaders who uphold these principles foster a positive organizational culture while making meaningful contributions to the well-being of individuals, the success of their organizations, and the betterment of society at large.

Values and ethical frameworks are integral components of leadership, providing a moral compass and a set of guiding principles that profoundly influence how leaders lead. These values, often stemming from deeply held personal beliefs, and ethical frameworks, which can draw from established ethical theories or organizational codes, play a pivotal role in shaping ethical leadership. They serve as decision-making aids, helping leaders navigate complex ethical dilemmas and make choices that align with their moral convictions.

Ethical decision-making is a cornerstone of leadership, and values and ethical frameworks play a central role in this process. Leaders reference these principles to assess the ethical implications of their decisions, ensuring alignment with their organization's ethical standards and culture. Consistency in ethical behavior builds trust and credibility, as leaders who consistently uphold their values earn the respect and confidence of their teams and stakeholders.

Values also exert a significant influence on organizational culture. Leaders who prioritize ethical values create an environment where ethical conduct is valued and expected, fostering an organizational culture rooted in ethical principles. This, in turn, encourages employees to adhere to similar values, reinforcing ethical behavior throughout the organization.

Leaders serve as ethical role models for their teams, and their embodiment of ethical behavior and commitment to values inspire and influence their employees to act ethically. This role modeling is a powerful tool for instilling and perpetuating ethical conduct within an organization.

Furthermore, ethical leadership extends to stakeholder relations, where it enhances trust and engagement with customers, investors, suppliers, and the broader community. Stakeholders are more likely to trust and collaborate with organizations led by individuals who prioritize values and ethical principles, resulting in positive reputational and financial outcomes.

Ethical leadership acts as a bulwark against ethical risks and misconduct. Leaders who are attuned to their values and ethical guidelines are better equipped to identify potential ethical pitfalls and proactively address them, thereby reducing the organization's exposure to ethical crises.

During periods of change and uncertainty, values and ethical frameworks provide leaders with a stable foundation. Leaders can rely on these principles to make decisions that prioritize the well-being of all stakeholders and uphold the organization's ethical standards, even in the face of significant challenges.

Moreover, ethical leadership ensures that organizational goals align with ethical considerations. Leaders who integrate their values and ethical frameworks into strategic planning ensure that business objectives are pursued in an ethical and responsible manner.

In an increasingly interconnected world, leaders with strong ethical foundations can navigate diverse cultural and ethical landscapes. They recognize the importance of respecting local customs and ethical norms while upholding universal ethical principles, thereby fostering global perspective and responsible leadership.

Values and ethical frameworks are indispensable elements of ethical leadership, guiding decision-making, shaping organizational culture, and influencing stakeholder relations. Leaders who not only understand the significance of these principles but also integrate them into their leadership approach contribute to the ethical and sustainable success of their organizations.

Ethical leaders are distinguished by their commitment to making decisions that are firmly grounded in moral principles. These leaders possess a clear understanding of their own values, such as honesty, fairness, and integrity, which serve as the bedrock of their ethical decision-making process. Importantly, they ensure that their personal values harmonize with the ethical standards of their organization, striving for alignment to maintain consistency in their leadership.

Ethical leaders approach decision-making with a sense of ethical reflection, taking the time to contemplate the moral implications of their choices. When faced with complex decisions, they carefully weigh the potential benefits and harms, recognizing the need to balance competing interests while upholding their moral principles. This deliberative process allows them to find ethical solutions that address both practical considerations and their commitment to moral integrity.

Transparency and openness are hallmarks of ethical leadership in decision-making. Ethical leaders communicate openly with their teams and stakeholders, sharing not only the outcomes but also the ethical reasoning behind their decisions. This transparency builds trust and demonstrates their unwavering dedication to ethical conduct.

Collaboration and consultation are common practices for ethical leaders. They actively seek input and diverse perspectives from others when making significant decisions, valuing the insights of their team members and stakeholders. Involving others in the decision-making process contributes to more ethical and well-rounded choices.

Ethical leaders adopt a long-term perspective when assessing the consequences of their decisions. They consider how their choices may impact the organization, its reputation, and its relationships with stakeholders over time. This forward-thinking approach underscores their commitment to sustainable and ethical outcomes, even if it requires short-term sacrifices.

Accountability is a fundamental aspect of ethical leadership. Leaders hold themselves accountable for the consequences of their decisions and actions, acknowledging that ethical leadership entails taking responsibility for both positive and negative outcomes. This accountability reinforces their dedication to moral principles.

When confronted with ethical dilemmas, ethical leaders explore alternative solutions that align with their values and ethical principles. They are willing to make difficult decisions that prioritize ethical integrity, even if those choices are challenging or may face resistance. This resolve in ethical dilemma resolution strengthens the ethical fabric of their leadership.

Moreover, ethical leaders are committed to continuous learning and improvement in their ethical decision-making skills. They recognize that ethical leadership is a dynamic process that can be honed over time. They actively seek opportunities for learning and growth to further enhance their ability to make principled decisions.

In essence, ethical leaders embody a principled approach to decision-making that reflects their commitment to moral values, transparency, accountability, and the well-being of all stakeholders. Through their ethical leadership, they foster a culture of integrity and ethical conduct within their organizations, influencing others to uphold similar ethical standards.

The alignment of personal values with those of an organization holds profound significance in the realm of leadership and organizational culture. When leaders find congruence between their personal values and the values espoused by the organization, it engenders authentic leadership. This authenticity, characterized by consistent and genuine behavior, cultivates trust and respect among team members and stakeholders.

Furthermore, the alignment of personal and organizational values contributes to the cohesion of the organizational culture. When individuals within the organization share similar values, it fosters a sense of unity, common purpose, and a shared ethical framework. This unity, in turn, serves as a unifying force that guides decision-making, behavior, and interactions throughout the organization.

Additionally, this alignment has a direct impact on employee engagement and commitment. Employees who perceive an alignment between their personal values and the values of the organization tend to be more motivated and engaged. They are driven by a sense of purpose and resonance with the organization's mission and goals, which fuels their dedication to their roles.

In the context of decision-making, leaders who make choices that align with their personal values and the organization's values are better equipped to navigate ethical dilemmas and complex decisions. This alignment provides clarity and a principled foundation for decision-making, ensuring that choices are consistent with both individual ethics and the organization's ethical framework.

Moreover, the alignment of personal and organizational values positively influences employee morale. When individuals feel that their personal values are acknowledged and respected within the organizational culture, it fosters higher levels of job satisfaction and contributes to a positive work environment.

Beyond the workplace, stakeholders such as customers, investors, and the community are more likely to trust and support organizations that demonstrate a clear alignment with ethical and socially responsible values. This trust can translate into enhanced reputation, brand loyalty, and sustained support from key stakeholders.

In terms of sustainability, organizations that prioritize values alignment are often more resilient and less susceptible to ethical crises, high turnover rates, and internal conflicts. This alignment creates an organizational environment characterized by stability and adaptability, enabling the organization to thrive over the long term.

Furthermore, values alignment plays a pivotal role in attracting and retaining top talent. Individuals are drawn to organizations that reflect their own values and offer an environment where they can contribute meaningfully. This, in turn, contributes to the organization's ability to build a skilled and motivated workforce.

Innovation and creativity are also fostered within a culture of values alignment. When individuals feel that their values are respected, they are more inclined to share diverse perspectives and ideas, leading to innovative solutions and approaches that can drive the organization's success.

Organizations with values alignment are often more adaptable and responsive to change. Employees and leaders who share common values can collectively work toward adapting to new challenges and seizing emerging opportunities, ensuring that the organization remains agile and forward-looking.

Strategic Synergy

To achieve and maintain alignment between personal and organizational values, leaders and organizations should engage in ongoing dialogue, articulate, and communicate their values clearly, and ensure that values are integrated into decision-making processes, policies, and practices. By emphasizing this alignment, organizations can build a culture of integrity, purpose, and ethical leadership that drives success and positively impacts all stakeholders.

The intricate interplay between ethical leadership, trust, and a positive organizational reputation forms the bedrock of organizational success and sustainability. Ethical leadership, characterized by unwavering adherence to moral principles and transparency, sets the stage for the establishment of trust within an organization. This trust is multifaceted, encompassing the belief in a leader's integrity and ethical commitment. Trust, in turn, is the linchpin that elevates an organization's reputation to a positive stature.

A positive organizational reputation is built upon the solid foundation of trust. Stakeholders, ranging from customers and investors to employees and the broader community, perceive organizations led by ethical leaders as credible, reliable, and morally upright. This enhanced trust contributes significantly to crafting a favorable reputation. Consequently, the organization is viewed favorably, and stakeholders are more inclined to engage with it positively.

The impact of trust and a positive reputation extends deeply into relationships with stakeholders. The trust nurtured by ethical leadership fosters loyalty among customers, instills confidence in investors, attracts top talent, and garners unwavering support from the community. This synergy between trust and reputation strengthens stakeholder engagement, reinforcing the organization's image as an ethical and reliable entity.

Furthermore, trust and reputation serve as resilient shields during turbulent times. Organizations with a strong reputation rooted in ethical leadership are better equipped to navigate crises and challenges.

Stakeholders tend to be more forgiving and supportive when they have witnessed the organization's consistent ethical conduct over time.

Ethical leaders who prioritize values alignment often draw like-minded stakeholders. This alignment deepens stakeholder engagement and further bolsters the organization's reputation as a champion of ethical behavior and social responsibility. It attracts individuals and entities that share similar ethical values, creating a mutually reinforcing relationship.

Moreover, the enduring sustainability of organizations is intricately linked to ethical leadership, trust, and a positive reputation. Sustainability here refers not only to financial stability but also to ethical and societal impact. Organizations that prioritize ethical principles tend to endure and flourish, cementing their status as industry leaders with a strong legacy.

In addition to sustainability, a positive reputation derived from ethical leadership provides a competitive edge. Stakeholders, be it customers, investors, or partners, gravitate toward organizations they trust and respect, endowing ethically led organizations with a distinct advantage in the marketplace.

Ethical leadership and a positive reputation also play a pivotal role in talent management. These attributes attract and retain top talent, as individuals are naturally drawn to organizations that prioritize ethical conduct and social responsibility. This, in turn, contributes to the organization's long-term success by fostering a committed and skilled workforce.

Ethical leaders, buoyed by trust and a positive reputation, are often more effective in embracing social responsibility initiatives. They are acutely aware of their role in giving back to communities and addressing societal challenges, further enhancing their reputation as socially conscious and responsible organizations.

Ihe intricate dance of ethical leadership, trust, and a positive organizational reputation forms a virtuous cycle that reinforces an organization's resilience, sustainability, competitive advantage, and societal impact. It positions the organization as a trusted and reputable entity in the eyes of its stakeholders and the broader public, reinforcing its status as a paragon of ethical conduct and responsible leadership.

Ethical lapses within an organization carry profound and far-reaching consequences, primarily affecting trust and reputation. One of the most significant repercussions is the erosion of trust among stakeholders, including employees, customers, investors, and the public. When these individuals witness unethical behavior or decisions, their confidence in the organization and its leadership deteriorates, often leading to lasting damage that is challenging to rectify.

Moreover, ethical lapses inflict considerable harm on an organization's reputation. Such lapses tarnish the organization's image, resulting in a negative reputation that can have severe consequences. A damaged reputation can lead to customer attrition, reduced investor confidence, and difficulty attracting top-tier talent. It also adversely impacts relationships with partners, suppliers, and regulatory bodies.

Ethical lapses can subject organizations to legal and regulatory consequences. This may entail investigations, fines, and lawsuits, culminating in financial losses and significant harm to the organization's reputation. In severe cases, legal actions can lead to criminal charges against individuals involved, exacerbating the crisis.

Internally, ethical lapses can trigger employee disengagement and reduced morale. When employees perceive unethical conduct within the organization, it undermines their commitment to the organization's values and mission. This can result in lower productivity, increased turnover, and challenges in attracting and retaining skilled employees.

Externally, customer and client loss are a common outcome of ethical lapses. Stakeholders who lose trust in the organization often opt to take their business elsewhere, leading to revenue loss that affects the organization's financial stability and long-term growth prospects.

Joel R. Klemmer

Attracting top talent can also become a daunting task for organizations marred by ethical lapses. Potential employees may be hesitant to join an organization with a compromised reputation, constraining the organization's ability to recruit qualified individuals.

Ethical lapses can strain partnerships and relationships with suppliers, contractors, and collaborators. Organizations may encounter difficulties securing new partnerships or maintaining existing ones when their ethical integrity is called into question.

Investor trust is another casualty of ethical lapses. Both institutional and individual investors may lose faith in the organization's leadership and governance, potentially resulting in divestment that impacts the organization's stock price and access to capital.

Recovering from the fallout of ethical lapses poses considerable challenges. Rebuilding trust and restoring a tarnished reputation is a protracted and labor-intensive process. Organizations often need to implement extensive reputation management and ethical reform efforts, which can strain financial resources and take years to yield results.

Ethical lapses trigger a cascade of adverse consequences that extend far beyond the immediate incident. They corrode trust, inflict damage on reputation, attract legal and regulatory scrutiny, and adversely affect a wide array of stakeholders, from employees and customers to investors and partners. Preventing and mitigating ethical lapses is imperative for an organization's long-term sustainability and success.

Ethical leadership serves as a cornerstone for enhancing employee engagement, job satisfaction, and overall well-being within an organization. At its core, ethical leadership is marked by trust and credibility. Leaders who consistently exhibit honesty, integrity, and transparency in their actions and decisions earn the trust and confidence of their employees. This trust forms the bedrock of employee engagement, as it instills a belief in leadership that, in turn, inspires employees to engage more deeply in their work.

Moreover, ethical leaders provide a clear sense of direction by communicating their values and principles. This clarity aligns employees with the organization's mission, fostering a sense of purpose and commitment that positively influences job satisfaction. Fairness and equality are also integral to ethical leadership. Leaders who prioritize these principles create a workplace where employees feel valued and respected, leading to higher job satisfaction. Ethical leaders additionally cultivate a culture that values work-life balance, further contributing to employee well-being.

Ethical leadership also empowers employees by entrusting them with responsibilities and decision-making authority, promoting a sense of autonomy and trust. This empowerment enhances job satisfaction as employees feel more engaged and invested in their roles. Furthermore, ethical leaders are dedicated to employee development, offering opportunities for skill enhancement, career advancement, and personal growth. This commitment to growth contributes significantly to job satisfaction and overall well-being.

Conflict resolution is another area where ethical leaders excel. They address workplace conflicts and challenges promptly and fairly, employing ethical principles in their resolution strategies. This approach fosters a harmonious work environment, reducing workplace stress and conflicts, which in turn positively impacts employee well-being.

Ethical leaders also promote open communication and value diverse perspectives, fostering an inclusive environment where employees feel comfortable sharing their ideas and concerns. This inclusivity enhances employee engagement by making employees feel heard and valued. Additionally, ethical leaders serve as role models, exemplifying ethical behavior and decision-making. When employees witness ethical leadership in action, it reinforces their commitment to ethical conduct and overall well-being.

Ethical leaders often align their leadership style with their personal values, resonating with employees who share similar principles. This alignment creates a sense of connection and resonance between personal and professional values, contributing to overall well-being. Organizations that prioritize ethical leadership tend to have more engaged, satisfied, and fulfilled employees. This, in turn, leads to increased productivity, higher retention rates, and overall organizational success.

Salesforce, a global leader in customer relationship management (CRM) software, stands out as an exemplary organization that places ethical leadership and employee welfare at the forefront of its corporate culture. Under the visionary leadership of CEO Marc Benioff, Salesforce has not only achieved remarkable success but has also set a standard for ethical conduct and social responsibility within the tech industry.

One of Salesforce's distinctive ethical practices is its unwavering commitment to pay equity. The company takes proactive steps to ensure that all employees, regardless of gender or other demographic factors, receive equal compensation for equivalent roles and responsibilities. This commitment to pay equity goes beyond mere rhetoric; Salesforce conducts regular audits of its compensation practices to identify and rectify any disparities. Such dedication to fairness not only aligns with ethical principles but also fosters a sense of trust and inclusivity among its workforces.

Salesforce's ethical leadership extends beyond its internal practices to encompass a broader commitment to social responsibility and philanthropy. The company has dedicated a significant portion of its resources to giving back to the community through its 1-1-1 model of philanthropy. This model involves donating 1% of Salesforce's equity, 1% of its product, and 1% of its employees' time to charitable causes. This approach resonates deeply with employees, as it empowers them to actively engage in volunteerism and community service, aligning their personal values with the company's mission.

Moreover, Salesforce's philanthropic efforts are not merely a corporate checkbox; they are deeply ingrained in the company's DNA. The Salesforce Foundation, now known as Salesforce.org, serves as the embodiment of the company's commitment to societal betterment. It provides grants, technology, and support to nonprofit organizations and educational institutions worldwide. This alignment between Salesforce's core values and its philanthropic endeavors creates a sense of purpose and meaning among its employees, contributing to their overall well-being and job satisfaction.

In Marc Benioff's leadership, Salesforce has demonstrated that ethical leadership and a commitment to employees' welfare are not only compatible but also integral to the company's enduring success. Salesforce's emphasis on pay equity and its philanthropic initiatives exemplify how ethical principles can be translated into concrete actions that benefit both employees and society at large. As a result, Salesforce has garnered not only recognition for its ethical leadership but also the unwavering loyalty and commitment of its employees, further solidifying its status as a model of responsible and purpose-driven business leadership.

Costco, under the steadfast leadership of CEO Craig Jelinek, stands out as a shining example of ethical leadership within the competitive retail industry. Jelinek's unwavering commitment to ethical values has profoundly influenced the company's corporate culture and practices, leading to an environment where employees flourish. A deeper examination of Costco's approach to employee welfare reveals the depth of its ethical leadership.

At the heart of Costco's ethical commitment is the principle of fair wages. The company has gained widespread acclaim for its dedication to paying employees above-average wages, bucking the industry trend of lower pay in the retail sector. This approach not only attracts top talent but also significantly reduces turnover rates, as employees are more likely to remain with a company that values their contributions and compensates them fairly.

Complementing its competitive wages, Costco provides its employees with comprehensive benefits packages. These encompass health insurance, dental and vision coverage, retirement plans, and opportunities for employee stock ownership. By prioritizing these benefits, Costco nurtures a sense of security and well-being among its workforce, allowing employees to focus on their roles without the added stress of healthcare or retirement concerns.

Furthermore, employee development and advancement are core tenets of Costco's ethical leadership. The company is renowned for its policy of promoting from within, offering employees a clear trajectory for career growth. This commitment not only enhances job satisfaction but also fosters loyalty, as employees recognize that their dedication can lead to meaningful career progression.

The result of Costco's ethical approach is notably high job satisfaction among its employees. The fair treatment, competitive compensation, and opportunities for personal and professional growth culminate in a content and motivated workforce. High job satisfaction not only boosts productivity but also enhances customer service quality and reduces turnover, yielding cost savings for the company.

Perhaps one of the most telling indicators of Costco's ethical success is its impressive employee retention rates, which significantly outshine industry averages in the retail sector. These retention rates are a testament to the efficacy of the company's ethical leadership and its unwavering focus on employee well-being. With low turnover costs and a highly experienced and dedicated workforce, Costco demonstrates how ethical principles can yield both a thriving and loyal employee base and long-term corporate success.

CEO Michele Buck has cultivated a culture of ethical leadership at The Hershey Company, placing a profound emphasis on both sustainability and the well-being of its employees. This ethical commitment underscores the company's core values and resonates through its multifaceted approach to creating a positive workplace culture.

Sustainability is a cornerstone of The Hershey Company's ethical strategy, particularly in the responsible sourcing of cocoa, a critical ingredient for its chocolate products. The company has taken substantial measures to ensure the ethical and sustainable management of its cocoa supply chain. This commitment aligns with ethical principles by upholding fair labor practices, environmental protection, and the empowerment of cocoa farmers and their communities.

Additionally, The Hershey Company's philanthropic endeavors, channeled through the Hershey Trust's initiatives, exemplify its dedication to giving back to society. These initiatives extend beyond charitable contributions; they are deeply integrated into the company's mission. The Hershey Trust focuses on programs related to education, community development, and the well-being of children. This alignment with societal betterment resonates with employees, as they actively engage in volunteerism and community service, knowing that their employer shares their commitment to making a positive impact.

In tandem with its ethical initiatives, The Hershey Company fosters a supportive work environment that prioritizes employee welfare. It goes beyond ethical principles by offering opportunities for career advancement and development, enabling its workforce to realize their full potential. These opportunities contribute not only to job satisfaction but also to a profound sense of loyalty, as employees recognize that The Hershey Company invests in their growth and professional well-being.

The Hershey Company's ethical leadership is not merely a matter of corporate philosophy; it is a tangible and integral aspect of its operations and values. Through its dedication to sustainability, responsible sourcing, and philanthropy, the company exemplifies how ethical principles can translate into meaningful actions that benefit both employees and society at large. Furthermore, its commitment to creating a supportive work environment and facilitating personal and professional development underscores the idea that ethical leadership is not only a moral imperative but also a catalyst for fostering employee well-being and engagement.

Ethical decision-making models offer structured approaches for individuals and organizations facing complex moral dilemmas. Two prominent models are the Ethical Decision-Making Framework and the Stakeholder Approach, each providing a comprehensive roadmap for ethical deliberation.

The Ethical Decision-Making Framework commences by identifying and defining the ethical issue at hand, necessitating a clear understanding of the conflicting values or principles involved. Subsequently, it involves gathering all pertinent information, including facts, stakeholders, and potential consequences. Stakeholder identification follows, determining those impacted by the decision. The model then guides individuals to brainstorm alternative courses of action and evaluate them against ethical principles, considering legality, fairness, and justice. Ultimately, a decision is made, implemented, and continuously monitored and reviewed for its ethical outcomes.

In contrast, the Stakeholder Approach centers on identifying and prioritizing stakeholders. Primary, secondary, and tertiary stakeholders are considered, recognizing their varying levels of importance and influence. Understanding the specific interests and expectations of each stakeholder group is crucial, as is the balancing of their interests and addressing conflicting concerns ethically. Decisions are made by considering stakeholders' well-being and the minimization of harm while maintaining transparent communication. Continuous evaluation is emphasized, allowing for adjustments when necessary based on stakeholder feedback and unforeseen consequences.

Both models underscore the significance of ethical principles, stakeholder engagement, and transparent communication in the decision-making process, offering valuable guidance for addressing intricate ethical challenges effectively and morally.

Ethical decision-making models play a crucial role in guiding leaders when they grapple with intricate ethical dilemmas. These models offer a structured pathway that enables leaders to navigate such challenges in a thoughtful and morally responsible manner. They provide a step-by-step approach to decision-making, ensuring that leaders can make well-informed and ethically sound choices.

The initial phase of these models involves the identification and definition of the ethical issue or dilemma at hand. This process encourages leaders to gain clarity about the fundamental nature of the problem, which often involves conflicting values, principles, or interests. It serves as a critical first step in understanding the ethical dimensions of the dilemma.

Once the issue is clearly defined, these models advocate for comprehensive information gathering. Ethical dilemmas often demand a deep understanding of the situation, including facts, stakeholders, and potential consequences. By systematically collecting all relevant information, leaders can ensure that they are well-equipped to make informed decisions, reducing the risk of making rash or uninformed choices.

The Stakeholder Approach, in particular, highlights the importance of considering the interests of stakeholders. It guides leaders in identifying and prioritizing these stakeholders, acknowledging their varying levels of significance and influence. Leaders are encouraged to delve into the specific interests, concerns, and expectations of each stakeholder group. This holistic perspective helps leaders recognize the broader impact of their decisions and the intricacies of stakeholder dynamics.

Balancing conflicting interests is another crucial aspect emphasized by the Stakeholder Approach. In complex ethical dilemmas, stakeholders may have divergent desires and concerns. Leaders can use this model to seek ethical solutions that align with principles like fairness and justice, fostering a collaborative approach to decision-making.

Both models underscore the significance of evaluating potential courses of action against ethical principles. Leaders are encouraged to assess the moral implications of each option, considering factors such as legality, fairness, and respect for individual rights. This systematic evaluation ensures that leaders make decisions that uphold ethical norms and standards.

Following this deliberation, leaders are guided to make a decision that reflects a thoughtful and principled approach. The chosen course of action should align with ethical considerations and be morally justifiable. Effective communication is highlighted in both models, emphasizing transparent and open dialogue with stakeholders. Leaders are encouraged to explain the rationale behind their decisions, fostering trust and ensuring that stakeholders understand the ethical reasoning that influenced the outcome.

Continuous evaluation and adaptation are integral to these models. Leaders are prompted to monitor the outcomes of their decisions, assessing their impact on stakeholders and the organization. They should be prepared to adjust their course if unforeseen consequences arise or if the decision does not yield the expected ethical results.

In essence, these ethical decision-making models serve as indispensable tools for leaders facing complex ethical dilemmas. They provide a structured framework that promotes clarity, comprehensive information gathering, stakeholder consideration, ethical evaluation, and transparent communication. By adhering to these models, leaders can navigate intricate ethical challenges with a systematic and morally responsible approach, prioritizing the welfare of all stakeholders involved.

Navigating challenging ethical dilemmas is a fundamental aspect of effective leadership. Leaders can approach these intricate situations by adhering to a set of guiding principles and practices that facilitate sound decision-making.

First and foremost, it is crucial to gain a comprehensive understanding of the ethical dilemma. Leaders should take the time to clarify the problem at hand, including identifying the conflicting values or principles that are central to the dilemma. Seeking input from various stakeholders and colleagues can provide valuable insights and diverse perspectives.

Ethical frameworks and principles play a pivotal role in ethical decision-making. Leaders should familiarize themselves with these frameworks, such as utilitarianism, deontology, virtue ethics, and the Stakeholder Approach. Applying these frameworks can help leaders analyze the situation and evaluate potential courses of action through an ethical lens.

Identifying stakeholders and their interests is another essential step. Leaders should consider all stakeholders, both directly and indirectly affected by the decision, and prioritize them based on their significance and influence in the context of the dilemma.

Gathering comprehensive information is paramount. Leaders should collect all relevant data, facts, and expert opinions to ensure they have a complete and accurate understanding of the issue. Assessing the credibility and reliability of information sources is crucial.

Generating a variety of alternatives is a creative and collaborative process. Leaders should brainstorm multiple solutions or courses of action to address the ethical dilemma, encouraging open discussion within their team or organization.

Each alternative should be rigorously evaluated, taking into account ethical implications, legal considerations, fairness, potential consequences, and alignment with ethical principles. It is essential to reflect on how each option affects stakeholders and whether it upholds their rights and dignity.

Seeking advice and collaboration is valuable. Leaders can consult with trusted colleagues, mentors, or ethics experts to gain guidance and diverse perspectives. Additionally, fostering open dialogue and collaboration within the team can lead to innovative ethical solutions.

Making a well-informed decision is the culmination of the process. Leaders should select the course of action that most closely aligns with ethical principles and respects the well-being of stakeholders. It is crucial to ensure that the decision is well-reasoned and ethically defensible.

Effective communication is essential in maintaining transparency. Leaders should clearly articulate their decision to stakeholders, providing a thorough explanation of the rationale and ethical considerations behind it. Addressing questions and concerns fosters an open and transparent environment.

Implementation and monitoring are integral to the process. Leaders should put their decision into action while closely monitoring its impact on stakeholders and the organization. Being prepared to adjust the approach if unforeseen ethical issues arise is essential.

Continuous learning and reflection are essential for ongoing improvement in ethical decision-making. Leaders should consistently evaluate the outcomes of their decisions and reflect on the ethical implications of their actions. Investing in professional development and staying informed about evolving ethical standards is also valuable.

Upholding personal and professional integrity is paramount. Leaders should set a high standard of integrity and ethical behavior, serving as a positive example for their team and organization. Accountability and a commitment to ethical culture are essential, as leaders strive to create an environment where ethical considerations are at the forefront of decision-making.

The Ford Pinto case of the 1970s delves into the intricate dynamics between ethics, corporate decision-making, and consumer safety. At its core, this case embodies a profound ethical dilemma that continues to be studied and discussed by scholars, ethicists, and business leaders.

In the context of the dilemma, Ford Motor Company was grappling with intense competition in the compact car market. To remain competitive, Ford was under tremendous pressure to control costs and deliver affordable vehicles. However, within this competitive landscape lurked a significant design flaw in the Ford Pinto's fuel tank. This flaw made the car prone to explosions in rear-end collisions, posing a substantial threat to consumer safety.

The pivotal decision not to recall and fix the Pinto initially was primarily driven by financial considerations. The costs associated with recalling and retrofitting the vehicles were substantial, and this weighed heavily on the minds of Ford's leadership. They faced a dilemma where prioritizing safety would entail significant expenses and potentially erode the company's financial performance.

Tragically, this initial decision led to a series of harrowing accidents and even fatalities. The public outcry and legal actions that followed cast a harsh spotlight on the company's ethical stance. As public sentiment turned against Ford, the ethical dilemma intensified. It became apparent that the company's reputation and financial standing were at stake, alongside the lives and safety of consumers.

Eventually, faced with mounting ethical and legal pressure, Ford reversed its course and initiated a recall of the Pinto. This decision was a turning point in the case and underscored the ethical principle that safety should always take precedence over financial considerations.

The enduring lesson of the Ford Pinto case is a stark reminder of the ethical responsibilities that corporations bear, particularly concerning consumer safety. It serves as a seminal example of the potential consequences when businesses prioritize short-term financial gains over long-term ethical integrity. Moreover, the case highlights the crucial role of ethical leadership and corporate accountability in safeguarding the well-being of consumers and upholding public trust in an organization. It remains a powerful case study in business ethics and a reference point for discussions on the ethical dimensions of corporate decision-making.

The Enron case of the early 2000s is a chilling example of an ethical dilemma that escalated into one of the most notorious corporate scandals in history, with far-reaching consequences.

At the heart of this dilemma was the staggering disconnect between Enron's outward appearance of financial prosperity and its internal reality of mounting debt and losses. Enron, once hailed as an innovative and successful company, was engaged in fraudulent accounting practices to conceal its financial troubles. The dilemma revolved around a critical choice facing the company's executives: whether to persist in manipulating financial records to maintain the illusion of profitability or to reveal the truth about Enron's precarious financial health.

The decision taken by Enron's leadership was nothing short of catastrophic. They opted to continue the unethical practices, choosing the path of deception and misinformation. This decision led to a series of events that eventually exposed the fraudulent activities, prompting investigations by regulators and law enforcement agencies.

The unraveling of the truth had severe consequences. Enron filed for bankruptcy, leading to colossal financial losses for investors, employees, and shareholders. The fallout from the scandal extended beyond the company itself, affecting the broader financial market and eroding public trust in corporate institutions.

The Enron case serves as a stark and enduring lesson in business ethics. It highlights the devastating repercussions of prioritizing short-term financial gains and the appearance of success over ethical integrity and transparency. The case underscores the critical importance of honesty, accountability, and ethical leadership in corporate governance.

Moreover, the Enron case triggered significant regulatory reforms and led to heightened scrutiny of corporate financial practices. It serves as a cautionary tale for leaders and organizations, emphasizing the lasting damage that can be inflicted when ethical principles are compromised for immediate financial objectives. Ultimately, the Enron case remains a powerful reminder of the imperative of ethical decision-making and the profound impact it can have on organizations, stakeholders, and the broader business landscape.

The Volkswagen (VW) emissions scandal, commonly referred to as "Dieselgate," stands as a compelling case study in ethical dilemmas, corporate misconduct, and the profound ramifications of decisions made by leadership.

At the core of this ethical dilemma was VW's deliberate use of software designed to manipulate emissions tests for its diesel vehicles. This software allowed the vehicles to appear environmentally friendly during regulatory testing while emitting significantly higher levels of harmful pollutants during regular driving conditions. This deception was a clear violation of environmental regulations and ethical principles, pitting short-term financial interests against honesty and compliance.

VW's leadership was confronted with a pivotal decision: whether to acknowledge and rectify the deception or perpetuate the fraud to protect the company's reputation and market share. Initially, the company's leaders chose the latter path, opting to conceal the issue and continue the fraudulent practices. They likely believed that admitting to the deception would result in significant damage to the company's image and potentially lead to financial losses.

However, as the scandal began to unravel and investigations intensified, the truth inevitably emerged. VW faced a devastating reckoning, including substantial legal penalties, fines, and a severe blow to its reputation. The financial consequences were staggering, and the scandal had far-reaching implications for the entire automotive industry, as it highlighted the importance of regulatory compliance and ethical practices.

Ultimately, VW's leadership reversed its course and acknowledged the wrongdoing. This change in direction underscored the lessons learned from the scandal. The case serves as a stark reminder of the dire consequences of prioritizing short-term financial gains and corporate image over ethical integrity and transparency.

Key lessons from the VW emissions scandal include the imperative of honesty and accountability in corporate governance, the lasting damage that unethical decisions can inflict on an organization's reputation and financial standing, and the critical role of ethical leadership in preserving trust among stakeholders. Additionally, the case highlights the significance of regulatory oversight and the need for robust ethical practices, not only within the automotive industry but across all sectors of business.

Corporate Social Responsibility (CSR) is a multifaceted concept that encompasses a company's commitment to ethical, sustainable, and socially responsible practices. It extends beyond profit generation and involves initiatives aimed at making a positive impact on various stakeholders, including employees, customers, communities, and the environment. Leaders play a pivotal role in championing CSR within their organizations. They can drive CSR efforts by promoting environmental sustainability, advocating for ethical business practices, fostering philanthropy and community engagement, and initiating social impact programs.

One critical aspect of CSR is environmental sustainability, where leaders can lead efforts to reduce resource consumption, minimize waste, and transition to renewable energy sources. Additionally, leaders should cultivate a culture of ethics and integrity within their organizations, encouraging fair labor practices, responsible sourcing, and transparency. Establishing codes of conduct and ethics training programs can help ensure high ethical standards are upheld.

CSR also involves philanthropy and community engagement, with leaders encouraging employees to volunteer, support local charities, and initiate community development projects. Furthermore, leaders can champion social impact initiatives that address societal challenges, such as poverty, education, and healthcare, through partnerships with nonprofits and social enterprises.

Promoting diversity and inclusion within the workplace is another crucial CSR element. Leaders can create inclusive hiring practices, diverse leadership teams, and policies that foster an inclusive culture, ultimately enhancing the company's reputation and improving employee satisfaction and innovation.

Supply chain responsibility is an often-overlooked aspect of CSR, where leaders ensure that suppliers adhere to ethical and sustainable practices. Monitoring suppliers for fair labor conditions, responsible sourcing, and environmental compliance is essential.

Transparency and reporting are vital components of CSR, with leaders being transparent about their CSR efforts and reporting on progress regularly. This transparency builds trust with stakeholders, including investors, customers, and employees, fostering accountability, and facilitating continuous improvement in CSR initiatives.

Leaders should embrace a long-term perspective on CSR, recognizing that the benefits may not yield immediate financial returns. Prioritizing sustainability and responsible practices contributes to the long-term success and resilience of the organization in a socially conscious marketplace. In essence, leaders are instrumental in embedding CSR into the organizational culture, promoting responsible business practices that extend beyond profit and toward creating a positive impact on society and the environment.

Larry Fink, Chairman and CEO of BlackRock, has emerged as a significant figure in the realm of responsible leadership and sustainable investing. His influence extends far beyond the financial sector, as he has passionately championed the integration of environmental, social, and governance (ESG) factors into investment strategies and advocated for responsible corporate behavior.

Under Fink's stewardship, BlackRock, one of the world's largest asset management firms, has undergone a transformation in its approach to investment. His commitment to ESG principles has been a driving force behind BlackRock's strategy. This shift involves considering not only financial returns but also the broader impact that investments have on society and the environment. BlackRock has integrated ESG considerations into its investment decisions, recognizing that companies with strong ESG performance are often better positioned for long-term success.

One of Fink's key contributions to responsible leadership is his annual letter to CEOs. In these letters, he has consistently emphasized the importance of sustainability, transparency, and ethical behavior in corporate governance. Fink has called on companies to articulate their purpose beyond profit and to take meaningful action on issues like climate change, diversity and inclusion, and social responsibility. These letters have had a significant ripple effect, encouraging other leaders and companies to reevaluate their own practices and priorities.

Fink's advocacy for sustainable investing goes beyond words. BlackRock has launched ESG-focused investment products and solutions, enabling clients to align their investments with their values and sustainability goals. This move has not only expanded the availability of responsible investment options but has also exerted pressure on companies to improve their ESG performance to attract investors.

Furthermore, Fink and BlackRock have engaged directly with companies in which they invest. They have used their influence as major shareholders to push for changes in corporate behavior, advocating for greater transparency, improved governance, and a commitment to sustainable practices. Fink's approach demonstrates that responsible leadership involves active engagement and accountability.

Larry Fink's impact on responsible leadership and sustainable investing is profound. He has redefined the role of asset management in shaping corporate behavior and influencing global financial markets. By integrating ESG considerations into investment decisions and advocating for responsible corporate practices, Fink and BlackRock have played a pivotal role in advancing the movement towards more sustainable and ethical business practices, making a lasting and positive impact on the financial industry and society as a whole.

Howard Schultz, the former CEO of Starbucks, is renowned for his visionary leadership that placed corporate social responsibility (CSR) at the heart of Starbucks' mission. Schultz's commitment to ethical and socially responsible business practices reshaped not only the coffee industry but also the broader landscape of corporate sustainability and employee well-being.

Schultz's leadership was marked by several pioneering initiatives that set industry standards for responsible business conduct. One of the most significant contributions was Starbucks' commitment to ethical sourcing of coffee beans. Under Schultz's guidance, the company established partnerships with coffee farmers worldwide, promoting fair trade and sustainable farming practices. This not only ensured a consistent supply of high-quality coffee beans but also improved the livelihoods of countless coffee growers and their communities.

Sustainability was another cornerstone of Schultz's leadership. Starbucks made substantial efforts to reduce its environmental footprint. The company implemented recycling programs, reduced water usage, and set targets for energy conservation. Schultz recognized the importance of sustainable business practices in mitigating climate change and conserving natural resources.

In addition to sustainability, Schultz prioritized the well-being of Starbucks employees. He introduced groundbreaking benefits such as comprehensive healthcare coverage, stock options, and even free college tuition for eligible employees. These initiatives aimed to improve the quality of life for Starbucks workers, promote employee retention, and set an example for the wider industry.

Beyond these tangible initiatives, Schultz's leadership was characterized by a strong sense of purpose and a commitment to social justice. He used Starbucks as a platform to engage in national conversations on issues like race relations and immigration. Starbucks stores became venues for open discussions and initiatives aimed at promoting diversity, equity, and inclusion.

Schultz's influence extended to the broader business world as well. His emphasis on ethical sourcing and CSR practices inspired other companies to consider the social and environmental impact of their operations seriously. Schultz demonstrated that a corporation could thrive financially while simultaneously making a positive contribution to society.

Furthermore, Schultz's commitment to social responsibility was not limited to the boardroom. He used his personal wealth and influence to support various philanthropic efforts, including initiatives to combat youth unemployment and provide aid to veterans.

Howard Schultz's tenure as the CEO of Starbucks was marked by a profound commitment to corporate social responsibility. His leadership set the bar for responsible business practices, from ethical sourcing and sustainability to employee benefits and social justice initiatives. Schultz's legacy is a testament to the transformative power of business leaders who prioritize ethical and socially responsible conduct, demonstrating that profitability and positive societal impact are not mutually exclusive but can indeed go hand in hand.

Paul Polman's tenure as the CEO of Unilever is a testament to the profound impact a leader can have when sustainability and responsible business practices are woven into the fabric of an organization. Polman's visionary leadership extended far beyond the confines of corporate profitability, placing sustainability, social responsibility, and ethical conduct at the core of Unilever's mission and operations.

At the heart of Polman's transformative leadership was the Sustainable Living Plan, a comprehensive and ambitious framework that redefined Unilever's approach to business. This plan was not just a corporate strategy; it was a commitment to reducing the company's environmental footprint while simultaneously improving global health and well-being and enhancing livelihoods in the communities where Unilever operated.

One of the most remarkable aspects of Polman's leadership was his unwavering dedication to sustainability. Under his guidance, Unilever made significant strides in reducing its environmental impact. The company set ambitious targets to achieve sustainability across its entire value chain. This included efforts to reduce water and energy consumption, decrease waste production, and source raw materials sustainably. Unilever's commitment to sourcing all of its agricultural raw materials sustainably was a groundbreaking industry standard.

Moreover, Polman recognized the interconnectedness of business and society. He understood that the success of Unilever was intrinsically linked to the well-being of communities, employees, and consumers. His dedication to improving global health was evident in initiatives such as the promotion of hygiene and sanitation through products like Lifebuoy soap. The company's commitment to enhancing livelihoods extended to efforts like empowering smallholder farmers and promoting inclusive business practices.

Polman's leadership also emphasized the importance of collaboration. He actively engaged with governments, NGOs, and other stakeholders to drive systemic change. Polman understood that addressing global challenges like climate change and poverty required collective action and a holistic approach.

Furthermore, Polman's commitment to sustainability went beyond rhetoric; he was willing to make bold decisions even if they might initially impact short-term profitability. He believed that a long-term perspective was essential for both business and society. His efforts to steer Unilever toward a more sustainable path demonstrated that profitability and sustainability were not mutually exclusive but could be mutually reinforcing.

The legacy of Paul Polman's leadership at Unilever is profound. He not only positioned the company as a global leader in sustainable consumer goods but also set an example for the entire corporate world. His tenure demonstrated that business can be a force for good, and that leaders who prioritize sustainability and social responsibility can drive positive change on a global scale. Paul Polman's impact transcends the boundaries of the corporate realm, serving as an enduring testament to the transformative potential of responsible and visionary leadership.

Leaders play a crucial role in spearheading sustainability efforts and advancing environmental responsibility within their organizations. To effectively lead sustainability initiatives, leaders should begin by articulating a compelling vision for sustainability that aligns with the organization's core values and mission. This vision should be supported by concrete and measurable sustainability goals, ensuring that the organization's progress can be tracked and assessed over time.

Leading by example is another fundamental aspect of sustainable leadership. Leaders should personally embrace and demonstrate sustainable practices in their daily decisions and actions. Their commitment to sustainability serves as a powerful motivator and sets the tone for the entire organization. Additionally, it is essential for leaders to integrate sustainability seamlessly into the organization's broader strategic planning and decision-making processes. Sustainability should not be viewed as a separate initiative but rather as an integral part of the overall business strategy.

Resource allocation is a critical aspect of sustainability leadership. Leaders must allocate sufficient resources, both in terms of budget and personnel, to support sustainability initiatives effectively. Adequate funding and staffing are necessary to ensure that sustainability programs can be implemented successfully and yield tangible results. Moreover, fostering a culture of sustainability is vital. Leaders can achieve this by recognizing and rewarding sustainability efforts, creating a supportive environment, and actively involving employees at all levels in sustainable practices.

Engaging stakeholders is another key responsibility for sustainability leaders. Effective communication and engagement with employees, customers, suppliers, investors, and local communities are essential for building support and garnering valuable input for sustainability initiatives. Furthermore, leaders should invest in sustainability education and training programs to enhance sustainability literacy among employees, ensuring that everyone understands the importance of sustainability and their role in contributing to it.

Innovation is a powerful driver of sustainability, and leaders should encourage it within their organizations. Investing in research and development efforts focused on sustainable products, processes, and technologies can lead to breakthroughs that reduce environmental impact. Additionally, leaders should evaluate and improve the sustainability of their supply chains by working closely with suppliers to ensure ethical and environmentally responsible practices.

Measuring and reporting progress is fundamental to sustainability leadership. Leaders should establish key performance indicators (KPIs) to quantitatively track sustainability progress and regularly communicate results to stakeholders. Transparency in reporting builds trust and demonstrates accountability. Furthermore, leaders can leverage their influence to advocate for policies and regulations that support sustainability and environmental protection at local, national, and global levels.

Leaders should also explore circular economy practices that emphasize reducing waste, reusing materials, and recycling to minimize environmental impact. Moreover, they can take concrete steps to reduce their organization's carbon footprint, such as transitioning to renewable energy sources, improving energy efficiency, and implementing transportation initiatives that reduce emissions.

Supporting conservation and biodiversity efforts is also important, as healthy ecosystems are integral to sustainability.

Collaboration and knowledge-sharing with other organizations and industry peers can amplify the impact of sustainability efforts. Leaders should actively engage in partnerships and networks to exchange best practices, leverage collective knowledge, and collectively address global sustainability challenges. In conclusion, leaders who embrace these multifaceted strategies can not only drive positive change within their organizations but also inspire a broader societal shift toward greater sustainability and environmental responsibility.

Incorporating sustainability into leadership practices offers a multitude of enduring benefits that extend beyond the immediate horizon. Firstly, it significantly enhances an organization's reputation and brand value. As consumers, investors, and stakeholders increasingly favor socially and environmentally responsible companies, a strong sustainability track record sets an organization apart and bolsters its long-term market position.

Secondly, sustainability-driven leadership serves as a potent risk mitigation strategy. By proactively addressing environmental, social, and governance (ESG) risks, organizations become better equipped to identify and manage potential challenges, regulatory shifts, and market fluctuations over time.

Thirdly, sustainability often leads to substantial cost savings in the long run. Initiatives focused on energy efficiency, waste reduction, and resource conservation translate into lowered operational expenses. Investments in renewable energy and sustainable technologies tend to yield returns by reducing reliance on costly fossil fuels.

Moreover, sustainability fosters a culture of innovation and continual improvement. Leaders who prioritize sustainability inspire creative thinking and drive product and process enhancements. This, in turn, enhances an organization's competitiveness by allowing it to stay ahead of evolving market dynamics and evolving consumer preferences.

Fifthly, incorporating sustainability into leadership practices has a positive impact on talent acquisition and retention. Younger generations of workers increasingly seek employers with robust sustainability commitments. Organizations that align with these values are more likely to attract and retain top talent, as employees are motivated when their work aligns with ethical and sustainable principles.

Additionally, sustainability initiatives facilitate meaningful engagement with stakeholders such as customers, suppliers, and local communities. These strong stakeholder relationships lead to increased customer loyalty, mutually beneficial supplier partnerships, and community support, all of which contribute to long-term organizational success.

Seventh, sustainability equips organizations with greater resilience in an ever-changing world. As environmental and social challenges intensify, organizations grounded in sustainable practices are better prepared to adapt and thrive. Challenges such as climate change, resource scarcity, and social inequality are global issues that can impact business operations. Sustainable practices help organizations build resilience in the face of such challenges.

Furthermore, sustainability practices often align with evolving regulatory requirements, keeping organizations ahead of regulatory changes and potential legal and financial penalties. Many regulations increasingly emphasize environmental and social responsibility, making sustainable leadership a proactive and strategic choice.

Access to capital is another significant advantage of incorporating sustainability into leadership practices. A growing number of investors consider environmental, social, and governance (ESG) factors when making investment decisions. Organizations that prioritize sustainability can attract socially responsible investors, broadening their access to capital.

Additionally, sustainability encourages long-term planning and decision-making. Sustainable leadership promotes a focus on the future, rather than short-term profit maximization. This long-term perspective leads to more prudent decisions and investments that contribute to the organization's long-term viability.

Lastly, sustainable leadership extends its positive influence to society as a whole. Organizations that prioritize sustainability contribute to addressing global challenges such as climate change, poverty, and inequality, making a meaningful and lasting impact on the world.

Incorporating sustainability into leadership practices is not a transient trend; it represents a strategic imperative for long-term success and resilience in an ever-evolving world. Leaders who prioritize sustainability contribute to a more sustainable planet and ensure the prosperity and adaptability of their organizations in the face of complex and interconnected global challenges.

Kofi Annan, the former Secretary-General of the United Nations, exemplified ethical leadership through his enduring commitment to promoting international peace, human rights, and global cooperation. Annan's ethical leadership was multifaceted, encompassing diplomatic finesse, unwavering integrity, and a profound sense of responsibility towards the world's most pressing issues. Notably, he played a pivotal role in the establishment of the United Nations Global Compact in 2000, a visionary initiative that urged businesses and organizations worldwide to align their strategies and operations with ten universal principles spanning human rights, labor, environment, and anti-corruption. Through the Global Compact, Annan underscored the pivotal role of corporations in addressing global challenges while adhering to ethical and sustainable business practices.

Furthermore, Kofi Annan's ethical leadership extended to the realm of peacekeeping and conflict resolution. During his tenure as Secretary-General, he navigated intricate international crises, including those in Kosovo, East Timor and Sierra Leone, with a steadfast commitment to peaceful resolutions, diplomacy, and the safeguarding of vulnerable populations. His dedication to upholding ethical principles in the arena of international relations was evident through his tireless efforts to mediate conflicts and promote peaceful coexistence.

Annan's advocacy for human rights left an indelible mark on the global stage. He actively championed the Responsibility to Protect (R2P) doctrine, a critical framework emphasizing the international community's obligation to prevent genocide, war crimes, ethnic cleansing, and crimes against humanity. Annan's ethical leadership was characterized by his unwavering commitment to safeguarding the dignity and rights of individuals worldwide.

Recognizing the intrinsic link between environmental sustainability and global peace, Kofi Annan emphasized the ethical imperative of addressing environmental challenges and climate change. He played a pivotal role in raising awareness about the environmental dimensions of international issues, highlighting the need for ethical stewardship of the planet.

Throughout his career, Annan consistently advocated for multilateralism and global cooperation as essential tools for addressing complex global challenges. His efforts to bolster the United Nations and enhance its effectiveness in advancing peace, development, and human rights underscored his dedication to ethical leadership on a global scale.

Even beyond his tenure as Secretary-General, Kofi Annan remained a tireless advocate for ethical leadership, peace, and human rights. He continued to engage in humanitarian and diplomatic endeavors, serving as a mediator in conflicts and championing critical causes such as the fight against HIV/AIDS. Annan's legacy serves as a powerful reminder of the profound and enduring impact of ethical leadership in tackling the world's most intricate challenges and advancing the principles of justice, diplomacy, and cooperation.

General Colin Powell's legacy stands as an enduring symbol of ethical leadership, etching a profound mark across the expanse of his illustrious military career and his pivotal role in the realm of politics. Serving as a Four-Star General and ascending to the esteemed position of Chairman of the Joint Chiefs of Staff during the Gulf War, Powell consistently showcased an unwavering dedication to ethical principles that permeated every facet of his military leadership. His approach to military strategy was not merely characterized by tactical acumen but also by an unyielding commitment to ethical conduct.

In the crucible of armed conflict, Powell's leadership shone brilliantly through a meticulous and principled approach to planning. His commitment to the ethical imperative of safeguarding civilian lives was unwavering, evident in his resolute efforts to minimize civilian casualties during military operations. Powell's actions mirrored a profound respect for international norms governing armed conflicts, reinforcing the ethos that ethical considerations must be at the forefront, even in the tumultuous theater of war.

What set Powell apart as an ethical leader within the military was his fervent emphasis on the principles of proportionality and discrimination in the use of force. These principles, deeply rooted in the laws of armed conflict, guided his decision-making, serving as moral compass points that illuminated the path toward minimizing harm and protecting the innocent. Powell's commitment to upholding these principles underscored his resolute dedication to the ethical duty of mitigating the human toll of warfare.

The principle of proportionality, as championed by Powell, is rooted in the fundamental tenet that the use of force in warfare must be proportionate to the military objectives pursued. In essence, it underscores the imperative to avoid excessive or indiscriminate force that could result in unnecessary harm to civilians and non-combatants.

Powell's steadfast adherence to this principle was manifested in his meticulous planning and execution of military operations during the Gulf War. His approach prioritized the protection of innocent lives and civilian infrastructure, even in the midst of intense combat. This ethical dedication ensured that the human toll of the conflict was minimized to the greatest extent possible, reflecting Powell's unwavering commitment to mitigating the suffering caused by armed conflict.

The principle of discrimination in the use of force, championed by Powell, is equally significant. It mandates that military actions must distinguish between combatants and non-combatants, with a categorical prohibition on targeting civilians intentionally. Powell's emphasis on this principle manifested in the precision and care with which military operations were conducted under his leadership. He took deliberate measures to ensure that civilian populations were shielded from harm, a testament to his ethical duty to protect the innocent.

Powell's commitment to upholding these principles underscores his profound dedication to the ethical duty of mitigating the human toll of warfare. His leadership was defined by the belief that ethical considerations were not mere afterthoughts in military operations but guiding principles that should be at the forefront of decision-making. In doing so, he exemplified the highest standards of ethical leadership in the military, emphasizing that even in the throes of conflict, the preservation of human dignity and the protection of civilians must remain paramount. Powell's legacy continues to resonate as a reminder that ethical leadership in the military entails not only strategic brilliance but also a profound commitment to humanitarian values.

Colin Powell's legacy in the military arena is, therefore, a testament to the profound intersection of leadership and ethics. His legacy underscores that ethical principles are not mere abstractions but guiding beacons that illuminate the path of leadership, even in the most challenging and high-stakes environments. Powell's unwavering commitment to ethical conduct serves as an enduring source of inspiration for leaders across domains, reaffirming that ethics are the cornerstone of responsible and compassionate leadership.

Colin Powell's transition to political leadership as the U.S. Secretary of State under President George W. Bush brought him face to face with one of the most challenging ethical dilemmas of his career—the case for military intervention in Iraq. Tasked with presenting this case to the United Nations Security Council, Powell delivered a high-stakes presentation that, in hindsight, contained information regarding Iraq's weapons of mass destruction that later proved inaccurate.

What distinguishes Powell as an exceptional ethical leader in this context is not the error itself but his subsequent response to it. In the aftermath of the presentation and as evidence mounted that the information was flawed, Powell did something remarkable—he publicly expressed deep regret and took responsibility for the inaccuracies. This act of self-accountability demonstrated his unshakable commitment to honesty and integrity, even when confronted with the crucible of intense political pressure.

Powell's willingness to admit to errors and shortcomings, despite his stature and the immense political ramifications, epitomizes the essence of ethical leadership. He embodied the principle that ethical leaders are not infallible but are defined by their willingness to acknowledge mistakes and rectify them. Powell's act of contrition underscored his unwavering dedication to the truth, transparency, and accountability, setting a profound example for leaders in the political arena and beyond.

Moreover, Powell's response also highlighted the ethical principle of moral courage. It showcased his willingness to stand firmly by his values, even when it meant acknowledging a significant failure. This demonstration of moral courage and ethical clarity reinforced his reputation as a leader who prioritized principles over political expediency, leaving an indelible mark on the ethics of leadership.

Powell's legacy serves as a timeless reminder that ethical leaders are those who not only adhere to high standards of conduct but also have the courage to confront and rectify ethical lapses, even when it is personally challenging.

Admiral Michelle Howard's legacy in the U.S. Navy is a testament to her trailblazing commitment to ethical leadership, diversity, and inclusion. Her historic appointment as the first female four-star admiral in the U.S. Navy's history signifies a pioneering spirit and determination that transcends gender barriers. Beyond this groundbreaking achievement, Admiral Howard's leadership carries enduring lessons in ethical values and leadership principles.

Throughout her career, Admiral Howard consistently championed diversity and inclusion within the armed forces. Her advocacy for equal opportunities and a more inclusive environment exemplified the ethical principle of fairness and the belief that every service member, regardless of gender or background, deserves equal recognition for their capabilities. Her leadership underscores the profound importance of diversity of thought and experiences in enhancing organizational effectiveness and promoting ethical values like respect and fairness.

Admiral Howard's commitment to ethical values in the military was unwavering. She recognized the weight of her leadership role and consistently emphasized the significance of ethical conduct, accountability, and transparency among her fellow service members. Her principled approach set a standard for integrity and ethical behavior within the U.S. Navy, serving as an example for others to follow.

Perhaps one of the most enduring aspects of Admiral Howard's legacy is her inspiration to future leaders. Her journey, from breaking gender barriers to attaining the rank of four-star admiral, serves as a powerful illustration of how ethical leadership can transcend obstacles and drive positive change. Her legacy continues to illuminate the path toward a more inclusive, equitable, and principled military and society, leaving an indelible mark on the ethics of leadership.

The Body Shop, under the influence of Anita Roddick, the founder of The Body Shop, extended far beyond its ethical transformation, deeply impacting both the company's culture and financial performance. Under her ethical leadership, The Body Shop underwent a profound cultural shift, with Roddick's personal values and convictions permeating the organization. This transformation created a unique corporate culture characterized by a commitment to social and environmental responsibility. Within the company, employees became not just workers but passionate advocates for ethical consumerism, fostering a sense of purpose that transcended traditional job roles. This culture of purpose-driven work and activism set The Body Shop apart in the cosmetics industry, reflecting Roddick's unwavering dedication to her ethical vision.

Furthermore, Anita Roddick's ethical leadership extended to the realm of consumer engagement. Her values deeply resonated with consumers who increasingly sought products aligned with their ethical beliefs. The Body Shop's retail outlets evolved into more than just places to purchase cosmetics; they became community hubs for social and environmental activism. Customers felt empowered by supporting a brand that shared their ethical principles, contributing to a sense of loyalty and trust. The Body Shop's stores served as platforms for educating the public about ethical consumer choices and driving social change, solidifying the brand's position as a company with a devoted and passionate customer base.

Despite conventional business wisdom, The Body Shop's ethical approach was not just a moral stance; it also proved to be a profitable strategy. Anita Roddick's commitment to cruelty-free products, fair trade sourcing, and environmental sustainability attracted customers willing to pay a premium for products that reflected their values. This demand, combined with the brand's ethical image, drove robust sales and expansion. The Body Shop's financial success stood as a testament to the idea that ethical leadership could be a competitive advantage in the marketplace, underscoring the enduring legacy of Anita Roddick's ethical vision within the company and beyond.

Strategic Synergy

Ben Cohen and Jerry Greenfield, co-founders of Ben & Jerry's, left an indelible mark on the ice cream industry through their unwavering commitment to ethical leadership. Their impact went beyond superficial gestures, leading to a profound transformation in the company's culture and financial performance.

At the heart of this transformation was a values-driven approach that prioritized social responsibility from the company's inception. Cohen and Greenfield actively championed causes such as fair trade, environmental sustainability, and community engagement. These ethical values were not mere slogans but integral components of the company's identity and mission.

What set Ben & Jerry's apart was the unique corporate culture cultivated under their ethical leadership. The co-founders were resolute in engaging employees in their ethical mission, encouraging active participation in community initiatives and sustainability efforts. This approach did not just create a workplace; it fostered a shared sense of purpose and social responsibility among the company's workforce. Employees were not just doing a job but contributing to a larger, meaningful cause.

The financial outcomes of Ben & Jerry's ethical leadership were remarkable. Their dedication to using high-quality ingredients, ethical sourcing, and active community involvement struck a chord with consumers. Beyond the delectable ice cream, customers embraced the company's commitment to ethical practices. This resonated so deeply that it cultivated a fiercely loyal customer base. Even after Ben & Jerry's acquisition by Unilever, the commitment to these ethical principles remained intact, demonstrating that ethical leadership and financial success need not be at odds. Instead, they can form a mutually reinforcing relationship where ethical values enhance brand appeal, contributing to sustained financial growth.

In essence, Ben Cohen and Jerry Greenfield's ethical leadership at Ben & Jerry's offers a profound lesson: ethical principles can be the cornerstone of business success, shaping culture, engaging employees, and driving financial prosperity. Their legacy endures as a testament to the transformative power of ethical leadership in the corporate world.

Blake Mycoskie's ethical leadership at TOMS Shoes reflects not only a philanthropic endeavor but a profound transformation that encompasses the company's culture and financial performance.

At the heart of this transformation lies TOMS' innovative one-for-one model, pioneered by Mycoskie. For each pair of shoes sold, TOMS donates a pair to a child in need. This ethical approach goes beyond a traditional business strategy; it addresses a pressing social issue while authentically aligning the company's values with its products and mission. This integration of ethics into the core of the business is a testament to Mycoskie's visionary leadership.

TOMS' corporate culture mirrors Mycoskie's ethical convictions, firmly grounded in values and social responsibility. Employees are not just part of a workforce but active participants in a mission to make a positive impact. This shared ethos fosters a deep sense of pride and engagement among the workforce, making TOMS a place where employees are driven by a greater purpose.

Despite the significant portion of its products that TOMS donates, the company's ethical business model has demonstrated impressive financial sustainability. TOMS has successfully cultivated a dedicated customer base that resonates with its mission-driven approach. This highlights a fundamental lesson in business: ethical leadership and a steadfast commitment to social responsibility can coexist with profitability. TOMS' journey showcases that being ethically driven can not only create positive change but also contribute to financial success.

Blake Mycoskie's ethical leadership at TOMS Shoes stands as a compelling example of how a values-driven business model can lead to transformative cultural shifts and financial prosperity. The company's commitment to making a difference resonates deeply with both employees and customers, illustrating the enduring impact of ethical leadership in the corporate world.

Strategic Synergy

Ethical leadership and social responsibility are not just buzzwords but essential guiding principles for leaders in the modern business world. Leaders who uphold high ethical standards and prioritize social responsibility not only achieve success but also contribute positively to their organizations and society at large. As you continue your leadership journey, remember that ethical leadership is a continuous commitment to doing what is right, even when faced with difficult choices.

Chapter 11

Global Leadership Perspectives

"Effective leadership on a global scale demands
the wisdom to see beyond borders and the courage
to unite nations."

—Joel R. Klemmer

Chapter 11
Global Leadership Perspectives

L eading in a global context is a complex and multifaceted endeavor, shaped by the intricate interplay of diverse cultures, values, and expectations that define the leadership landscape. Successful global leaders must possess a profound understanding of the nuanced relationship between leadership styles and the unique challenges they encounter across various cultural contexts.

Cultural sensitivity is at the heart of effective global leadership. Leaders must not only acknowledge but deeply respect the values, traditions, and norms of the cultures they engage with. What constitutes effective leadership in one cultural setting may be perceived differently elsewhere. For instance, a directive leadership style may be appreciated in some cultures, while others may prefer a more participative and consensus-driven approach. Global leaders must skillfully adapt their leadership styles to align with cultural expectations while upholding their core values.

Communication presents a significant challenge in the global arena. Language barriers, distinct communication styles, and varying non-verbal cues can lead to misunderstandings and misinterpretations. Global leaders must excel in cross-cultural communication, which entails not only mastering different languages but also comprehending the cultural subtleties of communication. This includes recognizing the significance of gestures, eye contact, and even the use of silence in different cultural contexts.

Diversity and inclusion are pivotal for global leaders. They must embrace diversity as a source of strength, fostering an inclusive environment where every voice is valued. While diverse teams offer a wealth of perspectives and ideas, they also demand adept leadership to manage potential conflicts arising from cultural differences. Building diverse teams, nurturing a culture of inclusion, and effectively addressing cultural diversity become essential aspects of global leadership.

Adaptability and flexibility are crucial traits for global leaders. They must remain open to change and be willing to modify their leadership approach in response to the evolving global landscape. Staying attuned to global trends, emerging markets, and geopolitical shifts that can impact their organization is vital. The ability to pivot and make informed decisions in the face of changing circumstances is a hallmark of effective global leadership.

Ethical considerations in global leadership extend beyond what is encountered in domestic leadership contexts. Global leaders often navigate intricate ethical dilemmas influenced by complex legal, ethical, and cultural factors, sometimes with conflicting expectations. To navigate these complexities, leaders must establish a robust ethical framework that guides their decision-making, transcending cultural boundaries while respecting local customs and laws.

Global leadership often involves managing teams and operations across different time zones and vast geographical distances. This necessitates effective time management, leveraging technology, and a willingness to accommodate different work hours to facilitate collaboration and communication. Additionally, it involves understanding the impact of geographical dispersion on team dynamics and productivity.

Strategic Synergy

Effective global leadership demands a profound understanding of the intricacies arising from cultural diversity, communication challenges, diversity and inclusion, adaptability, ethical considerations, and the practical aspects of managing global teams and operations. Leaders who navigate these complexities with cultural sensitivity and a commitment to inclusive and ethical leadership are best positioned to succeed in the intricate and dynamic global landscape.

The influence of culture on leadership is multifaceted and deep-rooted. Leadership styles are intricately intertwined with cultural norms and expectations. In cultures where authoritarianism is valued, leaders are often expected to wield directive authority and make decisions unilaterally. Conversely, collectivist cultures emphasize group harmony and consensus, promoting participative and democratic leadership styles where decisions are collectively reached.

Communication patterns are equally shaped by culture, leading to varying degrees of directness. Some cultures prioritize explicit, unambiguous communication, leaving little room for interpretation. In contrast, others favor indirect communication, relying on context, non-verbal cues, and subtle nuances to convey meaning. High-context cultures, characterized by shared context and non-verbal cues, require a keen understanding of unspoken communication. In contrast, low-context cultures place a premium on explicit verbal communication, necessitating clarity and transparency.

Listening styles further exemplify cultural diversity. In some cultures, active engagement during conversations, including frequent interjections, is seen as a sign of attentiveness and engagement. These cultures value dynamic, interactive discourse. On the other hand, some cultures prize reflective listening, where pauses for contemplation and considered responses are highly regarded.

Understanding these cultural nuances is paramount for effective leadership, especially in global and diverse settings. Leaders must navigate these complexities by adapting their leadership styles and communication approaches to align with cultural expectations. This cultural intelligence not only fosters cross-cultural collaboration but also enhances leadership effectiveness by promoting mutual respect and understanding within culturally diverse organizations and societies.

The intricacies of decision-making processes in diverse cultural contexts highlight the multifaceted nature of leadership. Cultural norms play a pivotal role in shaping these processes. In some cultures, decisions are reached through extensive group consultation, emphasizing consensus and collective agreement. This approach requires patience and inclusivity, as decisions may take time to evolve, but it fosters a sense of ownership among team members. Conversely, other cultures favor autocratic decision-making, where a single leader holds the authority to make decisions unilaterally. This method prioritizes efficiency but can lead to reduced team involvement.

Cultural attitudes towards risk significantly impact decision-making. In risk-averse cultures, decision-makers may lean towards cautious, incremental approaches, focusing on minimizing potential negative outcomes. In contrast, cultures that embrace risk may encourage bolder, innovative decision-making, often resulting in more rapid progress but potentially higher levels of uncertainty.

Relationship dynamics also vary according to cultural norms. Some cultures prioritize the cultivation of long-term bonds, where trust and loyalty are paramount. In such contexts, relationship-building may require time and investment, but the resulting connections tend to be enduring and deeply rooted. In contrast, cultures that lean towards shorter-term, transactional relationships may prioritize efficiency and pragmatism. These connections are often goal-oriented and may not require the same level of time investment.

Navigating these cultural nuances is an essential aspect of effective leadership in a global context. Leaders must be attuned to cultural attitudes towards decision-making, risk, and relationship-building to make informed choices that align with both their leadership goals and the cultural expectations of their teams or stakeholders. This cultural sensitivity not only enhances leadership effectiveness but also promotes harmonious collaboration and mutual respect within diverse organizations and societies.

Conflict resolution is a critical aspect of leadership in culturally diverse contexts, and the strategies employed can significantly impact team dynamics and organizational harmony. Cultural differences are particularly pronounced in how conflicts are approached and resolved.

In cultures that favor direct confrontation and open discourse, addressing conflicts head-on is seen as a sign of transparency and sincerity. Leaders in such cultures are expected to facilitate open dialogues and encourage team members to express their concerns openly. Conflict resolution processes may involve team discussions, debates, and problem-solving sessions, with an emphasis on reaching a resolution that is satisfactory to all parties.

Conversely, cultures that prioritize indirect conflict resolution methods often aim to mitigate loss of face and preserve harmony. In these contexts, leaders may need to exercise subtlety and diplomacy when addressing conflicts. Conflict resolution strategies may involve behind-the-scenes negotiations, mediation by trusted individuals, or the use of indirect language to convey concerns without causing direct offense.

Effective leadership in multicultural settings requires leaders to possess cultural acumen, allowing them to navigate these differences adeptly. Leaders must adapt their leadership styles, communication strategies, and conflict resolution approaches to align with cultural norms and expectations. This not only enhances leadership effectiveness but also promotes cross-cultural collaboration, fostering an environment where diverse perspectives are respected and valued. Cultivating this cultural sensitivity is a crucial skill for leaders aiming to navigate the complex landscape of multicultural organizations and societies successfully.

Culture exerts a profound influence on leadership styles, communication practices, and decision-making processes. Leadership styles vary across cultures, with some favoring hierarchical and authoritarian approaches, while others prioritize participative and democratic leadership. Collectivist cultures emphasize group harmony and consensus in decision-making, whereas individualistic cultures focus on personal autonomy and achievement.

Communication styles within different cultures vary significantly and can be categorized as high-context or low-context, each with its unique characteristics.

In high-context cultures, communication is a multifaceted and intricate process that goes beyond mere words. Non-verbal cues, such as facial expressions, body language, and even silence, play a pivotal role in conveying meaning. These cues are often deeply ingrained in the culture and carry significant weight in interpreting messages.

Shared context is another critical aspect of communication in high-context cultures. People within these societies often have a rich history and collective experiences that serve as a backdrop for conversations. This shared history forms a common ground upon which communication takes place, allowing individuals to make assumptions about what is unsaid. However, it can also pose challenges for those outside the culture, as they may lack the necessary context to fully understand the message.

In high-context cultures, the status and relationships of the individuals involved are paramount. Hierarchy and social position heavily influence communication dynamics. The speaker's authority, age, or position within the group can shape how their message is received. Respect for authority and deference to elders are common norms, impacting how individuals interact within society.

Indirect language and subtle hints are tools often used in high-context communication. Rather than stating a request or opinion explicitly, individuals may employ tactful strategies to convey their message while preserving social harmony. This indirectness allows for face-saving, avoiding embarrassment or confrontation.

Overall, high-context cultures prioritize the maintenance of social harmony, group cohesion, and face-saving in their communication. Understanding these nuances is vital for effective leadership and cross-cultural interactions, as misinterpreting non-verbal cues or failing to grasp the underlying context can lead to misunderstandings and strained relationships. Leaders in high-context cultures need to navigate this intricate web of communication to build trust and rapport successfully.

For example, Japan is a classic example of a high-context culture. Japanese communication relies heavily on non-verbal cues, such as bowing, eye contact, and subtle facial expressions. The use of indirect language is common, and people often employ the practice of "reading the air" (kuuki wo yomu), which involves understanding the unspoken feelings and intentions of others. In business settings, hierarchical relationships are emphasized, with seniority and rank playing a significant role in communication dynamics.

Middle Eastern cultures, including those in countries like Saudi Arabia and the United Arab Emirates, place a strong emphasis on relationships and hospitality. Communication often involves extensive greetings and inquiries about one's well-being before moving on to business matters. Politeness and respect are paramount, and indirect communication is preferred to avoid causing offense. Non-verbal cues, like handshakes and gestures, convey important messages.

Latin American cultures, including those in countries like Mexico and Brazil, are known for their warmth and expressiveness. Communication is often characterized by animated gestures, physical touch, and a focus on building personal relationships. People may use indirect language to convey messages politely, and social status and hierarchy can influence communication dynamics. Family bonds are strong, and conversations often revolve around personal matters and shared experiences.

China is an interesting example of a high-context culture that also incorporates some low-context elements due to its size and diversity.

While modern business communication in China may appear more direct, especially in urban areas, traditional Chinese culture places a significant emphasis on hierarchy, respect for authority, and saving face. Indirect language and non-verbal cues like facial expressions are still important in many contexts.

In South Korea, hierarchical relationships and respect for age and authority are deeply ingrained in the culture. Communication often involves indirect language, where requests or disagreements may be couched in polite phrases. Bowing and other non-verbal cues are common, and silence can carry meaning, allowing individuals to reflect and avoid confrontation.

Conversely, low-context cultures, such as those prevalent in Western countries like the United States, exhibit distinct communication patterns that prioritize explicit verbal communication. In these cultures, directness and clarity are highly valued, with an expectation that messages should be transparent and leave little room for interpretation or ambiguity. Communication is straightforward, encouraging individuals to express thoughts, opinions, and intentions explicitly. Transparency is a fundamental principle, with individuals expected to provide all relevant information during conversations to foster trust and accountability. While non-verbal cues like body language and facial expressions still play a role, they are considered secondary to the spoken word. Conversations follow structured and linear formats, progressing logically with points presented systematically. Individuals in low-context cultures often proactively seek clarification and ask questions to ensure understanding, and open confrontation and addressing conflicts directly are common approaches. Overall, low-context cultures emphasize individual expression, autonomy, and a proactive approach to communication, fostering clear and direct exchanges in various contexts, including business and interpersonal interactions.

In low-context cultures, precision in communication is paramount, and messages are expected to be clear and explicit. To avoid misunderstandings, individuals often go to great lengths to ensure their messages are well-understood, including providing comprehensive background information or context when necessary. This emphasis on precision extends to professional settings, where clarity in communication can significantly impact decision-making and project outcomes. Additionally, low-context cultures celebrate individualism and personal expression, encouraging people to voice their opinions even if they differ from the prevailing consensus. This promotes diversity of thought and the open exchange of ideas.

Structured presentation is highly valued in low-context cultures, especially in professional and academic contexts. Meetings, presentations, and written documents tend to follow a logical and organized format, with an expectation that information will be presented in a clear and linear manner. Feedback in these cultures is explicit and specific, whether it is in the form of performance evaluations or project assessments, aiming to provide a clear understanding of strengths and areas for improvement. This clarity in communication contributes to efficient decision-making processes, as stakeholders expect well-defined proposals, rationale, and options for consideration.

Open debate and discussion are encouraged in settings like academic institutions and workplaces in low-context cultures. Individuals are comfortable challenging ideas and engaging in critical thinking, leading to more robust problem-solving and decision-making. While directness is valued, individuals in low-context cultures also learn to balance assertiveness with diplomacy, expressing opinions and concerns openly but with a level of respect and professionalism. Preparation and planning are vital due to the structured nature of communication, with individuals investing time in getting ready for meetings, presentations, and negotiations to ensure a well-organized and clear exchange of information. Understanding these nuances of low-context communication is essential in today's globalized world, where cross-cultural interactions are common. Leaders and professionals from low-context cultures should recognize that their communication style may differ significantly from that of high-context cultures, and adapting to different cultural norms is key to effective cross-cultural collaboration and leadership.

The United States is often cited as a quintessential example of a low-context culture. Americans generally value direct and explicit communication, with a strong emphasis on clarity and transparency in both personal and professional interactions. Meetings and presentations in the U.S. tend to follow structured formats, and individuals are encouraged to express their opinions openly.

Germany is another country characterized by low-context communication. Germans are known for their direct and precise communication style. They place a high value on honesty and clarity in conversations, whether in business negotiations or social interactions. German workplaces often prioritize efficiency and professionalism.

The Swiss culture also leans toward low-context communication. Swiss people value punctuality, precision, and straightforwardness. In both personal and professional settings, the Swiss tend to be explicit in their communication and appreciate thoroughness in discussions and decision-making.

Dutch culture is often associated with low-context communication norms. Dutch people are known for their open and direct communication style. They value honesty, egalitarianism, and the exchange of straightforward feedback, making the Netherlands a place where clear and explicit communication is highly regarded.

Scandinavian Countries (e.g., Sweden, Norway, Denmark): Scandinavian cultures generally exhibit low-context communication patterns. People in these countries prioritize honesty, individual expression, and open dialogue. Meetings and work environments in Scandinavia tend to be characterized by direct communication and a focus on efficiency.

Australia is often considered a low-context communication culture. Australians appreciate clear and concise communication, whether in daily conversations or professional settings. They value individualism, egalitarianism, and the ability to express one's thoughts openly.

Canadian culture reflects low-context communication tendencies. Canadians typically value politeness, directness, and clarity in their interactions. In business, clear and well-structured communication is essential for effective collaboration.

Understanding these cultural differences in communication patterns is crucial for effective leadership, particularly in multicultural environments. Leaders operating in high-context cultures may need to pay careful attention to non-verbal cues, subtle messages, and the cultural context of interactions. In contrast, leaders in low-context cultures should prioritize clarity and directness in their communication to ensure that their messages are understood as intended. Cultural sensitivity and adaptability in communication can foster cross-cultural understanding and collaboration, enhancing leadership effectiveness in diverse settings.

Decision-making processes in diverse cultural contexts can exhibit a wide range of approaches and attitudes, which can significantly influence leadership and organizational outcomes.

In many collectivist cultures, particularly in East Asian countries like Japan and South Korea, decision-making often follows a consensus-driven approach. This means that decisions are made collectively, with extensive group consultation and consensus-building. In such cultures, harmony within the group and preserving face are highly valued, and decisions aim to maintain this harmony. While this process can be time-consuming, it often results in strong group cohesion and buy-in.

In contrast, some cultures, like certain Middle Eastern and African societies, may lean towards autocratic decision-making. In these contexts, a single leader or authority figure holds significant power and makes decisions unilaterally. Decisions are typically not subject to extensive consultation or discussion, and the leader's authority is unquestioned. While this approach can lead to swift decision-making, it may also stifle creativity and input from others.

Cultural attitudes towards risk play a substantial role in decision-making. Some cultures, like the United States, tend to have a more risk-tolerant approach. This means they are more open to taking calculated risks and embracing innovation. In such cultures, decisions may prioritize potential rewards and opportunities over avoiding risk.

On the other hand, cultures like those in many European countries, particularly in Northern Europe, often exhibit a more cautious and incremental approach to decision-making. These cultures may be risk-averse and prioritize stability and gradual progress. Decisions are carefully considered, and the potential downsides of actions are weighed heavily.

Effective global leaders understand these cultural nuances and adapt their decision-making processes accordingly when working across cultures. They recognize that what works in one cultural context may not be suitable in another. This adaptability and cultural sensitivity are crucial for successful leadership in diverse, multicultural environments.

In today's interconnected world, leaders often encounter hybrid approaches to decision-making that blend elements from various cultural norms. These approaches reflect the realities of globalization and the influence of cross-cultural interactions. Leaders who can navigate and facilitate decision-making in such hybrid contexts demonstrate flexibility and effectiveness in their leadership roles.

Understanding these diverse cultural approaches to decision-making is essential for leaders who operate in global or multicultural settings. It enables them to build trust, make informed decisions, and foster collaboration across cultural boundaries, ultimately contributing to their effectiveness as global leaders.

Conflict resolution strategies across diverse cultural contexts are vital considerations for effective leadership, as they significantly impact how conflicts are managed, relationships are maintained, and organizations operate within multicultural settings.

In various cultural contexts, the approach to conflict resolution can differ significantly. Some cultures, such as those in Western countries like the United States, tend to favor direct confrontation and open discourse when addressing conflicts. They value frankness, transparency, and addressing issues head-on. In these cultures, it is common to express concerns openly and seek resolutions through straightforward communication.

Conversely, many Eastern and collectivist cultures, including those in Japan and China, tend to adopt indirect methods when dealing with conflicts. These cultures prioritize harmony, face-saving, and the preservation of relationships. In such contexts, openly confronting conflicts can be seen as disruptive and damaging to social bonds. Therefore, indirect approaches like using intermediaries, non-verbal cues, or gradual, subtle discussions are often preferred.

Effective leadership in multicultural contexts demands a high degree of adaptability. Leaders must be adept at recognizing and respecting these cultural preferences for conflict resolution. This means adjusting their leadership styles, communication strategies, and decision-making frameworks to align with cultural norms and expectations.

Leaders who possess cultural acumen can effectively navigate conflicts in a way that is sensitive to cultural nuances. They understand that what might be a respectful and effective way to address a conflict in one culture could be seen as confrontational or disrespectful in another. This awareness enables leaders to choose the most appropriate conflict resolution strategies based on the cultural context.

The ability to harmonize conflict resolution styles across cultures is not only about avoiding misunderstandings but also about fostering cross-cultural collaboration. When leaders demonstrate an understanding of different cultural approaches to conflict, it fosters an environment where team members from diverse backgrounds feel heard and valued. This, in turn, contributes to enhanced collaboration, creativity, and productivity within multicultural teams.

Finally, promoting mutual comprehension within culturally diverse organizations and societies is a key outcome of effective cross-cultural conflict resolution. When conflicts are resolved in ways that respect cultural values and norms, it promotes mutual understanding and respect among team members, which is essential for long-term cooperation and organizational success.

Culture plays a profound role in shaping leadership styles, communication patterns, and decision-making processes across different societies and organizations. Understanding these cultural influences is essential for leaders operating in multicultural contexts, as it can significantly impact leadership effectiveness and organizational outcomes.

In collectivist cultures, such as many Asian societies, leadership tends to be more team-oriented and consensus-driven. Leaders in these cultures often emphasize group harmony and cohesion. In contrast, individualistic cultures, like those in Western countries, may favor a more assertive and autonomous leadership style, where leaders make decisions independently.

Leadership styles can also vary in terms of authority. Some cultures, like those in the Middle East, may prefer authoritative leadership, where leaders have significant control and decision-making power. Others, such as Scandinavian cultures, may prefer a more participative leadership style, where decision-making is more decentralized and collaborative.

Cultural norms also influence the directness of communication. Some cultures, such as the Dutch or Germans, tend to communicate very directly, stating opinions and feedback explicitly. In contrast, cultures like the Japanese or Chinese may use more indirect language to convey messages, relying on subtlety and context.

Decision-making processes range from consensus-driven approaches, often seen in collectivist cultures like Japan, where extensive group consultation is common, to autocratic methods prevalent in some Middle Eastern cultures, where a single leader makes decisions unilaterally.

Cultural attitudes towards risk also influence decision-making. Some cultures, like the United States, may have a more risk-tolerant approach, embracing innovation and calculated risks. In contrast, many European cultures may lean towards cautious and incremental decision-making, prioritizing stability.

The approach to resolving conflicts can vary widely. Some cultures, such as those in the United States, may favor direct confrontation and open discourse to address conflicts. Others, like many Asian cultures, may adopt more indirect methods to mitigate the loss of face or preserve harmony.

Culture exerts a profound influence on leadership styles, communication patterns, and decision-making processes. Effective leaders in multicultural contexts need to be culturally sensitive, adaptable, and aware of these influences to navigate the complexities of leadership successfully. Recognizing and respecting diverse cultural norms and expectations fosters mutual understanding, cross-cultural collaboration, and ultimately, effective leadership in today's globalized world.

Hofstede's cultural dimensions, developed by Dutch psychologist Geert Hofstede, offer a valuable framework for comprehending how culture shapes leadership practices, communication patterns, and decision-making processes across different societies. These dimensions provide insights into the cultural influences that affect leadership in various global contexts. The six dimensions are as follows:

Power Distance (PD): This dimension measures how societies perceive and accept unequal power distribution. In cultures with high Power Distance, leaders often wield substantial authority, and hierarchical structures are common. In contrast, low Power Distance cultures lean towards more egalitarian leadership styles with reduced hierarchy.

Individualism vs. Collectivism (IDV): Individualism vs. Collectivism measures whether societies prioritize personal autonomy or group cohesion. In individualistic cultures, leaders may adopt independent and autonomous leadership styles. In collectivist cultures, leadership often revolves around team harmony and consensus-building.

Masculinity vs. Femininity (MAS): This dimension assesses whether a culture values assertiveness, competitiveness, and success (masculinity) or nurturing, quality of life, and caring (femininity). Leadership in masculine cultures may prioritize achievement and assertiveness, whereas leadership in feminine cultures emphasizes empathy, relationships, and work-life balance.

Uncertainty Avoidance (UAI): Uncertainty Avoidance indicates a culture's tolerance for ambiguity and risk. High Uncertainty Avoidance cultures prefer rules and structure to minimize uncertainty, while low Uncertainty Avoidance cultures accept ambiguity. Leaders in high Uncertainty Avoidance cultures may favor cautious decision-making, while those in low Uncertainty Avoidance cultures may embrace experimentation and risk-taking.

Long-Term Orientation vs. Short-Term Orientation (LTO): This dimension gauges whether a culture focuses on future-oriented thinking, perseverance, and thriftiness (long-term orientation) or immediate results, tradition, and social obligations (short-term orientation). Leaders in long-term orientation cultures may emphasize sustainable strategies and future investment, while those in short-term orientation cultures prioritize immediate outcomes and adherence to tradition.

Indulgence vs. Restraint (IND): Indulgence vs. Restraint reflects a culture's willingness to gratify human desires and enjoy life (indulgence) or regulate desires and impulses (restraint). Leadership in indulgence cultures may accommodate personal desires and enjoyment, whereas leaders in restraint cultures may emphasize discipline and self-control.

Comprehending these cultural dimensions enables leaders to adapt their leadership styles, communication approaches, and decision-making methods to align with the cultural norms and expectations of diverse individuals and organizations. This cultural acumen enhances leadership effectiveness in a globally interconnected world, fostering cross-cultural collaboration and mutual understanding.

As we are uncovering leadership styles vary significantly across cultural contexts, reflecting the values, norms, and expectations inherent to each society. Let us explore some more notable leadership styles prevalent in different cultural regions.

Paternalistic leadership is widespread in many Asian cultures, including China, Japan, and South Korea. In this leadership style, leaders assume a parental role, providing guidance, support, and protection to their subordinates. Paternalistic leaders are expected to make decisions for the group's benefit, and loyalty and respect towards authority figures are highly valued. Subordinates often defer to their leaders' wisdom and experience.

Many Middle Eastern cultures exhibit authoritarian leadership styles. Leaders in these contexts often wield substantial power and make decisions without extensive consultation. Respect for authority and hierarchy is paramount, and subordinates are expected to follow directives without questioning them openly. This style may reflect the region's historical and cultural reverence for strong leadership.

Scandinavian countries, such as Sweden, Norway, and Denmark, are known for their participative and democratic leadership styles. These societies emphasize egalitarianism, open communication, and consensus-building. Leaders often involve employees in decision-making processes and value input from all team members. This approach aligns with the culture's emphasis on equality and inclusivity.

Western European cultures, including France and Belgium, often exhibit laissez-faire leadership styles. Laissez-faire leaders grant considerable autonomy to their subordinates, allowing them to make decisions independently. These leaders provide guidance when needed but generally adopt a hands-off approach. This style aligns with the region's value for individual freedom and autonomy.

In North America, particularly the United States, transformational leadership is prevalent. Transformational leaders inspire and motivate their teams by setting a compelling vision and fostering innovation and personal growth. They encourage creativity and often lead by example, expecting their teams to be proactive and take ownership of their work.

Some African cultures embrace servant leadership, which emphasizes leaders' responsibility to serve and empower their followers. Leaders prioritize the well-being and development of their teams and often engage in acts of humility and selflessness. This style aligns with communal values and the importance of collective welfare in many African societies.

In various Indigenous cultures worldwide, consensus-based leadership prevails. Decisions are made collectively through discussions and deliberations, with a focus on achieving unanimous agreement. This approach reflects the communal values and egalitarian principles of many Indigenous societies.

In multinational corporations and organizations with diverse workforces, leaders often adopt adaptive leadership styles. They recognize the need to adjust their leadership approaches to accommodate varying cultural norms and expectations within their teams, aiming for inclusivity and effectiveness.

Understanding and respecting these diverse leadership styles is essential for effective leadership in a multicultural world. Leaders who can adapt their approaches to align with the cultural contexts they operate in are more likely to build trust, collaboration, and success within their teams and organizations.

Leadership approaches vary in their strengths and weaknesses, and their effectiveness often depends on the specific context and the leader's ability to adapt. Autocratic leadership, for example, allows for quick decision-making and clear directions, which can be effective in crisis situations but may stifle creativity and hinder morale. In contrast, democratic leadership involves team members in decision-making, fostering inclusivity and motivation, but it can be time-consuming and may not work well in situations requiring swift action.

Transformational leadership inspires and motivates teams to excel, encouraging innovation and commitment. However, it can sometimes focus more on vision than execution. Transactional leadership establishes clear roles and expectations, creating efficiency and stability, but it may lack innovation and lead to dissatisfaction if rewards are perceived as unfair.

Servant leadership prioritizes the well-being of team members, fostering trust and a positive work environment. Yet, it may impede assertiveness in some situations. Laissez-faire leadership empowers team members by granting autonomy, boosting creativity and initiative, but it may result in confusion and inefficiency if not managed well.

Paternalistic leadership provides support and guidance, building trust and commitment. However, it can hinder independence and critical thinking if overused. Adaptive leadership tailors the approach to specific needs, effectively navigating complex challenges. Still, it demands significant flexibility and adaptability.

Effective leaders often employ a combination of these styles, adapting to the situation and the team's needs. The key lies in recognizing the strengths and weaknesses of each approach and using them strategically to achieve organizational goals while considering the well-being and development of team members.

Effective communication in multicultural teams and organizations can be challenging due to various factors. One significant challenge is language barriers. Team members from different cultural backgrounds may have varying levels of proficiency in the common language, leading to misunderstandings, misinterpretations, and reduced efficiency in communication.

Cultural differences in communication styles also pose challenges. High-context cultures, which rely on non-verbal cues and shared context, may perceive low-context communication as overly direct or even rude. Conversely, low-context communicators may find high-context communication vague or unclear. These differences can lead to frustration and miscommunication.

Differing norms regarding hierarchy and authority can affect communication dynamics. In hierarchical cultures, team members may hesitate to express their opinions openly to superiors, inhibiting open dialogue. In contrast, egalitarian cultures may encourage more open and direct communication, which hierarchical team members may perceive as disrespectful.

Time orientation is another factor. Some cultures emphasize punctuality and efficiency, while others prioritize relationship-building and may view strict adherence to schedules as inflexible. This can lead to conflicts and misunderstandings regarding deadlines and time management.

Cultural differences in feedback and criticism also play a role. Some cultures value direct and constructive feedback, while others prefer indirect and subtle approaches to avoid causing embarrassment or loss of face. These differences can hinder the effectiveness of performance evaluations and hinder personal and professional growth.

Finally, cultural diversity can result in varying communication expectations. Team members may have different norms regarding email etiquette, meeting formats, or the use of technology in communication, leading to confusion and inefficiencies.

Navigating these challenges requires cultural sensitivity, effective cross-cultural training, and open communication. Leaders and team members must be aware of these dynamics and actively work to create a communication-friendly environment that respects cultural differences while promoting clarity and understanding.

Improving cross-cultural communication skills is a critical component of effective collaboration in today's diverse teams and organizations. To navigate the complexities of cross-cultural interactions successfully, several strategies can be employed. Firstly, promoting cultural awareness and education is essential. Providing team members with cultural awareness training helps them gain insights into the values, norms, and communication styles of different cultures. Encouraging curiosity about other cultures fosters a more inclusive and empathetic work environment.

Active listening is another fundamental skill for cross-cultural communication. Team members should be trained in active listening techniques to ensure that they fully understand and engage with what others are saying. This involves paraphrasing and asking clarifying questions to confirm comprehension, which helps prevent misunderstandings.

Non-verbal communication plays a significant role in cross-cultural interactions. Acknowledging the importance of non-verbal cues, such as body language, gestures, and facial expressions, helps team members interpret messages accurately. Moreover, individuals should be conscious of their own non-verbal communication to avoid unintentional misinterpretations.

Creating an environment of open and inclusive communication is paramount. Encouraging all team members to share their perspectives freely contributes to a more inclusive workplace. Open dialogues and regular feedback sessions can help address concerns and improve communication.

Flexibility and adaptability in communication styles are essential. Team members should be encouraged to adjust their communication approaches to accommodate the preferences of others. Cultivating a growth mindset that values learning from diverse communication experiences is also beneficial.

In cases where language proficiency is a barrier, organizations should invest in language training programs. Offering resources for improving language skills and utilizing bilingual or multilingual tools can help bridge language gaps.

Cross-cultural teams can be particularly effective in promoting intercultural communication and collaboration. These teams bring together individuals from different cultural backgrounds, facilitating the exchange of ideas and perspectives. Additionally, rotating team members among different projects or teams increases exposure to diverse viewpoints.

Cultural mentoring can also be beneficial. Pairing team members with mentors from different cultural backgrounds allows for guidance and insights that bridge cultural gaps and promote understanding.

Promoting a culture of respect and sensitivity toward cultural differences is essential. Addressing incidents of bias or discrimination promptly and decisively ensures a safe and inclusive environment for all team members.

Leveraging technology wisely is another crucial aspect of cross-cultural communication. Video conferencing, instant messaging, and collaboration tools can facilitate communication, especially in virtual teams. Ensuring that team members are comfortable with these tools and understand their cultural implications is vital.

Finally, patience and perseverance are key. Building cross-cultural communication skills takes time, and learning from mistakes is part of the process. Encouraging team members to seek feedback on their communication experiences and regularly evaluating and refining cross-cultural communication strategies can lead to continuous improvement in this important area.

Cultural intelligence, often abbreviated as CQ, is a fundamental concept that holds great significance for global leaders and individuals working in diverse, multicultural environments. It goes beyond mere cultural awareness and delves into the capability to effectively understand, adapt to, and interact with people hailing from various cultural backgrounds. In essence, cultural intelligence empowers leaders with the skills and insights necessary to navigate the complex web of cultural nuances, communicate sensitively, and make informed decisions in multicultural contexts.

The importance of cultural intelligence for global leaders cannot be overstated for several compelling reasons. Firstly, effective global leadership increasingly involves operating in international or multicultural settings. In such scenarios, leaders must be adept at building trust, managing conflicts, and motivating teams across diverse cultural landscapes. Cultural intelligence equips them with the tools to excel in these critical areas.

Secondly, communication lies at the heart of leadership, and cultural intelligence plays a pivotal role in this regard. Leaders with high CQ are well-equipped to grasp how different cultures may perceive and respond to various communication styles, ensuring that their messages are not only clear but also culturally sensitive. This, in turn, reduces the likelihood of misunderstandings and misinterpretations in cross-cultural interactions.

Moreover, cultural intelligence has also proven invaluable when it comes to conflict resolution. Cultural disparities can sometimes lead to disputes or misunderstandings within diverse teams. Leaders with a strong cultural intelligence quotient are better positioned to identify the root causes of conflicts, effectively mediate disputes, and foster a harmonious work environment where diverse perspectives are valued.

Furthermore, cultural intelligence enhances decision-making capabilities. Global leaders frequently encounter complex, culturally influenced decision-making scenarios. CQ enables them to consider the cultural factors at play when making choices, resulting in more informed and culturally sensitive decisions that resonate with stakeholders from diverse backgrounds.

Cultural adaptability is another key facet of leadership in today's globalized world. Leaders who operate in various regions or oversee multinational operations need to flexibly adjust their leadership styles and strategies to align with the cultural preferences of their teams and stakeholders. Cultural intelligence empowers them to do just that.

Additionally, the ability to harness the creativity and innovation inherent in diverse teams is a hallmark of effective leadership. Cultural intelligence fosters the inclusion of varied perspectives and ideas, ultimately leading to novel solutions and enhanced creativity within organizations.

Moreover, global leaders with high cultural intelligence are better poised to build positive relationships with stakeholders, partners, and customers worldwide. This can significantly bolster an organization's global reputation and competitive edge in the international market.

Lastly, in the realm of talent attraction and retention, leaders who possess cultural intelligence can create inclusive, welcoming workplaces where individuals from diverse backgrounds feel valued and motivated. This not only attracts top talent but also improves employee retention rates, contributing to overall organizational success.

To develop and enhance cultural intelligence, leaders can engage in dedicated training and education focused on intercultural competence, actively seek cross-cultural experiences, leverage mentorship from individuals with diverse backgrounds, and engage in continuous self-reflection to uncover and address their own cultural biases and assumptions. As the world continues to grow increasingly interconnected, cultural intelligence is rapidly evolving into an indispensable skillset for leaders aspiring to excel in the complex, globalized landscape of modern business.

Developing cultural intelligence (CQ) is imperative for leaders in today's interconnected and diverse global landscape. To enhance CQ, leaders should first cultivate cultural awareness by acknowledging its significance and recognizing their own cultural biases and assumptions. Self-awareness lays the foundation for improvement. Leaders should then invest in education by proactively learning about various cultures, their customs, traditions, and values. This involves reading extensively, watching documentaries, and attending diversity training.

Building relationships across cultures is another vital step. Leaders should actively seek opportunities to engage with people from different cultural backgrounds, whether by joining international organizations, attending multicultural events, or forming diverse teams within their organizations. Active listening plays a crucial role in CQ development. Leaders should practice this skill when interacting with individuals from diverse backgrounds, asking open-ended questions and seeking clarification to ensure mutual understanding.

Observation and adaptation are essential in cross-cultural interactions. Leaders should pay attention to non-verbal cues, body language, and communication styles, adjusting their approach to align with the cultural norms of their audience.

Empathy is also critical; leaders should strive to understand others' experiences and emotions, fostering a deeper connection.

Learning the local language, even at a basic level, demonstrates respect and cultural sensitivity. Traveling and immersing oneself in different cultures is an invaluable experience that can broaden perspectives and deepen understanding. Seeking feedback from colleagues and team members on cross-cultural interactions can highlight areas for improvement.

Mentorship and coaching can provide valuable guidance from experienced cross-cultural leaders. Cultural adaptability is a skill to hone, as leaders experiment with adjusting their leadership style to align with the preferences of their team members from different cultures. Staying informed about global trends, geopolitical events, and cultural developments is crucial for informed decision-making.

Leaders should lead by example, fostering a culture of diversity, inclusion, and cultural sensitivity within their organizations. Periodic evaluation and reflection help track progress in developing cultural intelligence, and setting specific goals ensures a structured approach to improvement. Cultivating cultural intelligence is an ongoing journey that demands a commitment to continuous learning and self-improvement. By following these practical steps, leaders can develop the skills and mindset necessary to navigate the complexities of multicultural leadership effectively.

Carlos Ghosn, the former CEO of the Nissan-Renault-Mitsubishi Alliance, provides a remarkable case study in the intricacies of cross-cultural leadership and the significance of cultural intelligence in a global business context. Ghosn's background, with Brazilian, Lebanese, and French heritage, made him uniquely qualified to lead an automotive alliance that encompassed diverse cultural backgrounds, most notably the distinct corporate cultures of France and Japan.

Ghosn's leadership acumen rested on his adept navigation of the nuanced cultural dynamics within the organization. When he assumed leadership at Nissan, he demonstrated an acute awareness of the Japanese corporate culture, characterized by deeply ingrained traditions, a hierarchical structure, and a penchant for consensus-based decision-making. Rather than imposing Western management practices, Ghosn adopted a balanced approach that honored Japanese values while simultaneously introducing crucial reforms to address Nissan's financial challenges. This nuanced cultural sensitivity played a pivotal role in establishing trust and garnering support from Japanese employees and stakeholders.

Crucially, Ghosn exhibited a genuine respect for Japanese traditions, a cornerstone of his leadership style. He actively participated in and demonstrated respect for traditional ceremonies, thereby fostering a sense of inclusion and appreciation for local customs. This approach not only underscored his cultural intelligence but also showcased his commitment to assimilating into the Japanese corporate milieu, a vital aspect of building relationships and ensuring the success of the transformative changes he spearheaded.

While honoring Japanese traditions, Ghosn remained cognizant of the imperative for change to resuscitate the company. He implemented a series of sweeping reforms, including stringent cost-cutting measures and the introduction of a more performance-oriented culture. His ability to communicate the necessity of these changes within a culturally sensitive framework was instrumental in overcoming resistance and propelling the transformation of Nissan.

Ghosn's leadership purview extended beyond Japan, encompassing a global scale. His leadership spanned continents, and he demonstrated a remarkable capacity to adapt his leadership style to suit the diverse cultural contexts inherent to the alliance. His multicultural background and keen understanding of cultural disparities allowed him to foster a collaborative ethos among heterogeneous teams, ensuring the harmonious functioning of the alliance on a global stage.

Carlos Ghosn's tenure as a cross-cultural leader serves as an exemplar of the paramount importance of cultural intelligence in the context of today's intricately interconnected business landscape. His ability to seamlessly blend respect for cultural traditions with an unyielding commitment to catalyzing change provides a model for leaders confronted with the multifaceted challenges of navigating diverse cultural environments. Ghosn's leadership legacy highlights the pivotal role of leaders who can adeptly bridge cultural divides, thereby harnessing the richness of diversity to propel innovation, expansion, and triumph within multinational organizations.

Jack Ma, the co-founder of Alibaba Group, offers another compelling case study in the intricacies of global expansion and the critical role of cultural intelligence in driving the international success of a business empire. Ma, a Chinese entrepreneur with a visionary outlook, recognized that the path to transforming Alibaba into a global e-commerce giant was paved with the need for a deep understanding of diverse markets and the ability to seamlessly adapt the company's business model to suit local conditions.

One of the key facets of Jack Ma's leadership was his cultural intelligence, which served as the linchpin of Alibaba's international triumph. Ma understood that each market possessed its unique cultural nuances, preferences, and business practices. Rather than imposing a standardized global approach, he exhibited an extraordinary capacity to bridge cultural gaps, adapting Alibaba's strategies to align with the specific needs and sensibilities of each region. This ability to appreciate and respect the cultural diversity of markets became a hallmark of Ma's leadership.

A striking example of Jack Ma's cultural intelligence is Alibaba's foray into the Southeast Asian market. When expanding into countries like Indonesia, where e-commerce was still emerging and traditional retail was dominant, Ma recognized that the company needed to tailor its approach to gain a foothold. Alibaba invested in local talent, formed strategic partnerships, and developed innovative solutions like mobile payment platforms that catered to the unique conditions of the market. This adaptability and willingness to immerse Alibaba in the cultural fabric of each region were instrumental in the company's rapid ascent to dominance in Southeast Asia.

Furthermore, Ma's leadership was characterized by a profound respect for local cultures and traditions. He understood that fostering trust and building relationships were paramount in international business. Ma often emphasized the importance of "eating the local food" and "speaking the local language" as symbolic gestures of respect and solidarity with the communities Alibaba served. This demonstrated commitment to assimilating into local cultures not only endeared the company to consumers but also facilitated smoother operations and regulatory compliance.

Jack Ma's cultural intelligence not only enabled Alibaba's global expansion but also played a pivotal role in positioning the company as a bridge between China and the rest of the world. His leadership was instrumental in fostering international trade and cooperation, with Alibaba serving as a conduit for connecting Chinese manufacturers and entrepreneurs with markets worldwide. Ma's vision transcended borders, emphasizing the importance of globalization and the interconnectedness of businesses and cultures.

Jack Ma's leadership legacy underscores the paramount significance of cultural intelligence in the realm of global business. His ability to navigate cultural diversity, adapt to local conditions, and bridge cultural gaps was pivotal in Alibaba's transformation into a global e-commerce behemoth. Ma's leadership serves as a testament to the idea that cultural sensitivity and adaptability are not just desirable attributes but fundamental prerequisites for international success in today's interconnected world. His legacy continues to inspire leaders seeking to navigate the complex landscape of global business with acumen and respect for diverse cultures.

Christine Lagarde, the President of the European Central Bank, and a prominent figure in international finance, offers a remarkable case study in the realm of cultural intelligence and its profound impact on the world of global finance. As a French lawyer who previously served as the Managing Director of the International Monetary Fund (IMF), Lagarde's leadership demonstrated exceptional cultural intelligence as she navigated the intricate terrain of financial negotiations involving countries with vastly different economic systems, political dynamics, and cultural backgrounds.

One of the most striking facets of Christine Lagarde's leadership was her adeptness at communication, which extended far beyond language proficiency. She understood that effective communication in international finance involved not only conveying information but also grasping the cultural nuances that underpinned financial diplomacy. Her ability to listen actively, empathize with diverse perspectives, and adapt her communication style to resonate with different audiences proved to be a linchpin of her success.

Lagarde's leadership style was characterized by a deep appreciation for cultural diversity. She recognized that each nation brought its unique economic traditions, regulatory frameworks, and financial sensitivities to the table. Instead of imposing a one-size-fits-all approach, she displayed a keen understanding of the importance of accommodating these differences. Whether negotiating financial assistance programs, debt restructuring, or economic policy recommendations, Lagarde's cultural intelligence allowed her to tailor solutions that respected the individuality of each country while working toward common financial goals.

One of the most notable examples of Lagarde's cultural intelligence was her leadership during the Greek financial crisis. Greece's economic woes and negotiations for bailout programs involved high-stakes discussions with complex cultural and political dimensions. Lagarde's ability to engage with Greek officials, understand their perspective, and communicate the IMF's position effectively played a pivotal role in achieving consensus and financial stability.

Furthermore, Lagarde's cultural intelligence extended to her ability to forge relationships based on trust and mutual respect. She recognized that building relationships was foundational to successful financial diplomacy. Her willingness to engage in dialogue, build personal rapport with leaders from diverse backgrounds, and appreciate the cultural sensitivities of her counterparts fostered an environment of collaboration and cooperation on the international stage.

Christine Lagarde's leadership legacy in international finance underscores the paramount importance of cultural intelligence in managing the complexities of a global financial landscape. Her ability to navigate cultural diversity, communicate effectively, and build trust with leaders from around the world was instrumental in resolving financial crises, promoting economic stability, and advancing global financial cooperation. Her leadership serves as a compelling testament to the indispensable role of cultural intelligence in the realm of international finance and diplomacy.

In fact, there are so many leadership lessons from renowned global leaders. These lessons have created profound impacts on their nations and organizations.

Nelson Mandela, the former President of South Africa, taught us the power of forgiveness, reconciliation, and inclusivity. His unwavering commitment to ending apartheid through peaceful negotiations showcased the strength of moral authority.

Mandela's leadership not only led to the end of apartheid but also prevented a potential civil war. His approach to forgiveness and inclusivity helped heal a deeply divided nation and establish a foundation for a more equitable South Africa.

Winston Churchill, the former Prime Minister of the United Kingdom during World War II, demonstrated the importance of resilience, courage, and effective communication. His steadfast resolve in the face of adversity inspired a nation.

Churchill's leadership played a pivotal role in rallying the British people during a challenging time in history. His speeches and determination helped Britain endure the war and maintain its sovereignty, earning him a place in history as one of the most iconic leaders.

Angela Merkel, the former Chancellor of Germany, exemplified the importance of steady and pragmatic leadership. Her ability to navigate complex issues, such as the European financial crisis and the refugee crisis, highlighted the value of thoughtful decision-making.

Merkel's leadership stabilized Germany's economy during the financial crisis and showcased compassion in welcoming refugees. Her leadership in the European Union contributed to the stability and cohesion of the region, making her one of the world's most respected leaders.

Lee Kuan Yew, the founding Prime Minister of Singapore, emphasized the significance of visionary leadership, pragmatism, and long-term planning. His policies transformed Singapore from a struggling nation into a global economic powerhouse.

Lee's leadership is credited with turning Singapore into a prosperous and highly developed country within a single generation. His focus on education, clean governance, and strategic economic policies laid the foundation for Singapore's success as a global financial hub.

Mahatma Gandhi, a key figure in India's struggle for independence, taught us the power of nonviolent resistance, civil disobedience, and moral leadership. His humility and commitment to justice continue to inspire movements worldwide.

Gandhi's leadership led to India's independence from British colonial rule and inspired civil rights movements across the globe. His principles of nonviolence and moral leadership remain influential in advocating for social justice and human rights.

In analyzing these global leaders' approaches and impacts, we learn valuable lessons about the diverse qualities and styles that effective leadership can encompass. From Mandela's message of reconciliation to Churchill's resilience, Merkel's pragmatism, Lee's vision, and Gandhi's moral authority, these leaders offer a rich wealth of leadership insights that continue to guide nations and organizations toward progress and positive change.

Global leadership is a multifaceted journey that requires an understanding of cultural dynamics, effective communication, and adaptability. Leaders who can navigate the complexities of global leadership contribute to organizational success and foster international cooperation. As you continue your leadership journey, remember that global perspectives enrich your leadership skills and enable you to thrive in an interconnected world.

Chapter 12

The Future of Leadership

"Leadership guides us towards a future where our
actions today create ripples of positive change for
generations to come."

—Joel R. Klemmer

Chapter 12
The Future of Leadership

We will now embark on a journey into the future of leadership. Let us explore emerging trends, challenges, and opportunities that leaders are likely to encounter in a rapidly evolving world. As the business landscape continues to change at an unprecedented pace, it is essential for leaders to be forward-thinking and innovative in their approach. We will speculate on future leadership trends and inspire readers to embrace the evolving landscape of leadership.

Technology is at the forefront of change, with innovations like artificial intelligence, automation, the Internet of Things, and blockchain reshaping industries. These advancements are not only enhancing operational efficiency but also transforming customer experiences. Businesses are increasingly adopting digitalization to stay competitive, adapt to evolving technologies, and meet the demands of the digital age.

Changing demographics are influencing both consumer preferences and the composition of the workforce. An aging population in certain regions and the emergence of millennials and Generation Z are driving shifts in demand for products and services. Businesses must tailor their offerings to suit the needs and expectations of diverse demographic groups while also adapting their workplace practices to attract and retain a multi-generational workforce.

Globalization continues to open up new markets and opportunities for businesses. Companies are expanding internationally to tap into emerging economies and diverse consumer bases. This expansion comes with challenges, including managing complex global supply chains and addressing international regulatory differences, all of which require strategic planning and cross-border expertise.

Environmental concerns, such as climate change and resource depletion, are pushing businesses to adopt sustainable practices. Consumers are increasingly conscious of the environmental impact of products and services. To meet these expectations and remain socially responsible, businesses are implementing sustainability initiatives, rethinking supply chain management, and developing eco-friendly products.

Work models are evolving rapidly. The rise of remote work, the gig economy, and flexible work arrangements are changing the traditional employment landscape. Businesses are adapting by embracing remote work technologies, reevaluating workplace policies, and offering flexible work options to attract and retain talent in a changing labor market.

Consumer behavior is continuously shifting, influenced by digital experiences, social media, and increased awareness of sustainability and ethical considerations. As a result, businesses need to stay agile and responsive to rapidly changing consumer preferences and demands, which often require adjustments in marketing strategies and product development.

Regulatory environments are becoming increasingly complex, especially in areas like data privacy, cybersecurity, and ethical considerations. Businesses face the challenge of navigating these regulatory landscapes, ensuring compliance, and safeguarding customer data while maintaining ethical business practices to protect their reputation.

Geopolitical tensions and trade disputes can disrupt global supply chains and impact international business operations. Businesses need to assess geopolitical risks and develop strategies to mitigate the potential impacts of such uncertainties on their operations, including diversifying supply sources.

Recent global health crises, notably the COVID-19 pandemic, have underscored the importance of robust healthcare systems and crisis management plans. Businesses are reassessing their strategies and preparedness for health-related crises to minimize disruptions and ensure employee safety.

The era of big data has ushered in a data-driven decision-making process for businesses. By investing in data analytics and artificial intelligence, companies can gain valuable insights into customer behavior, streamline operations, and enhance competitiveness in an increasingly data-centric business environment.

In this dynamic and rapidly evolving landscape, businesses that proactively embrace change, innovation, and adaptability are better positioned to thrive. The ability to anticipate and respond effectively to these driving forces of change is crucial for sustained success in the modern business world.

Adaptability and forward thinking have become indispensable traits for effective leadership in today's rapidly evolving business landscape. The reasons behind this shift are multifaceted. Firstly, the pace of change in the modern business environment is unprecedented, with technology, market dynamics, and global events capable of disrupting industries overnight. Leaders who can swiftly adapt to new circumstances and seize emerging opportunities are better positioned for success.

Secondly, the prevalence of uncertainty and complexity in business today necessitates adaptability. Leaders often encounter ambiguity, must make decisions in rapidly changing situations, and manage diverse challenges. Adaptability allows leaders to pivot and adjust strategies when faced with uncertainty.

Globalization is another driving force behind the importance of adaptability and forward thinking. Businesses frequently operate across borders, engaging with diverse cultures, markets, and regulations. Forward-thinking leaders anticipate global trends and understand the intricacies of international business, while adaptability helps them navigate different cultural norms and address geopolitical challenges.

Technological disruption is a hallmark of the modern era, with technology constantly reshaping industries and creating new business models. Leaders must embrace digital transformation and harness technology to remain competitive. Forward thinking enables leaders to anticipate technological trends and integrate them into their strategies.

The evolving workforce also demands adaptability in leadership. Generational shifts, remote work trends, and the growth of the gig economy have altered the employment landscape. Leaders who can adapt their leadership styles and create an appealing work environment for diverse talent are more likely to attract and retain top employees.

Ethical and sustainable practices are gaining prominence, and leaders who are forward thinking recognize the significance of corporate social responsibility, environmental sustainability, and ethical conduct. They align their organizations with these principles to meet changing consumer and investor expectations.

Moreover, customer behavior and preferences evolve rapidly. Leaders who can adapt their products, services, and customer experiences to meet changing demands are better positioned for success. Forward-thinking leaders anticipate customer needs and stay ahead of market trends.

Effective crisis management is another area where adaptability and forward thinking come into play. Unexpected crises, such as pandemics or geopolitical conflicts, can disrupt business operations. Leaders who possess these traits have crisis management plans in place and can respond effectively to protect their organizations and stakeholders.

Innovation is a key driver of competitiveness, and leaders who foster a culture of innovation and are open to disruptive ideas can create a sustainable competitive advantage. Forward thinking involves identifying future opportunities for innovation.

Finally, long-term sustainability is a critical consideration. Leaders who focus solely on short-term gains without considering future trends and challenges may jeopardize their organizations' viability. In conclusion, adaptability and forward thinking have evolved from advantageous qualities to essential attributes for leadership in the 21st century's dynamic and complex business landscape.

Emerging leadership trends are fundamentally reshaping the way leaders and organizations operate in today's fast-paced and ever-evolving business landscape. Three prominent trends—remote leadership, digital transformation, and the ascendancy of purpose-driven leadership—bear significant implications for both leaders and the organizations they guide.

Firstly, the rise of remote leadership is compelling leaders to redefine their roles and adapt to managing teams spread across diverse locations and time zones. Effective communication and the cultivation of trust have emerged as central tenets, necessitating leaders to harness technology for staying closely connected with their geographically dispersed teams. Organizations, in turn, must invest in the requisite infrastructure for remote work, furnish leaders with training for managing remote teams, and establish clear-cut remote work policies to balance flexibility and accountability effectively.

Secondly, digital transformation is revolutionizing business operations across the board, compelling leaders to not only embrace digital literacy but also lead their organizations through intricate digital transformation journeys that often entail substantial cultural and operational shifts. Staying attuned to technological advancements becomes pivotal for leaders as they spearhead digital transformation initiatives to bolster organizational efficiency, competitive positioning, and customer experience.

Lastly, purpose-driven leadership is gaining traction as leaders and organizations increasingly recognize the significance of aligning corporate objectives with a higher sense of purpose that transcends mere profitability. Leaders are tasked with embodying and articulating their organization's purpose to inspire and engage their teams. Consequently, organizations must intricately weave a clear sense of purpose into their mission and values, as such purpose-driven entities tend to draw top talent and loyal clientele while making positive societal contributions.

These trends intersect and intersect to pose several significant implications for leaders and organizations. Adaptive leadership proves indispensable in navigating these trends effectively, demanding leaders to display agility, openness to change, a propensity for learning, and a readiness to experiment with novel approaches.

Effectively managing remote workforces necessitates a focus on productivity outcomes rather than tracking hours worked. Cultivating a culture of trust, communicating clear expectations, and furnishing remote employees with the essential tools and support are vital components of effective remote leadership.

When it comes to technology integration and digital transformation, leaders must not merely shepherd the adoption of new technologies but also foster an innovation-centric culture within their organizations. This entails championing technology adoption while addressing the potential challenges and risks that accompany such profound change.

Furthermore, ethical, and sustainable leadership aligns harmoniously with purpose-driven approaches, emphasizing the social and environmental impact of decisions and fostering cultures rooted in responsibility and integrity. Prioritizing employee well-being, regardless of the work environment—be it remote or digital—is an integral facet of leadership strategies, encompassing considerations such as mental health, work-life balance, and fostering a sense of belonging.

Lastly, leaders and organizations must prioritize resilience and effective change management capabilities, given the rapid pace of change in today's business world. Building resilience and adeptly guiding teams through uncertainty represent vital leadership competencies.

Emerging leadership trends reflect the evolving nature of work and business. Leaders who wholeheartedly embrace remote leadership, digital transformation, and purpose-driven approaches position their organizations for success in a dynamic, competitive, and ever-changing landscape. Organizations that wholeheartedly adapt to these trends are better poised to attract and retain top talent, foster innovation, and thrive in the years ahead.

Technology has significantly transformed leadership practices, reshaping how leaders communicate, make decisions, and drive innovation within organizations. The integration of digital tools has become pivotal for leaders to enhance their effectiveness and achieve positive outcomes.

Firstly, in the realm of communication, digital technology has revolutionized the way leaders connect with their teams, stakeholders, and peers. Leaders now have access to a plethora of digital platforms such as video conferencing, email, and instant messaging, enabling efficient and inclusive real-time communication. These virtual communication tools transcend geographical boundaries and time zones, fostering collaboration and maintaining open and transparent lines of communication. Leaders are required to master effective virtual communication skills, actively listen, and adapt their communication style to suit different contexts to maximize the impact of digital communication.

Secondly, technology plays a crucial role in decision-making by providing leaders with access to vast amounts of data and advanced analytics tools. This enables leaders to make data-driven decisions, gaining valuable insights into market trends, customer preferences, and operational efficiency. Artificial intelligence (AI) and machine learning algorithms assist in processing data rapidly and generating actionable recommendations. It is essential, however, that leaders exercise discernment and ethical judgment when making data-driven decisions, ensuring alignment with the organization's values and long-term goals.

Lastly, technology fosters innovation by streamlining idea generation, collaboration, and prototyping. Leaders can leverage innovation management platforms and crowdsourcing tools to collect ideas from employees and external sources. Virtual collaboration platforms facilitate seamless cross-functional teamwork, promoting creativity and problem-solving. To encourage innovation, leaders should cultivate an environment where failure is perceived as a learning opportunity, leveraging digital tools for rapid testing and validation of new concepts.

To effectively harness digital tools in their leadership practices, leaders should consider several strategies. Firstly, staying technologically proficient is crucial, necessitating an investment in digital literacy and staying informed about emerging technologies and industry-relevant trends. Secondly, leaders must commit to continuous learning as technology evolves rapidly, participating in technology-related courses, workshops, and seminars. Thirdly, promoting digital inclusivity is vital, ensuring that digital tools are accessible and user-friendly for all employees, accommodating diverse skill levels and abilities.

Additionally, leaders should strike a balance between virtual and face-to-face interactions, recognizing the importance of in-person engagements for relationship building, addressing sensitive issues, or conveying complex messages. Moreover, cybersecurity and data privacy should be prioritized to protect sensitive information. Leaders should be vigilant regarding potential cybersecurity threats and comply with data protection regulations. Finally, adaptability is crucial as leaders integrate new technologies into their leadership practices, requiring flexibility and openness to change in the digital age.

Technology has become an integral part of modern leadership, offering opportunities to enhance communication, decision-making, and innovation. Effective leaders leverage digital tools judiciously, continually expand their technological proficiency, and foster a digital-savvy organizational culture that adapts to the evolving digital landscape.

Emotional intelligence retains its fundamental importance in the realm of leadership, and its relevance persists in today's rapidly evolving work environments. It encompasses the ability to recognize, comprehend, manage, and leverage emotions, both one's own and those of others. Leaders possessing a high degree of emotional intelligence can cultivate trust, nurture positive workplace relationships, and navigate intricate challenges with greater effectiveness.

In the context of virtual and diverse work environments, the application of emotional intelligence assumes an even more significant role. Leaders must apply emotional intelligence in various ways:

Firstly, in virtual settings, leaders should exercise empathy. With remote work becoming increasingly prevalent, it can be challenging to discern emotions due to physical separation. Leaders can demonstrate empathy by actively listening to their team members' concerns, validating their emotions, and providing support when needed. Regular one-on-one virtual meetings and team gatherings offer opportunities for open communication and emotional connection.

Secondly, cultural sensitivity is vital in diverse work settings. Leaders must acquaint themselves with their team members' cultural backgrounds, encompassing norms, values, and communication styles. By being culturally intelligent, leaders can navigate potential misunderstandings, circumvent inadvertent offense, and advance inclusivity.

Additionally, self-regulation is a pivotal component of emotional intelligence. In virtual work environments, where self-discipline and time management are crucial, leaders can set an example. They can manage their emotions effectively, exhibit resilience in the face of challenges, and maintain a positive demeanor, thereby motivating team members through their own actions.

Social awareness also assumes great significance. In virtual settings, leaders should be astute observers, capable of discerning non-verbal cues, tone of voice, and subtle shifts in team members' behavior during virtual meetings or written communications. Such attentiveness enables leaders to identify potential issues early and address them proactively.

Furthermore, conflict resolution plays a critical role, especially in diverse teams. Differences in perspectives and cultural backgrounds can lead to conflicts. Leaders proficient in emotional intelligence can foster constructive conflict resolution by creating a safe space for open dialogue, promoting empathy among team members, and seeking mutually beneficial resolutions.

Moreover, feedback and recognition are crucial in virtual work environments. Applying emotional intelligence, leaders can deliver feedback empathetically and sensitively, focusing on constructive improvement rather than criticism. Acknowledging and celebrating diverse achievements and contributions fosters a sense of belonging and motivation.

Lastly, adaptability and flexibility are indispensable traits, particularly in virtual and diverse work settings where unexpected challenges and changes are commonplace. Emotional intelligence empowers leaders to remain flexible, resilient, and adaptable in the face of uncertainty, thereby inspiring confidence, and trust among team members.

Emotional intelligence continues to be an invaluable asset in leadership, allowing leaders to build robust, inclusive, and high-performing teams in virtual and diverse work environments. Through practices like empathy, cultural sensitivity, self-regulation, and effective communication, leaders can create workspaces where team members feel valued, comprehended, and driven to excel.

Purpose-driven leadership is a philosophy that centers leadership practices and organizational strategies around a higher purpose beyond profit. It emphasizes a commitment to social and environmental responsibility, striving to create a positive impact on society and the planet while pursuing business goals. Purpose-driven leaders prioritize values, ethics, and corporate social responsibility in their decision-making, fostering a sense of meaning and fulfillment within their organizations. There are so many examples of organizations exemplify purpose-driven leadership.

Co-founders Neil Blumenthal and Dave Gilboa established Warby Parker with a purpose-driven approach. Their "Buy a Pair, Give a Pair" program donates eyeglasses to those in need for every pair sold. The company prioritizes affordable eyewear, social responsibility, and environmental sustainability.

New Belgium Brewing, a craft brewery, known for brands like Fat Tire, has a strong commitment to sustainability and environmental responsibility. New Belgium Brewing has implemented various green initiatives, including using wind power, recycling, and reducing its carbon footprint.

REI is a retail cooperative specializing in outdoor gear and clothing. The company prioritizes sustainability and environmental protection. REI's purpose-driven approach includes supporting outdoor conservation efforts and promoting responsible outdoor recreation.

These examples illustrate that purpose-driven leadership goes beyond profit and strives to create a positive societal and environmental impact. Purpose-driven leaders inspire employees, customers, and stakeholders by aligning business success with a broader mission to make the world a better place. Their commitment to social and environmental responsibility is a driving force for change in the business world, demonstrating that profitability and positive impact can coexist.

Resilience and adaptability stand as indispensable leadership traits, especially in today's rapidly changing and uncertain world. These qualities are essential for leaders to effectively guide their teams and organizations through various challenges. Resilience allows leaders to remain steady and composed during turbulent times, instilling confidence in their teams. It enables leaders to view obstacles as opportunities for growth, fostering problem-solving skills and innovation. Emotional intelligence, a component of resilience, helps leaders manage their own and their team's emotions, providing stability during crises.

Moreover, resilience directly impacts employee well-being. Leaders who can navigate uncertainty with grace and resilience are better positioned to support their team members' emotional and psychological needs, thereby maintaining high morale and productivity during difficult periods. Resilience also leads to more adaptive and effective leadership, allowing leaders to pivot their strategies when circumstances demand it.

To build personal and organizational resilience, leaders should employ several key strategies. Self-care is paramount, as leaders must prioritize their own well-being to effectively support others. Adaptive leadership, which embraces change and feedback, is crucial in times of uncertainty. Clear and transparent communication helps alleviate anxiety among team members by keeping them informed and engaged.

Scenario planning, or preparing for various contingencies, reduces fear of the unknown. Seeking mentorship and coaching from experienced leaders is another valuable strategy. Leaders should foster a culture of continuous learning, encouraging their teams to learn from setbacks and failures. Creating a supportive workplace environment where employees feel safe and supported is equally vital. Leaders should also be flexible in their leadership styles, adapting them to different situations and individuals. Investing in crisis management training can further prepare leadership teams to tackle unexpected challenges effectively. Finally, promoting a growth mindset within the organization encourages employees to perceive challenges as opportunities for learning and improvement.

Ethical leadership in our interconnected world presents leaders with a complex landscape of challenges and responsibilities. One prominent challenge is the relentless public scrutiny facilitated by the rise of social media and digital communication channels. Leaders' actions and decisions, whether ethical or unethical, can rapidly become widely known, intensifying the pressure to consistently make ethically sound choices.

The globalization of businesses and organizations further compounds the challenges of ethical leadership. Leaders often operate within a global context, where their decisions and policies can impact diverse cultures and communities. This necessitates a profound understanding of various ethical norms, values, and cultural perspectives, demanding heightened cultural sensitivity and adaptability.

In today's world, supply chains are intricate and interconnected across borders. Ensuring ethical practices throughout these global supply chains can be a significant challenge. Leaders bear the responsibility of overseeing that their organizations source materials and labor ethically, even in regions with differing standards and practices.

The environmental dimension adds another layer of complexity. Leaders are increasingly expected to make ethical decisions regarding sustainability, environmental responsibility, and the mitigation of their organizations' carbon footprints. The ethical imperative to engage in responsible resource management and address environmental concerns is now a central aspect of leadership.

In the digital age, data privacy and security have become paramount ethical concerns. Leaders must navigate the complex terrain of ethical data handling, safeguarding sensitive customer and employee information, and addressing cybersecurity challenges.

Promoting diversity and inclusion is another ethical dimension. Leaders are called upon to foster diverse and inclusive workplaces, which involves confronting and rectifying bias, discrimination, and inequities within their organizations.

Global crises, such as the COVID-19 pandemic, present leaders with profound ethical dilemmas. Balancing public health imperatives, economic impact, and individual rights requires ethical decision-making under intense pressure and scrutiny.

Moreover, leaders face ethical quandaries driven by political and economic forces. Decisions related to lobbying, campaign donations, and corporate tax practices can be ethically intricate, as they often involve navigating the interests of multiple stakeholders and adhering to broader societal expectations.

Despite these formidable challenges, numerous leaders have exemplified ethical leadership by successfully navigating complex ethical dilemmas with unwavering integrity. For instance, Jamie Dimon, CEO of JPMorgan Chase, openly acknowledged the bank's mistakes in the wake of the 2008 financial crisis, working diligently to rebuild trust. Similarly, Mary Barra, CEO of General Motors, confronted an ethical crisis concerning vehicle recalls by assuming responsibility, implementing organizational reforms, and prioritizing safety and transparency.

Leaders hold a pivotal role in cultivating innovation and creativity within organizations. They are responsible for setting the stage, nurturing an environment, and instilling expectations that either promote or hinder innovative thinking and actions. This leadership role encompasses various crucial aspects.

Firstly, leaders must articulate a compelling vision that underscores the significance of innovation and aligns it with the organization's mission and long-term objectives. This communicates that innovation is not merely a luxury but a strategic imperative.

Secondly, cultivating a culture of psychological safety is essential. Innovation often involves risk-taking and embraces failure as part of the learning process. Leaders should foster a culture where employees feel safe to voice their ideas, take calculated risks, and learn from both successes and setbacks without the fear of punitive measures.

Thirdly, providing resources is a fundamental responsibility of leaders. This includes allocating financial, human, and technological resources to support innovative endeavors, ensuring there is a tangible commitment to innovation.

Encouraging cross-functional collaboration is another key dimension of leadership in innovation. Innovation thrives when individuals with diverse perspectives collaborate. Leaders should promote cross-functional teams and open lines of communication, dismantling silos that can stifle creativity.

Leading by example is also critical. When leaders actively engage in brainstorming sessions, experimentation, and the pursuit of novel ideas, it sends a clear message to the organization about the importance of innovation.

Furthermore, recognizing and rewarding innovation is essential. Whether through financial incentives, promotions, public acknowledgment, or professional development opportunities, these rewards serve as positive reinforcement, motivating employees to continue innovating.

Lastly, leaders must identify and eliminate barriers to innovation, whether they are bureaucratic, cultural, or procedural. This involves streamlining processes, revisiting outdated policies, and challenging the status quo.

A culture of innovation offers numerous benefits, including a competitive advantage, enhanced problem-solving abilities, attraction and retention of top talent, increased productivity, improved customer satisfaction, business growth, and long-term sustainability. Innovative organizations are more adaptable to changes in the business landscape, respond effectively to market shifts, and are better poised for growth and relevance in the long run.

Intrapreneurship, a concept rooted in encouraging employees to act like entrepreneurs within their organization, involves cultivating an environment where employees are not only allowed but also empowered to innovate, take calculated risks, and develop new ideas or solutions. Intrapreneurs, in this context, are individuals who exhibit entrepreneurial qualities such as creativity, initiative, and a willingness to challenge conventional norms, all while operating within the boundaries of the existing organization's structure.

The impact of intrapreneurship on organizational innovation can be profound, encompassing several critical aspects. First and foremost, intrapreneurship tends to enhance innovation within the organization. Intrapreneurs often bring fresh perspectives, unconventional ideas, and creative approaches to long-standing challenges, spurring innovative products, services, or processes.

Furthermore, intrapreneurship contributes to improving a company's competitive advantage. Organizations that actively encourage and support intrapreneurial initiatives tend to remain ahead of the competition. By consistently adapting and evolving, they develop a sustainable edge over their peers.

Intrapreneurship also has a significant influence on employee engagement and job satisfaction. When employees are granted the autonomy to pursue their ideas, and these ideas are genuinely valued, they become more motivated, engaged, and committed to their work.

From a risk management perspective, intrapreneurship enables organizations to explore new opportunities and markets while effectively managing risks. It can be less risky than external entrepreneurship because it leverages existing resources, infrastructure, and industry expertise.

Moreover, intrapreneurship supports talent retention efforts. Companies that actively promote intrapreneurial culture are often more appealing to top talent. Employees who possess a strong desire for innovation and personal growth tend to remain loyal to organizations that foster and support their aspirations.

To empower employees to become intrapreneurs, leaders must take concrete steps. They need to cultivate a culture that not only values innovation but also rewards it. This includes creating an environment that encourages experimentation, embraces the notion of learning from failure, and celebrates successful innovations.

Additionally, leaders should ensure that employees have access to essential resources—whether it is time, budgets, or specialized tools—to facilitate the development and testing of their ideas. Clear communication of the organization's strategic goals and objectives is vital to align intrapreneurial initiatives with the broader mission.

Cross-functional collaboration should be encouraged, as it brings diverse perspectives to intrapreneurial projects. Leaders must also implement reward systems that recognize and incentivize employees displaying intrapreneurial behavior. This can include promotions, bonuses, or various forms of recognition.

Training programs and skill development opportunities should be made available to help employees enhance their entrepreneurial abilities. Leaders should convey that calculated risks are not only acceptable but also encouraged, with failure viewed as a valuable learning experience rather than a detriment to one's career.

Ultimately, leaders must lead by example, actively participating in innovation efforts and demonstrating a willingness to take risks themselves. In conclusion, intrapreneurship is a potent catalyst for organizational innovation. Leaders play a pivotal role in creating an environment where employees feel empowered to be intrapreneurs, fostering a culture of innovation, providing resources, and recognizing and rewarding innovative efforts. This approach not only leads to a more agile, competitive, and engaged workforce but also promotes a continuous culture of innovation within the organization.

The future of leadership is both exciting and challenging. Leaders who embrace change, prioritize adaptability, and lead with purpose will be well-positioned to thrive in the evolving landscape. As you continue your leadership journey, remember that leadership is not static; it is a dynamic practice that requires continuous learning, innovation, and a commitment to positive impact.

Chapter 13

Conclusion

Becoming a Transformational Leader

"Become the transformational leader, transform the
vision into an everlasting legacy."

−Joel R. Klemmer

Chapter 13
Conclusion: Becoming a Transformational Leader

In this final chapter, we now bring together the key insights and lessons from this book to empower you on your journey to becoming a transformational leader. We have explored the multifaceted world of leadership, from understanding its history to anticipating its future. Now, it is time to summarize the key takeaways and inspire you to embrace your role as a transformational leader with confidence.

Effective leaders possess a unique blend of qualities that set them apart in the ever-evolving landscape of leadership. Vision, the ability to articulate a compelling and inspiring future, is at the forefront. Leaders envision a path forward and inspire others to join them on the journey.

Empathy is another crucial trait. Leaders understand and connect with the emotions, needs, and perspectives of those they lead. This empathetic connection builds trust and fosters collaboration.

Integrity is the foundation of leadership. Leaders act with honesty and consistency, adhering to strong moral and ethical principles. Their actions align with their words, and they are trusted to do what is right, even in challenging situations.

Adaptability is a hallmark of effective leaders. In a dynamic world, leaders must navigate change, learn from setbacks, and embrace new ideas. They remain open to growth and consistently evolve their leadership style.

As you reflect on your own leadership journey, consider how these qualities have influenced your growth. How has your vision evolved? In what ways have you deepened your empathy? What experiences have tested your integrity and solidified your commitment to it? How have you adapted and thrived in the face of change?

Leadership is a journey of continuous development, shaped by experiences, challenges, and personal growth. Embrace these core qualities, nurture them, and allow them to guide you on your path to becoming an even more effective leader.

Leadership encompasses a wide spectrum of styles, each with its own strengths and applications. At one end, there's authoritative leadership, characterized by a clear vision and a directive approach. Authoritative leaders set the course and make decisions with authority, providing clarity and structure in times of uncertainty.

On the other end lies servant leadership, which prioritizes serving the needs of others and empowering the team. Servant leaders are empathetic, collaborative, and focused on facilitating the growth and success of their team members.

Aligning your leadership style with your values and context is essential for effective leadership. Your style should be a reflection of your core principles and beliefs. It should also adapt to the specific circumstances and needs of your team or organization. A versatile leader knows when to be authoritative and when to be a servant, finding the right balance for optimal results.

In the journey of leadership, several skills stand out as fundamental. Effective communication is paramount, as it fosters understanding, trust, and collaboration. Decision-making skills, including the ability to analyze situations and make informed choices, are crucial for steering the course. Team management involves creating an environment where team members can thrive, leveraging their strengths and promoting a sense of unity.

By recognizing the diversity of leadership styles, aligning your style with your values, and mastering these essential skills, you can become a versatile and effective leader capable of navigating various challenges and contexts.

Continuous skill development is the lifeblood of effective leadership. In a rapidly evolving world, leaders must adapt and refine their skills to meet new challenges and seize emerging opportunities. The journey of leadership is an ongoing process of growth and learning, where each experience and lesson contributes to your development.

Ethical leadership and social responsibility are the cornerstones of sustainable leadership. Leaders are not just responsible for their organizations' success but also for the well-being of their teams and the impact they have on society. By leading with integrity, making ethical decisions, and embracing social responsibility, leaders contribute to a better world while earning the trust and respect of their teams and communities.

Leadership is a dynamic journey that requires continuous skill development and a commitment to ethical principles and social responsibility. By embracing these ideals and focusing on personal growth, leaders can make a positive impact on their organizations and the world at large.

Leading with a sense of purpose that goes beyond profit is not just a choice; it is a responsibility we bear as leaders. When we recognize our capacity to influence and impact the lives of others and the world, it becomes apparent that our leadership should be guided by a higher purpose.

By striving for a purpose-driven leadership style, we can inspire our teams, foster innovation, and create a positive impact on society.

It is about aligning our values and actions to contribute meaningfully to the greater good. When we lead with purpose, we not only enhance our organizations but also make a difference in the lives of our employees, customers, and communities.

So, I encourage you to embrace purpose-driven leadership. Seek to understand how your leadership can be a force for positive change in the world, and let that purpose guide your actions and decisions. By doing so, you will not only achieve success in your professional life but also leave a lasting legacy that benefits society as a whole.

Leading in a rapidly changing world presents both challenges and opportunities for leaders. On one hand, the pace of change can be overwhelming, requiring leaders to adapt quickly and make informed decisions in uncertain environments. This demands resilience, agility, and the ability to manage ambiguity. Additionally, the need for continuous skill development is crucial to keep up with evolving technologies and trends.

On the other hand, these dynamic circumstances offer opportunities for innovation and growth. Leaders can harness the power of digital transformation to streamline processes, enhance communication, and drive organizational efficiency. Embracing diversity and inclusion can foster creativity and attract a broader talent pool. Furthermore, the emphasis on ethical leadership and social responsibility allows leaders to contribute positively to society.

In essence, leading in a rapidly changing world necessitates a balance between addressing challenges and leveraging opportunities. It calls for visionary, adaptable, and socially responsible leadership that can thrive amidst complexity and drive organizations toward a brighter future.

As future leaders, it is crucial to recognize that adaptability and innovation will be your guiding principles in a constantly evolving world. The ability to embrace change, learn from it, and pivot when necessary, will define your success. Innovation will drive your organization's growth and competitive edge, as well as your personal development.

Remember that leadership is not a static concept; it is a journey of continuous learning and growth. By cultivating adaptability and a mindset of innovation, you will not only navigate the challenges of tomorrow but also lead your teams and organizations to new heights of success. Embrace change, foster creativity, and never stop exploring new ways to make a positive impact on your organization and society.

As transformational leaders, you have the incredible power to inspire positive change in your organizations, communities, and the world at large. Embrace this role with enthusiasm and purpose, recognizing that your actions and decisions can shape a brighter future.

Lead with vision, empathy, and integrity. Be adaptable and open to new ideas. Cultivate a culture of innovation and ethical responsibility. Understand that your journey as a leader is a continuous learning process.

Every day, strive to make a positive impact, both personally and professionally. Encourage those around you to do the same. By fostering a sense of purpose that transcends profit and contributes to the betterment of society, you can truly lead the way toward a brighter and more sustainable future.

Becoming an effective leader involves several key strategies, starting with setting meaningful and achievable goals. To begin, it is essential to define your long-term vision as a leader, considering where you envision yourself and your organization in the future. Utilize the SMART goal framework, ensuring that your objectives are Specific, Measurable, Achievable, Relevant, and Time-bound. Prioritize a select number of goals at a time to maintain focus, and break larger goals into smaller, manageable steps to facilitate tracking and motivation.

Seeking mentorship is another valuable aspect of leadership development. Identify potential mentors from whom possess the experience and expertise you can benefit. Approach them thoughtfully, explaining your goals and what you hope to gain from the mentorship. Actively participate in discussions, ask questions, and be receptive to constructive criticism. Nurture mentor-mentee relationships and stay connected, as mentors can continue to provide insights throughout your career.

Continuous learning and growth are essential to adapt to a rapidly changing world. Stay informed about industry trends, technological advancements, and global developments relevant to your field. Invest in professional development through workshops, conferences, and training programs. Consider pursuing advanced degrees or certifications to enhance your skills. Seek feedback regularly from peers and reflect on your leadership style and areas for improvement. Embrace failures as opportunities for learning and adjust your strategies accordingly.

Leadership development is an ongoing journey. Patience and commitment are key. By setting clear goals, engaging in mentorship, and embracing continuous learning, you will not only become a more effective leader but also contribute positively to your organization and the broader community.

Consider the impact you want to have on your organization, your team, and the world around you. Reflect on the values and principles that guide your leadership style and decision-making.

Think about the positive changes you can bring about and the difference you can make in the lives of those you lead. Your legacy as a leader is not just about the results you achieve but also the way you inspire and empower others. Consider the long-term effects of your actions, decisions, and the culture you foster within your organization.

Remember that your legacy is not set in stone; it is something you actively shape through your daily actions and choices. Strive to leave a legacy of ethical leadership, positive impact, and continuous improvement. Inspire others to follow in your footsteps and carry forward the values and principles that define your leadership style.

The legacy you leave as a leader is a testament to your dedication, integrity, and commitment to making the world a better place. So, take the time to reflect on your leadership journey and envision the legacy you want to create—it will guide your actions and inspire those around you to reach their full potential.

Ethical, empathetic, and purpose-driven leadership have a profound and enduring impact on various aspects of organizations and society. These leadership qualities set the foundation for an organization's culture by promoting integrity, trust, and accountability. Over time, they contribute to a workplace environment characterized by loyalty, motivation, and increased employee engagement, fostering long-term commitment among the workforces.

Furthermore, leaders who prioritize empathy and employee well-being create a positive work culture that endures and continues to inspire innovation. When employees understand the broader mission and purpose of their work, they are more likely to generate creative solutions and actively contribute to the organization's long-term success.

Purpose-driven leadership transcends profit motives and underscores an organization's responsibility to make a positive impact on society. This commitment to social responsibility often includes philanthropic efforts and sustainable practices, leaving a lasting legacy of ethical and socially conscious business practices.

The impact of ethical, empathetic, and purpose-driven leadership extends to an organization's reputation and brand image. Such leaders contribute to building a positive reputation, attracting customers, partners, and investors who share the organization's values. Their influence also reaches succession planning, as they focus on mentoring and developing the next generation of leaders, ensuring the continuity of ethical principles within the organization.

Beyond the confines of the organization, these leadership qualities have a broader societal impact. Ethical leaders advocate for social justice, environmental sustainability, and ethical business practices, contributing to positive changes in society. They inspire individuals and communities to align with similar values-driven leadership, creating a ripple effect of positive influence.

As you have journeyed through the pages of this book, I encourage you to translate knowledge into action, turning insights into real-world leadership. Leadership is not an abstract concept; it is a practice that thrives through implementation.

Begin with self-reflection, delving into your unique leadership journey. Understand your strengths, pinpoint areas for growth, and align your values with your leadership style. Self-awareness serves as the bedrock of effective leadership.

Establish clear leadership goals. Define the kind of leader you aspire to be and the impact you aim to make within your organization or community. Setting concrete objectives provides direction and purpose.

Seek out mentorship and guidance from those who embody the leadership qualities you admire. Learn from experienced leaders, leveraging their insights to accelerate your growth.

Commit to continuous learning. Leadership is an ever-evolving field; staying current requires ongoing education. Read more books, attend seminars, and stay informed about the latest leadership trends and practices.

Apply ethical principles consistently. Make decisions grounded in integrity, transparency, and accountability. Be a model of ethical conduct, both in your workplace and the broader sphere.

Embrace empathetic leadership by understanding your team members' needs and perspectives. Demonstrate authentic care for their personal and professional well-being.

Find a deeper purpose in your leadership role. Explore how your actions can contribute to a greater good. Ensure that your endeavors resonate with meaningful values and missions.

Inspire others to excel. Great leaders motivate and empower their teams to reach their full potential. Recognize and celebrate their achievements to foster a positive work environment.

Stay adaptable and open to change. The business landscape is continually shifting, and adaptability is a hallmark of effective leadership.

Proactively seek leadership opportunities. Do not wait for titles; seize chances to lead by volunteering for challenging projects, proposing innovative solutions, and showcasing your leadership potential.

Extend your leadership influence beyond the workplace. Engage with your community, support social and environmental causes, and become a catalyst for positive change.

Consider the legacy you wish to leave as a leader. Reflect on how you would like to be remembered by those you have led and impacted. Your actions today shape the legacy you leave behind.

Remember, leadership transcends titles—it is about the impact you have on others and the positive changes you bring about. Whether leading a team, an organization, or a community, your leadership is consequential. By translating insights into action, you can make a substantial difference in the world through your leadership. Commence your journey today and be the catalyst for inspiring positive transformation.

Each stride you take brings you closer to realizing your vision of becoming a transformational leader. In our fast-paced world, adaptability, and a willingness to embrace change are fundamental. Being open to new ideas, emerging technologies, and innovative approaches is not just advantageous but essential in your leadership journey. It enables you to stay relevant and responsive in a rapidly evolving landscape.

Challenges and setbacks are inherent in leadership. However, they are not obstacles but rather opportunities for growth and development. Resilience is a vital quality to cultivate as it allows you to learn from adversity, bounce back from setbacks, and emerge from difficulties stronger and more resilient. Purpose is the compass that guides your leadership journey. It is essential to keep your values and the positive impact you want to create at the forefront of your leadership. Leaders who lead with a clear sense of purpose are not only more focused but also more inspiring to their teams and organizations.

Empathy is the cornerstone of effective leadership. It is the ability to understand and connect with others on a deeper level. Practicing active listening, seeking to understand diverse perspectives, and demonstrating genuine care for others are key components of being an empathetic leader.

Leadership is not just about words; it is about actions. Effective leaders lead by example, showcasing the values and behaviors they expect from their teams. Being a role model is a powerful way to influence and inspire positive change. Commit to lifelong learning and personal growth. Regularly assess your leadership skills, seek feedback from peers and mentors, and take concrete steps to develop and refine your abilities. Leaders who continuously invest in their growth are better equipped to adapt to changing circumstances and lead effectively. Transformational leaders have a unique ability to inspire and motivate those around them. Encourage and uplift your team members, helping them recognize their own potential and inspiring them to reach their goals. By empowering others, you create a culture of motivation and growth.

Cultivate relationships based on trust, respect, and collaboration. Strong interpersonal connections can be a cornerstone of effective leadership. Building and nurturing meaningful relationships with your team members, colleagues, and stakeholders fosters a positive and supportive work environment. Acknowledging and celebrating the accomplishments of your team and colleagues is crucial. Recognition not only boosts morale but also reinforces a culture of appreciation and motivation. By celebrating achievements, you create a sense of pride and purpose within your team.

Consider the legacy you want to leave as a leader. The impact you make today can resonate far into the future, influencing others and contributing to a better world. Thoughtfully crafting your leadership legacy is a profound way to ensure that your influence endures. As you progress in your leadership journey, remember that you possess the capacity to inspire change, empower others, and shape a more positive and inclusive future. Each step you take brings you closer to realizing your vision of transformational leadership. Continue moving forward with purpose, resilience, and the unwavering belief that your leadership can make a meaningful and enduring difference in the world.

Leadership is a dynamic and ever-evolving journey that requires dedication, self-reflection, and a commitment to growth. By embracing the qualities of effective leadership, navigating the challenges of the modern world, and envisioning a future of positive change, you have the power to become a transformational leader who inspires others and shapes a better future.

As you embark on your leadership journey, remember that leadership is not defined by a title but by your actions, your impact, and your unwavering commitment to making a difference in the lives of others and the organizations you lead.

Thank you for joining us on this exploration of leadership and may your path as a transformational leader be marked by purpose, empathy, and innovation.

10322678R00203